Embraced

by God

Praise for *Embraced by God*

"Babbie Mason has thrown down the gauntlet. Could you or I possibly be the apple of God's eye? Could we be a favorite child of the King, top of the heap? Could He actually delight in us, warts and all? *Embraced by God* is a powerful exercise for the willing—especially the reluctant or weary of heart. We find time for a 21-day diet or 21 days to 'find fulfillment.' Why not give God 21 days to reveal a deeper understanding of His unchangeable passion for you? Tenderly and powerfully Babbie's book quiets our secret fears, the voices of 'not enough,' and leads us into true places of self-worth and possibility. Twenty-one days of *Embraced by God* will astonish and release one from the grip of lies and pour in a flood of Scripture-drenched truths. Take the challenge! Twenty-one days later you will see a refreshed, beloved face in your mirror!"
—Bonnie Keen, author/speaker/recording artist
www.bonniekeen.com

"Babbie Mason's *Embraced by God* is the encouragement you need to experience the richness of God's love for you. As Babbie highlights this message, you'll discover God's love will lighten your load as it lights the way through this journey called life."
—Linda Evans Shepherd, Author of *When You Don't Know What to Pray and How to Talk to God About Anything.*
Founder of Advanced Writers and Speakers Association

CELEBRATING WHO AND
WHOSE YOU ARE

Embraced
by God

BABBIE MASON

Abingdon Press
Nashville

Embraced by God

Celebrating Who and Whose You Are

This book is printed on acid-free paper.

Library of Congress Cataloging-in-Publication Data

Mason, Babbie.
  Embraced by God : celebrating who and whose you are / Babbie Mason.
    p. cm.
  ISBN 978-1-4267-4134-0 (book - hardback / adhesive casebound : alk. paper) 1. Christian women—Religious life. 2. God (Christianity)—Love. 3. Self-acceptance—Religious aspects—Christianity. 4. Mason, Babbie. I. Title.
  BV4527.M268 2012
  248.8'43--dc23

2011050127

12 13 14 15 16 17 18 19 20 21—10 9 8 7 6 5 4 3 2

MANUFACTURED IN THE UNITED STATES OF AMERICA

IN LOVING MEMORY
OF MY FATHER,
THE REVEREND GEORGE W. WADE,
1922–1987

TO MY MOTHER,
GEORGIA WADE . . .

Who can find a virtuous woman? for her price is far above rubies.
The heart of her husband doth safely trust in her, so that he shall
have no need of spoil. She will do him good and not evil all the
days of her life. She seeketh wool, and flax, and worketh willingly
with her hands. She is like the merchants' ships; she bringeth her
food from afar. She riseth also while it is yet night, and giveth meat
to her household, and a portion to her maidens. She considereth a
field, and buyeth it: with the fruit of her hands she planteth a vine-
yard. . . . Her husband is known in the gates, when he sitteth
among the elders of the land. She maketh fine linen, and selleth it;
and delivereth girdles unto the merchant. Strength and honour are
her clothing; and she shall rejoice in time to come. She openeth
her mouth with wisdom; and in her tongue is the law of kindness.
. . . Her children arise up, and call her blessed; her husband also,
and he praiseth her. Many daughters have done virtuously, but
thou excellest them all. Favour is deceitful, and beauty is vain: but
a woman that feareth the LORD, she shall be praised.

—*Proverbs 31:10-30*

ACKNOWLEDGMENTS

I owe a deep debt of gratitude to some very special people who walked alongside me during the course of writing this book. You cheered me on, you ran with me, and you prayed me through. Because of your constant encouragement, loving support, and prayerful insight many, many hearts and lives will be touched and changed.

First and foremost, to my Lord and Savior, Jesus Christ— Thank You for embracing me the way You do! This newfound joy of discovering another dimension of Your deep, sweet love for me has changed my life forever.

To my husband, Charles—You have always been there for me, oftentimes setting your own dreams aside to help me pursue my own. Thanks for the days and nights you ate and slept alone while I stayed tethered to the computer. You, my love, are the best!

To our sons, Jerry and Chaz—Thanks for the joy and inspiration you always bring to me. May you always know that you are God's favorites. Mine too.

To my personal assistant, Kimberly, and her husband, Rick— Thanks for dreaming with me and investing your lives to help me run with this *Embraced By God* vision, both in the office and on the road. I couldn't do it without you.

To my brothers and sister, Ben, Al, Benita, and Matt—You are all brilliant! I'm so grateful to God for each one of "Reverend Wade's children." March forth.

To Ruth, Donna, Barb, Tracy, Becky, Glenda, Nancy, April, Allison, and Sisters of the Pink Sneaks for standing in the gap for me.

To Pamela—Thank you for believing in me! Your genuine care, insight, wisdom, and feedback are invaluable. You are a cheerleader in the truest form.

To Paula—Thank you not just for the fine editing job, but for much, much more. I sensed your prayerful support during this entire process. What a blessing you are to me.

To Johnny—I praise God for the day you picked up the phone and called me.

And to you, dear reader—Many thanks for choosing to read this book. May your life be changed by the eternal truth that you are chosen, accepted, and loved unconditionally by God.

CONTENTS

BEFORE YOU BEGIN
THE OVERTURE

Have you ever pondered, *Does God really love me? Does He accept me unconditionally? Is He concerned about my problems? Do I really matter to Him?* If these thoughts have ever crossed your mind, take comfort, you are not alone. You join millions of people who, throughout the ages, have asked these same questions.

I can admit that I have joined these ranks, and I've been a Christian most of my life. In fact, I was raised in church. I'm a preacher's daughter turned Christian singer, songwriter, and recording artist. Still, I have dealt with these very thoughts at different points during my life's journey. And I have found that God's love for me never changes.

If you sometimes question God's love for you, consider this: I believe God allows us to experience these longings so that we will have a hunger for Him. I believe we long to be with Him and desire to be loved completely by Him so that we will stay in His presence—where He desires for us to be.

I accepted Christ when I was eight years old, and in another year I will celebrate what I call my "Year of Jubilee," fifty years of knowing Christ as my Lord and Savior. Yet just a couple of years ago my eyes were opened to a new awareness of God's love when I heard my good friend Dr. Tony Ashmore, pastor of the Life Gate Church in Villa Rica, Georgia, preach a life-changing sermon. On that Sunday morning he instructed each person in the congregation to turn to one's neighbor and say, "I am God's favorite."

My friend's words troubled me at first. Initially I thought, *How could I be God's favorite? I have a past filled with mistakes. I have issues and challenges in my life. There are so many people who must stand ahead of me in line for that prize.*

Don't get me wrong. I have always known that God loves me, and honestly speaking, just knowing this was enough for me. I was satisfied with that. But to consider that I could *ever* be God's favorite? That seemed to be overstepping a boundary, even a bit presumptuous. I reasoned to myself that if God had favorites, then I certainly couldn't be one of them.

This motivated me to seek God and the truth of His word. As I studied the Scriptures, two passages stood out to me. In John 17:22-23, Jesus said, "I have given them the glory you gave me, so they may be one as we are one. I am in them and you are in me. May they experience such perfect unity that the world will know that you sent me and that you love them as much as you love me" (NLT). Romans 8:17a adds, "Since we are his children, we are his heirs. In fact, together with Christ we are heirs of God's glory" (NLT).

Suddenly, God quickened my heart. I realized that God not only loves me; He loves me just as much as He loves His own Son, Jesus. I also became more deeply aware that everything God gave to Jesus, He has also given to me! This has taken my love relationship with Him to another level. *The realization of these promises has made me more keenly aware of God's loving presence and purpose in my life.* I now have a little better understanding of how David felt when he wrote these timeless words in Psalm 139:6 (NIV):

> Such knowledge is too wonderful for me,
> too lofty for me to attain.

In other words, the knowledge of this truth rocked his world! I can identify with King David. The knowledge of this truth has rocked my world as well! So I have concluded that if I, a Christian for nearly fifty years, could come to a profoundly new understanding of God's love, then maybe you could too. This book, *Embraced by God*, is the result of that discovery.

Come with Me, Experience His Embrace . . .

Allow me to invite you to a special event, a symphony of sorts, for which this introduction serves as an *overture*: the first orchestral movement in exploring the depths of God's amazing love. I have already asked the Holy Spirit to set the stage, paint the scenes, tune the music to your key, adjust the sound, and focus the spotlight. Each time the curtain opens, I'll be here, making wonderful discoveries with you. During these daily concerts of love, I'll share my experiences, insights, highlights, and even the secrets of my heart. Sometimes I'll share a few verses of a song.

Don't get too comfortable in your seat, though, because you're the reason why this "Embrace" celebration is about to begin. I encourage you to participate fully, completely, and without reservation. I have also asked Someone very special to join us during this encounter, and He is the most exciting participant: *Jesus.* He is the Great Orchestrator. I am asking Him to lead us and accompany us according to Zephaniah 3:17, which says, "The LORD thy God in the midst of thee is mighty; he will save, he will rejoice over thee with joy; he will rest in his love, he will joy over thee with singing."

Get ready, my friend. Jesus is about to sing over you! This is a concert experience you don't want to miss! During each session, you'll learn how to live *loved* by your heavenly Father.

So, let our celebration begin! As we prepare for the downbeat of this experience, I want to serve as your trusted friend, encouraging you along the way, for I am someone whose life has been transformed by the power of God's amazing love. My prayer is that you, too, will be changed as you realize that God not only loves you, He loves you passionately and completely. He loves you without condition and without exception. He loves you as much as He loves Jesus.

As a matter of fact—*you* are His favorite as well. You see, this is not a message of favoritism for a select few. This symphony of love is for all of God's children. As you draw near to Him, you will experience your own unique place in His favor and grace. Your heavenly Father desires to have a deep and intimate relationship with you through His Son, Jesus Christ, and He wants His love to impact every area of your life. No matter what you are facing at this moment, *He wants to embrace you*: in your challenges, victories, or defeats, and in your strengths, weaknesses, or fears.

The world is in a love crisis. Many people suffer from a love deficiency, but not those who enjoy the rich and satisfying life that only Christ can give! If your "cup" is nearly empty, don't worry. As you come into His embrace you will receive refills over and over again. Oh yes, the refreshments at this event are always on the house. They have already been bought and paid for by our Sponsor. So take all you need whenever you need it. The more you enter in and receive Jesus' unconditional love, the more you will truly enjoy abundant life.

Enjoy Twenty-one Days of Love . . .

Research has proved that if you are not satisfied with your current life experience, you must examine your habits. Anything you repeatedly put into practice will become an integral part of your life, and these practices will influence the quality of your life. For this reason, developing good habits is fundamental and essential. Without them you will not enjoy success in the things you desire to accomplish.

Psychologists, counselors, and life coaches say it takes twenty-one days to develop a new habit. In light of this, for the next twenty-one days I encourage you to treat this book as more than just a daily devotional. Instead, use it as a manual to help you develop and deepen your spiritual love life—to understand with more clarity God's deep, sweet love for you.

Investing in your love walk with God will require a commitment on your part. I'll ask you to read a chapter a day. So, just as you have a designated place to park your car and a specific place to store your shoes, determine to meet with God at the same time, in the same quiet place, where you will not be distracted or disturbed. Try to find somewhere you would feel comfortable reading or praying out loud, or perhaps singing a verse or two of a beautiful hymn. Make your special time with the Lord a priority, and anticipate spending this time with Him daily.

Together, we will explore and experience that love is not a feeling. Love is much more than an emotion. *Love is a person.* Spending time with this person—*Jesus*—will be the respite you've needed for so long as you linger in His embrace. My hope and prayer are that your experience over the next twenty-one days will alter the course of your life and take your love relationship with the Lord to a new level, one that you've never known before.

Encounter Seven Promises from God's Heart

I have divided our daily concert experience into seven segments, each containing three devotions, which reflect God's promises to us as His beloved children. I refer to these segments as *themes* because each addresses a pertinent area in our love relationship with the Lord. As we move through each theme we will address, discuss, and reflect on it together. Then when a new theme begins, we will encounter a different area of your relationship with Jesus and see how His love covers it all. Let's start by taking a look at these seven wonderful promises:

> God's passion for you is unconditional.
> God's picture of you is beautiful.
> God's presence in you is perpetual.
> God's provision for you is immeasurable.
> God's plan for you is exceptional.
> God's power in you is accessible.
> God's promise in you is incomparable.

Each day's reading will close with a heartfelt prayer and give you four significant areas to consider and act upon. I call this closing section "Embrace Your Day" because as you put what you read into practice, you will live *loved* by God and be able to embrace all He has for you. Our daily love exercises include:

Think About His Love. This part of your daily reading will serve as a recap, encouraging you to really think about what you have read. It will challenge you to meditate on God's promise. It will help you consider how it relates to your life, so you will turn the promise over and over in your mind throughout the day. Write your thoughts down in a notebook to track your progress and your requests of the Lord. As you consider this section each day, remember that Psalm 119:105 says, "Thy word is a lamp unto my feet and a light unto my path."

Read About His Love. This section contains a theme scripture from each day's reading. One of the best habits you could establish is reading and memorizing God's word. It is active and powerful, transforming our minds, piercing our hearts, and exposing our deepest desires and intentions as it divides between soul and spirit (see Hebrews 4:12). As you work through this daily exercise, remember Psalm 119:11: "Thy word have I hid in mine heart, that I might not sin against thee."

Pray About His Love. Throughout our series of devotional gatherings we will talk to God often. I encourage you to talk to Him on your own, as well. As you spend time with the Lord, relax and enjoy your conversations with Him. You can be completely real. God loves conversing with you. So, talk with Him about everything. Candidly share your challenges, relationships, dreams, hopes, and aspirations. Tell God what you are experiencing as you learn to live *loved*. He already knows your experience—but you need to tell Him anyway. Just knowing that *He knows* will bring you great peace of mind, particularly when you are facing difficult challenges. As you take time with the Lord each day, let Psalm 5:1-2 guide you: "Give ear to my words, O LORD, consider my meditation. Hearken unto the voice of my cry, my King, and my God: for unto thee will I pray."

Be About His Love. You can expect your love walk with Jesus to bring about changes in your life! As a result, you will impact others as they experience His love through you. This section will help you put your love walk into action. Let this exercise challenge you to activate your faith daily according to Ephesians 5:2, which tells us, "Walk in love, as Christ also hath loved us, and hath given himself for us an offering and a sacrifice to God for a sweetsmelling savour."

Endeavor to Return His Embrace

My prayer is that this twenty-one-day encounter in God's embrace will increase your capacity to love Him and receive His love, allowing Him to impact every aspect of your life. Give God permission to transform your thinking and change any misconceptions you have about Him, or yourself, for that matter. No doubt, you will learn many new things about your loving heavenly Father. You may even make some surprisingly new discoveries about who *you* are.

My dear friend, let me encourage you to return His embrace. As we enjoy each concert in the Father's symphony of love, ask the Lord to form His will and purpose in you. When you emerge from this "Embrace" celebration, you will understand with more clarity *who you are in Him* and *who He is in you.* When our *Embraced by God* experience is complete, and we're on our feet asking for "The Encore" (at the end of this book), I pray you will have a new perspective concerning who and whose you are.

There is absolutely nothing more important than developing an intimate, life-changing relationship with the God who made you, loves you deeply, and knows you better than anyone else. He knows you more intimately than your mother, your father, or your best friend. He even knows you better than you know yourself. God knows everything about you—the good things printed in your résumé and other things nobody else knows—yet He loves you just the same. *Respond to His love. Return His embrace.*

Finally, before starting this special event together, let's set the record straight. ***If you have never received Jesus Christ as your Savior, this is the perfect opportunity to make that life-changing decision.*** Turn now to page 421, "The First Note: *How to Receive Christ as Savior.*" Using this prayer as your guide, you can take the first step in embracing all Father God has for you. As you pray this heartfelt prayer, He will plant the first beautiful note of His divine symphony in your heart. Now, you can share in the complete concert experience.

If you have given your life to Christ, this would be a great time to pause and pray a simple prayer asking the Lord to renew your Christian experience. Share openly from your heart with the Lord, surrendering to Him completely, trusting Him to complete the work He has started in your life. Now, you can relish twenty-one days in His embrace and enjoy His promises to the fullest.

Are you ready to get started? I'm excited as we begin this wonderful celebration for His glory! You could even ask a friend or a small group to join you. Your group could meet in a friend's home, at church, in a local coffee shop, or even get together in a conference call. However you choose to walk out twenty-one days of being *Embraced by God*, prepare your heart, arrange your thoughts, and get ready to find the *real love* you've been searching for.

Now, get comfortable in your seat and focus your eyes on the stage. Everything is ready behind the scenes. The curtain is about to open. Let's begin our journey of discovering what it means to be unconditionally loved, approved, accepted, forgiven, blessed, cherished, favored, and treasured by God!

GOD'S PASSION FOR YOU IS UNCONDITIONAL

Glory, glory everlasting
Be to Him who bore the cross,
Who redeemed our souls by tasting
Death, the death deserved by us.
Spread His glory,
Who redeemed His people thus!

His is love, 'tis love unbounded,
Without measure, without end;
Human thought is here confounded,
'Tis too vast to comprehend.
Praise the Savior!
Magnify the sinner's Friend!

While we tell the wondrous story
Of the Savior's cross and shame,
Sing we, Everlasting glory
Be to God and to the Lamb.
Hallelujah! Give ye glory to His Name![1]
—Thomas Kelly

Imagine the most wonderful love relationship you could ever experience here on earth. Envision a love without limits or conditions. Consider a relationship that is completely satisfying in every way. Now imagine multiplying that as high as you can calculate. If you could count all the way to infinity and beyond, your answer would still be far too small compared to how much God really loves you. His love for you is passionate, unconditional and far, far beyond any love you could ever experience with another human being.

Your heavenly Father wants you to see yourself as He sees you—loved beyond your capacity to imagine, saved from your sins, healed from all diseases, delivered from bondages, and free to live the life He has planned for you. As you take hold of this life-changing truth it will impact the way you think and ultimately the way you live. Not only does the God of the universe love you; He wants more than anything for you to love Him in return.

The overture has sounded. As we count down, preparing ourselves for the first downbeat of this encounter of being *Embraced by God*, let me encourage you to open the eyes of your heart and take a fresh new look at an age-old promise.

OVER THE NEXT THREE DAYS,
MEDITATE ON THIS PROMISE:

Because God loves me, He wants more than anything
for His love to influence my life in every way
and for me to love Him in return.

Day 1

YOU ARE GOD'S FAVORITE

To write the love of God above
Would drain the ocean dry
Nor could the scroll, contain the whole
Though stretched from sky to sky.[1]
—Frederick M. Lehman

For God so loved the world, that he gave his only begotten Son,
that whosoever believeth in him should not perish,
but have everlasting life.
—John 3:16

God loves you.

No doubt, you've heard these words before. Maybe you heard them as a child in Sunday school class. It's possible that you caught them as you surfed through the television channels. Perhaps you saw the words, *God Loves You* on a car bumper sticker during rush-hour traffic. Perhaps these familiar words are in a song that you know.

You might even be saying to yourself at this moment, *That's a really nice thought.* But have you truly considered what these timeless words really mean? Consider how a holy, perfect, infinite God could ever love someone who is sinful, unholy, severely imperfect, and hopelessly finite. This is hard to comprehend, but it's true. Not only does the God of the universe love the whole world . . . *He loves you.* The very same God who spoke heaven and earth into existence created *you*, loves *you*, and longs for *you* to know that *you* are completely and utterly treasured without measure or condition. First John 4:10a (NIV) makes this clear: "This is love: not that we loved God, but that he loved us."

God's love cannot be compared to any other love you have encountered. The way human beings love and the way God loves are two totally different things entirely.

Human love is temperamental. When humans love, the circumstances have to be just right. Feelings are subject to change without a moment's notice, and they hinge on conditions. God's love is unconditional. To Him, circumstances don't matter. In good times or bad, when we do wrong or when we do right, God's love is always constant. His love never changes.

Human love is temporary. It can be here one moment and gone the next. People change their minds. They discard relationships and move on. Not so with God. His love is eternal. From everlasting to everlasting, He has always loved you. God loves you more than you know right at this very moment. And He will love you for all time.

Human love is often tentative. People are capable of entering into relationships with caution, hesitancy, and uncertainty. Many times people give to get, having selfish ulterior motives. God's love is completely selfless. He is liberal with His affection, always giving His love sacrificially. Even now, your heavenly Father would give up everything and lay it all down, both joyfully and willingly, just for you.

God's Love for You Is Perfect

Perhaps you find it difficult to wrap your mind around the truth that God loves you without any conditions. You might be thinking, *How could the God of the universe love me unconditionally? I'm flawed and scarred. I don't measure up to God's standard of perfection. I have a past, and it's not pretty. I tend to be self-seeking and prideful, even hateful at times. I have a bad temper. I can be overindulgent and insensitive. There are times that my heart is filled with greed and envy.* The reasoning for not feeling good enough to receive God's love could go on and on.

Be encouraged. God knows everything about you—both good and bad—and He still loves you. He knows the areas in which you flourish and shine, and He knows where you are weak and vulnerable. Yet God loves you just the same. But that's not an excuse to become stagnant. Max Lucado said, "God loves you just the way you are, but he refuses to leave you that way. He wants you to be just like Jesus."[2]

You are God's favorite. That's right. I'll say it again: *you are God's favorite.* You are unique, special, irreplaceable, and incomparable in value to Him. God loves you more passionately than any human ever could. You might think of yourself as an unimportant, nameless face in a crowd of millions. You might even think, as I did in church that day, *God has His favorites and I certainly don't qualify to be one of them.*

Yes, God is all-powerful, and He needs help from no one. Yet without you, your heavenly Father's joy would never be complete. It breaks His heart when you resist His love. Worse yet, it grieves Him when you don't believe that He loves you. To think this way is to silently accuse God of having imperfect love. That kind of thinking is an insult to the work that Jesus completed on the cross for you.

In Galatians 2:6-9, the Apostle Paul speaks of Jesus' beloved disciples, Peter, James, and John. If anybody could claim to find a favorite place in God's heart, certainly these men would. John even considered himself to be "the disciple whom Jesus loved" (John 19:26). These great men walked with Jesus as His closest earthly friends. Each is considered a foundational pillar of the church. Yet the Apostle Paul said of these men:

> But from those who were of high reputation (what they were makes no difference to me; God shows no partiality)—well, those who were of reputation contributed nothing to me. (Galatians 2:6 NASB)[3]

The Bible says you are just as important to God as His beloved disciples, Peter, James, and John. Because of Christ's finished work, you qualify for God's favor just as much as they did. Let's think about this in human terms. If you had a broken leg, you would qualify to see a doctor, right? If your tooth ached, you would qualify to see a dentist. If your sink had a busted water pipe, you'd qualify to call a plumber—even if this emergency occurred in the middle of the night.

In the same manner, we as people are flawed and scarred. We don't measure up to God's perfect standards. We have a past that is not pretty. We are self-seeking and full of pride. We lose our temper and self-control. We have all sinned and missed God's mark of perfection. Figuratively speaking, we all have something in our lives that is *broken, aching,* and *busted.* So, every one of us qualifies for a Savior.

In your own strength you could never qualify to be God's favorite, but Jesus does. And because of what Jesus did for you at Calvary, He qualified you!

This may seem to be an amazing thought to grab hold of, but your heavenly Father delights in you. He loves you just as much as He loves His own Son, Jesus. What a great truth this is! Don't just hear this with your ears; embrace it with your heart. Read what Jesus prayed to the Father on your behalf:

> I am in them [*that includes you!*] and you are in me. May they experience such perfect unity that the world will know that you sent me and that you love them as much as you love me. (John 17:23 NLT, emphasis mine)

Some people think of God as an age-old ogre with a long beard, a perpetual scowl, and a pointy finger, who is distant, uncaring, and aloof. They picture God as being mean-spirited: Someone who can't wait for people to make a mistake so He can banish them eternally from His presence. That, my friend, only happens in the movies. It simply is not true in daily life.

Remember, God not only has the ability to love, *He is Love personified.* The very essence of our heavenly Father's character is love. As a matter of fact, His name is Love. Read 1 John 4:7-8 with me: "Beloved, let us love one another: for love is of God; and everyone that loveth is born of God and knoweth God. He that loveth not knoweth not God; for God is love."

From the very beginning, God wanted you to experience His love. He sent His Son, Jesus, to the world so you could understand more clearly what love looks like in flesh and blood. As you follow Jesus' example, you will experience *real love.*

Do you want to know what God is like? Look at Jesus. Do you want to know how to live life to the fullest? Look at Jesus. Do you want to experience love in a personal way? *Look to Jesus.* When you experience the Father's love through Him, with each new day you can discover real joy and the true meaning of life.

God's Love for You Is Like Precious Gold

Have you ever read John 3:16? Not just glanced over it in passing, but have you ever really read it? This passage is considered to be the "golden text" of the Bible: "For God so loved the world, that he gave his only begotten Son, that whosoever believeth in him should not perish, but have everlasting life."

The third chapter of the book of John opens with the story about Nicodemus, a very learned man and member of the Jewish council. He came to Jesus by night, knowing in his heart that Jesus must have been sent from God because of the miracles He performed. What intrigues me most about Nicodemus is his relentless curiosity. I believe Jesus was pleased not only to answer Nicodemus's questions, but to reveal to him the key that unlocks all of life.

This story is very familiar to a lot of people, including me. Like many others, I memorized John 3:16 as a small child. Growing up in the church my father pastored, it was expected of me (and every church member for that matter) to memorize Scripture. The church even held annual contests, giving awards to the person who had memorized the most passages. And yes, I won a few ribbons for displaying this skill.

I've known John 3:16 in its entirety for most of my life. However, over the years this passage became so familiar to me that I almost took it for granted. Recently, when I read this verse again that is the central theme of the Bible, I was impacted by its powerful truth. Suddenly, I began to gain a depth of meaning I hadn't realized before. As I pondered the words I was reading, I felt led to engage in a personal exercise.

Knowing that Christ died for me, I replaced the words *the world* and *whosoever* with my own name. Completing this exercise by speaking it aloud, I felt the weight of its meaning sink deeply into my heart: *For God so loved **Babbie**, that he gave his only begotten Son, that if **Babbie** believes in him, **Babbie** should not perish, but have everlasting life.*

My eyes were opened! I was stunned at how clearly I understood the message of God's love. *May I challenge you to do the same?* Right now, go ahead and fill in the blanks below with your own name; then read the sentence slowly. As you read, ask

God to make this age-old promise come alive in you with fresh, new meaning.

> *For God so loved* _____, *that he gave his only*
> *begotten Son, that if* _____ *believes in him,*
> _____ *should not perish, but have everlasting*
> *life.*

Take a moment to grasp the implications of this passage a little more firmly. The God of the universe loves you so much that He surrendered His most prized possession, the life of His own Son, as a supreme sacrifice for your sin.

I am the mother of two wonderful sons, and my mind cannot conceive of such a selfless act! God gave up the life of His only Son, and Jesus laid down His own life, completely paying the penalty for your sin once and for all. God's only Son was crucified, put to death on a cruel, bloody cross. What a beautiful demonstration of just how much He loves you.

Think of the price that was paid for your sin. You and I should have been on that cross, but Jesus took our place. As you ponder this great exchange, repeat these words aloud: *God loves me.* Now say with emphasis: *I am God's favorite.* You may even want to make it a practice today by saying these words aloud, repeatedly, throughout the day. Find a mirror, look yourself in the eye, and say them over and over again. Let these powerful truths sink deeply into your heart.

Now say it once more, slowly this time: "*God loves me . . . I am His favorite.*"

It's amazing. Whenever I ask the Holy Spirit to help me understand the Scriptures, He does exactly that. You will find this to be true as well. Ask the Holy Spirit to give you an understanding of the Scriptures, and you will begin to realize new revelation from God's word—no matter how familiar you may already be with certain passages.

God Loves You So Much

On another occasion, I read John 3:16 again and the same thing happened. As I read, slowly and deliberately, a tiny word seemed to leap off the page. In and of itself, this word doesn't appear to mean much. At first glance, it can even seem to be rather nondescript and insignificant. Not so!

This time as I read John 3:16, I was compelled to look up the definition of those two small letters cuddling closely to each other, and I found a huge meaning! By the way, the word I'm talking about is *so*. Think about its meaning and context as you read the definition: "To a great extent or degree; very, extremely; exceedingly, enormously, tremendously. To an immeasurable degree."[4]

Do you understand this passage a little more clearly now? God loved you so very much—to such an extent, so extremely, enormously, and tremendously—that He sent Jesus to the ends of the earth and back again, conquering sin, death, hell, and the grave for one reason and one reason alone. *You*.

Rock 'n' roll legend Tina Turner's classic hit asks the question, "What's love got to do with it?" According to God's word, love has *everything* to do with it! Love has everything to do with the way God sees you. It has everything to do with the way you see your past, present, and future. Love has everything to do with the way you treat others, and yes, it even determines the way you see yourself.

Because God loves you, regardless of what your day holds in store—good or bad, the best and the rest—absolutely nothing can separate you from His love! Romans 8:38-39 explains this beautifully in *THE MESSAGE*:

> I'm absolutely convinced that nothing—nothing living or dead, angelic or demonic, today or tomorrow, high or low, thinkable or unthinkable—absolutely *nothing* can get between us and God's love because of the way that Jesus our Master has embraced us. (emphasis mine)

I'll say it again. God loves you. I challenge you to never get to the place where knowing this doesn't have a comforting, lingering affect on you. Don't ever take this eternal truth for granted. Never allow these three vitally important words to become old, cold, or so common that they no longer move you. As a matter of fact, my friend, as time passes you must allow them to do exactly the opposite. Let this life-changing phrase become like a magnet, always drawing you closer to your heavenly Father's heart.

As you come into a deeper understanding of the power this truth holds, it will not only change the way you perceive God's love for you. It will change *you*.

When I was in the third grade, I got my first love letter from a boy in my class. He sat two rows over. Billy (not his real name) wrote the letter in a way that only a third grader could do. Then he folded it up, origami-style, in the shape of a paper cup. Risking being caught and severely reprimanded by our teacher, he then carefully passed the letter to me when she turned her back to write on the chalkboard. I unfolded it and began to read. This is what it said:

Dear Babbie,
I love you.
Do you love me?
Yes or no?
Circle one.

Then, using a number two lead pencil, he signed his name . . .

Billy

I don't remember how I responded to Billy's proposition to be his sweetheart. But I do remember how it made me feel. I felt preferred and uniquely chosen, knowing that someone in that classroom thought I was special. Even though it was only a third grade crush, I clearly recall, even now, how it felt to know someone loved me. Even more, that someone thought enough of me to tell me so.

The Bible is God's love letter to you. From cover to cover, He's calling your name. From the table of contents all the way to the maps in the back of the Book, He's charting your life's course. From the words, "In the beginning God . . ." to "Behold, I am coming soon . . ." God desires to write His love story on the tablets of your heart. Oh, yes, from the first *hallelujah* to the last *amen*, God is singing your victory song.

Can you hear it? I heard it one day and captured these words in a beautiful song, "I Love You, I Do." Listen with your heart and experience God's eternal love for you:

> *I love you, I love you, I love you, I do*
> *I love you through the darkest of night*
> *And in the daytime too*
> *Just as roses are red and the violets are blue*
> *Never doubt for one moment that My love is true*
> *And if you need to be reminded of how I feel about you*
> *I'll tell you again, I love you, I do . . .* [5]

God really, really loves you! Yes, He does! Each page of the Bible is engraved with an invitation from Jesus to come and drink from the water of life freely (Revelation 21:6; 22:17). He signed it with His precious blood, sealed it with His perfect love, and delivered it straight to *the very center of your heart*.

Always remember, day in and day out, *you* are the object of His deep, sweet love.

It was for *you* that Jesus came into the world. For *you*, Jesus was born. It was for *you* that He lived, sinlessly, perfectly, joyfully, and willingly laying His life on the line. It was for *you* that He was crucified, died on the cross, and was laid in another man's tomb. For *you*, my dear friend, Jesus rose from the grave. And if you were the only person on earth, He would still have done it all, *just for you*.

The next time you hear the words, "God loves you," don't just think, *Isn't that nice?* and walk away unaffected, living far beneath your privilege. Instead, as a blood-bought, born-again child of God, receive His promise and return His embrace. Begin living as one who knows that *this promise* (and countless others) in His eternal Book of love *belongs to you.* In fact, 2 Corinthians 1:20 says, "All the promises of God in him are yea, and in him Amen, unto the glory of God by us."

Turn this fundamental truth over and over in your mind, and let it sink to the very depths of your soul. God *so* loves you and He wants you to *so* love Him in return. When you make it a practice to rehearse this powerful promise from John 3:16, like Nicodemus, you will begin to discover what many people fail to notice. *Everything begins with God's love.*

EMBRACE YOUR DAY

As we bring the lights down on the stage for today, let me encourage you to think about the things we've discussed. Make a real effort to reflect on them throughout the day. The greatest human discovery is to find God. The greatest human achievement is to know God. The greatest adventure is to walk with God, and the greatest romance is to fall in love with God.

Remember, God loves you and wants you to love Him in return. There is absolutely nothing more important in the world than developing an intimate, life-changing relationship with Him.

From the beginning of time, you have been a part of God's great big love story. Although you may not fully understand how a perfect God could love imperfect people, always keep in mind that only Jesus makes this love relationship even possible. Don't wait for your emotions to tell you God loves you deeply. Whether you feel like it or not, His love for you is real.

Endeavor to keep in the forefront of your mind, dear friend, that love is not a feeling. Love is not an emotional urge or a physical desire. *Love is a person*, and that person is Jesus. You could look inside yourself and try to find real love, but you will come up empty every time. You could look to others for the affirmation you crave, but you will be disappointed. Right now, in the seat where you are sitting, stop and think about one fact: *the love you crave and long for is personified in the loving, perfect, sinless Lamb of God—Jesus Christ.*

We're off to a wonderful start. Tomorrow, we'll continue taking hold of this incredible promise and discover that every day can be brand new in Christ. So meet me tomorrow, same time and same place, to experience Day 2.

I think this would be a good moment to pause and offer a prayer of thanks to God for His passionate love toward us.

Would you pray with me?

Dear heavenly Father,

I am overwhelmed by how much You love me. Thank You for caring for me the way You do. What a blessing it is to know that being a recipient of Your love doesn't depend, not even for a moment, on me. I know now that I could never do anything to earn Your love. It is a free gift. So today, anew and afresh, I will receive Your gift of love and enjoy it. I know now that it's not about me. It's about what You, through Your precious Son, Jesus, did for me. It's so good to know that nothing I have ever done or ever could do will separate me from Your love. Today, regardless of how I feel, I will determine to live like the child of God I know that I am. Help me, Lord, to never take this powerful truth for granted. In Jesus' name,

Amen.

Think About His Love

Reflect for a few moments on what you have read today. Think about what God's great love means to you personally. Determine that it will impact how you embrace Him today. As suggested in this session, remind yourself throughout the day of this timeless promise by saying, "I am God's favorite."

Read About His Love

"For God so loved the world, that he gave his only begotten Son, that whosoever believeth in him should not perish, but have everlasting life" (John 3:16). If you haven't yet committed this verse to memory, just close your eyes after reading it and repeat it a few times. Then, remind yourself again that you are God's favorite. This time, personalize it even more by adding this passage. Say, "I am God's favorite *because* '. . . God so loved _____ that he gave his only begotten Son. . . .' " Say the promise in its entirety. Wonderful results will be yours.

Pray About His Love

Talk to God throughout the day today. Repeatedly and in your own words, thank Him for His great love that is extended to you. Ask Him to increase your understanding of His love and help you to love Him on a deeper, more intimate level.

Be About His Love

Love is contagious. Your love walk with God will cause others to experience His love through you. Since His perfect love is making all the difference in your life, what will you do differently today to share this love with others? Before the day is over, spend a few moments writing about how you have been impacted by God's love today and have been able to share this wonderful experience.

DAY 2

YOU CAN START AGAIN

*This is how grace works. It enters the soul,
penetrates the heart, saturates the conscience,
abides in the memory, affects the affections, gives understanding
to the understanding, and imparts real life to the heart,
which is the seat of life.*[1]
—Charles Haddon Spurgeon

*If any man be in Christ, he is a new creature:
old things are passed away; behold, all things are become new.*
—2 Corinthians 5:17

No matter how many times you have failed, you can always begin again.

Everybody knows what it's like to make mistakes and need an opportunity to start over. Have you ever come to the point where you were just sick and tired of the situation you were in? We've all been there. Keep reading and listen to one young lady's story.

Like most good Christian kids who have been raised by parents who love God, Becca accepted Christ as a young girl and was involved in a lot of church activities growing up. She sang in the choir as a youth and later played piano and directed the choir in her pastor-father's growing church. Every once in a while she would even step in to teach Sunday school when one of the regular teachers was absent.

Becca was an excellent student, hung out with other nice Christian kids, and even worked a part-time job after school. But as she reached her late teenage years and graduated from high school, her heart began to wander, and her walk with God suffered because of it. As a freshman at a nearby community college she met new friends—kids who hadn't been raised in Christian homes. These new friends influenced Becca to hang out in places where she had never hung out before. In the past, Saturday nights had been spent at home with family preparing for early Sunday church services. But Becca's new friends convinced her that Saturday nights were better spent partying in local bars and clubs.

Although the taste of alcohol never appealed to her, she'd never tell her friends for fear that she'd look foolish: like a square peg in a round hole. Becca was afraid that she wouldn't fit in and that her friends wouldn't accept her. As a matter of fact, hanging out in smoky, noisy bars didn't appeal to Becca at all, but she felt this route was the road that would lead to the realization of her big dream. She thought this was just the price she would have to pay to get signed to a secular record company, like Motown Records, and become an overnight R&B singing sensation.

Becca could easily justify her decisions. When the club's house band would take their breaks during intermissions, the friends in their small group would urge her to go to the piano and sing. And they didn't want her to sing church songs either! Becca was happy to oblige them. She would sit behind the old upright piano situated under the bright spotlights on that smoke-filled bar room platform. And she didn't have to be coaxed.

She longed for this moment—the opportunity to get to the piano and perform the hit songs everybody loved to hear. Belting out the soulful melodies and lyrics made famous by lady soul singers of that day, Becca charmed her audiences with the songs by Aretha Franklin, Gladys Knight, and Roberta Flack. She wanted nothing more than to hear the applause and the cheers that came flooding back to her from the audience after her performances. Becca didn't care that she wasn't getting paid. She loved performing so much that she would have gladly sung for free.

And who knew? Maybe, just maybe, one night soon there would be someone in the audience who would love her voice enough to sign her to that record contract she longed for.

After a while, singing in the bar and experimenting with alcohol on Saturday nights, while playing for her father's church on Sundays, caused Becca's heart to grow increasingly troubled. She had become a young Christian who was caught between a rock and a hard place. Each time she would darken the door of the club on Saturday nights, pangs of guilt would grip her heart like a vice because deep inside Becca knew that "light" could have no fellowship with "darkness" (2 Corinthians 6:14). Then on Sunday mornings, while singing gospel songs, she'd wrestle with the wrenching clutches of conviction when she recalled where she had been the night before.

Becca's heart had become divided; she no longer fully enjoyed either opportunity.

Deep inside, compromise was ruling her life. Restless with guilt and anxiety, Becca remembered the words of her mother: "You can't run with the devil and walk with God." Now she realized just how true this was, for Becca had come to the place where she had too much world for the church and too much church for the world. She was living in two totally different worlds, and they were about to collide.

Becca played a good game, but in her heart she knew the truth. She was a hypocrite. And the lifestyle she thought would help her fit in actually made her feel isolated and alone.

We'll leave Becca's story for a moment and come back to it a little bit later in this chapter.

Do You Need to Start Over?

Now, my friend, what about you? Does hearing this young lady's story make you think of your own? Got failures from your past? If you are anything like Becca, you can still see vivid details of your life's story that reveal selfish decisions to go it on your own and do things your own way. If you think about it, there have probably been times in your life when you took a wrong turn that led to some bad decisions. And like Becca, you could have even been a practicing Christian and still ended up making the wrong choice to do things your way.

Making the choice to do things your way is what the Bible calls *sin*. Sin is any word, thought, or act that is against the laws and precepts of God. Everyone has sinned. The Bible confirms in

Romans 3:23: "For all have sinned and fall short of the glory of God" (NIV).

It doesn't matter who you are or what your story may be. Jesus will forgive every mistake, and He can satisfy every longing you have, if you ask Him. Everybody can use a do-over every now and then: another opportunity to get things right with the Lord. Life in Christ is the only road to discovering what *true life* really is. Jesus promises the forgiveness you need, the peace you long for, the acceptance you crave, and the love you deeply hunger for. I find real encouragement in Ephesians 2:4-5:

> But God's mercy is great, and he loved us very much. Though we were spiritually dead because of the things we did against God, he gave us new life with Christ. (NCV)

Learning to live "freely and lightly" means letting go of the past, living in the moment, and looking ahead to the future. You must not let mistakes from your past keep you from moving forward and embracing all that God has in store for you. Your best days are still ahead of you.

The great American writer Mark Twain said, "Twenty years from now you will be more disappointed by the things you didn't do than by the ones you did do. So throw off the bowlines. Sail away from the safe harbor. Catch the trade winds in your sails. Explore. Dream. Discover."[2]

No one knows what starting over means better than a farmer. He knows what it's like each year to begin again. Whenever a farmer wants to plant a new field of crops at the beginning of a brand-new season, there are many things that he knows he must do to guarantee a successful harvest. Jesus uses the art of comparison as He tells the story of the sower (farmer) in Matthew 13. As you read this powerful passage use your spiritual eyes to see how this truth applies to you.

A Farmer's Story

On the same day Jesus went out of the house and sat by the sea. And great multitudes were gathered together to Him, so that He got into a boat and sat; and the whole multitude stood on the shore. Then He spoke many things to them in parables, saying: "Behold, a sower went out to sow. And as he sowed, some seed fell by the wayside; and the birds came and devoured them. Some fell on stony places, where they did not have much earth; and they immediately sprang up because they had no depth of earth. But when the sun was up they were scorched, and because they had no root they withered away. And some fell among thorns, and the thorns sprang up and choked them. But others fell on good ground and yielded a crop: some a hundredfold, some sixty, some thirty. He who has ears to hear, let him hear!" (vv. 1-9 NKJV)

Every human being is born with a heart condition. In Becca's story, she had made the choice to compromise. Although she knew *in her head* the right thing to do, *her heart* had become hardened to the things of God. We all, just like Becca, make the decision to do things our own way, perceiving in our hearts that we know best. But we must always remember Jeremiah 17:9. Read along with me: "The heart is deceitful above all things, and desperately wicked: who can know it?"

This is why Proverbs 4:23 tells us, "Above all else, guard your heart, for it is the wellspring of life" (NIV). Becca had grown up in the things of God, but she had a lot to learn about true life in Christ. Isn't that the case for most of us? If we want to experience life abundantly, we must continually guard (protect, maintain) our hearts by going to the One from whom *real life* flows . . . Jesus. I think farmers have a heads-up when it comes to understanding this process.

I don't know a whole lot about soil, seeds, and farming conditions. What little I do know, I have learned by observing my husband. Charles is not a commercial farmer, but he is a *serious* farmer. He can hardly wait to get his hands in the dirt when the early spring season comes around. For more than three decades I have observed how my husband goes through the annual task of preparing and tending his huge vegetable garden. It's an arduous task, but I will be the first to tell you the rewards are absolutely wonderful.

Long before he plants a single seed in the garden, Charles prepares the soil. By tilling the soil, the ground is loosened and aerated, turning over useless debris such as weeds, rocks, and old vegetation. I have watched my husband go up and down each row of impacted soil, laid bare and hardened by the harsh winds of winter. The tiller turns over the soil, exposing it to fresh air, moisture, and sunshine—the very things it needs to grow and thrive.

The do-over you need in order to change and grow happens the same way. The process of growing up spiritually doesn't just happen routinely or mindlessly. It requires *a decision* on your part. You must decide for yourself that you need to grow and change. No one can make that decision for you. You must determine in your own heart that you want, more than anything, to live a life that is pleasing to God. Along with this, you must make a conscious effort to submit to Him and change.

My sweet friend, if you are standing at a distance from God you must come to the place where what used to sustain you is no longer enough: where you know it cannot carry you through to the new season of life you long for. Decide that you want more and won't be satisfied with less. Remember, you cannot do this on your own. Jesus will help you.

The Parable of the Sower Explained

Later in this parable of the sower, a farmer's story, Jesus shared the rest of what happened to the crowds who gathered, longing to hear what He had to say:

> Hear the parable of the sower: When anyone hears the word of the kingdom, and does not understand it, then the wicked one comes and snatches away what was sown in his heart. This is he who received seed by the wayside. But he who received the seed on stony places, this is he who hears the word and immediately receives it with joy; yet he has no root in himself, but endures only for a while. For when tribulation or persecution arises

because of the word, immediately he stumbles. Now he who received seed among the thorns is he who hears the word, and the cares of this world and the deceitfulness of riches choke the word, and he becomes unfruitful. But he who received seed on the good ground is he who hears the word and understands it, who indeed bears fruit and produces: some a hundredfold, some sixty, some thirty. (Matthew 13:18-23 NKJV)

I love how the word of God is so simple. Jesus breaks it down in terms we can easily understand. *First, He speaks about the person who hears the word of God, but does not ask the Holy Spirit to help him understand it.* So, because of ignorance and a lack of discipline, the wicked one comes along and snatches the word that was sown in that person's heart.

Second, He tells of the person who hears the word, but has a stony heart. When that person hears the word, he gets excited in the moment. But because he is a shallow Christian, he doesn't have much depth in his relationship with God. Then the cares of the world and the issues in his own life *beat him up* and then *beat him down.* He goes to worship service on Sunday, and by the same time the next Sunday morning, he has stumbled—most likely feeling weary and defeated.

Third, there is the one who hears the word, but whose heart is filled with compromise. The word of God is crowded out by paying too much attention to the things of the world, like getting rich, consuming wealth, gaining popularity, and getting ahead. The result of this worldly way of life is fruitlessness.

But the heart God wants us all to possess, the kind of soil we all need to grow and be fruitful for God, is found in Jesus' fourth example. This person represents the heart that possesses good ground. *He hears the word of the Lord and understands it.* He does what it says and produces not only enough fruit to feed himself, but has such an abundance of fruit that he is able to be a blessing: to his family, friends, coworkers, and the world around him.

Do You Want More of God?

If you want to experience more of God's blessing in your life—more of His love, His peace, His grace and favor—then you must decide to do things God's way. Make room in your heart to receive more of Him. You make room for more of Christ by first letting go of more of *you*. By relinquishing your old ideas, habits, and ways of thinking you're making room to live more fully, joyfully, and productively. Ask the Lord to help you guard your heart: to make it "good soil" that readily receives and understands His word and then bears an abundance of fruit for His glory. God will overflow you with the true, abundant life only He can supply.

I know letting go isn't easy, but you can do this with the help of Jesus. Like Becca, the girl in our story at the beginning of this chapter, you may have even tried to reason with yourself by justifying your present situation. Perhaps you have concluded that what you've been holding on to is working, when you know deep down in your heart it's not.

This mind-set is just what your adversary, the devil, wants you to have! The adversary wants you to be satisfied with just enough. The enemy of your soul wants you to be satisfied with *good*, when *the best* is just a step away. Hear me, my friend. You do not have to settle for average when "a more excellent way" is available to you (see 1 Corinthians 12:31). If he can, the enemy will convince you that what you have in your hand is all there is. He will tell you that you have messed up too much in your life and can only expect to live a limited, frustrating, miserable existence.

It is so imperative for you to hear and understand God's word, the Bible. Jesus promises that what He has waiting for you is far better than what you're holding on to right now! Let's read Ephesians 3:20 from *THE MESSAGE*:

> God can do anything, you know—far more than you could ever imagine or guess or request in your wildest dreams! He does it not by pushing us around but by working within us, his Spirit deeply and gently within us.

Just as it is with Charles's garden, so it is within your own heart. God wants you to grow. He desires that you would be mature and complete, "lacking nothing" (James 1:4 NJKV). He wants to give you more of Himself.

The key to growth and maturity is diligence. I call it good, old-fashioned stick-to-it-iveness. One more illustration from Charles will help me explain.

Once, during the gardening season, Charles had a problem with deer. They were having a field day with his field peas. One weekend, while we were on the road doing a concert, the deer came in and nibbled a portion of Charles's tender crop of peas right down to the ground. Charles was disgusted by the damage they had done.

His buddies who are also farmers offered suggestions. "Put a sofa in your pea patch," one of them said. Another neighbor suggested, "Yeah, and go to the barber and get some hair and sprinkle the hair on the sofa. And while you're at it, sprinkle some cologne on that sofa." Still another friend said, "Put a radio in the pea patch and turn it to a hard rock station. The deer don't like the noise. That'll keep them out."

The next weekend, before we left for another concert, Charles did all that his fellow farmers had suggested. When we got home the following Monday, we immediately went to inspect the garden and found that the deer had come in and ravaged the entire pea patch and most of his watermelon crop. I think I saw a tear well up in my sweet husband's eyes. Later that day, I heard Charles on the phone telling one of his friends about the damage the deer had done. He said, "I can see those deer now, having a party in my garden. I'll bet they were sitting on the sofa, smelling good, getting haircuts, and some of them were probably dancing to the hard rock music."

Charles had to laugh to keep from crying. But he got smart. He planted more peas and watermelons. He also put up a tall chain-link fence around the perimeter of his garden. *That kept the deer out once and for all!*

In the same way, you must put a spiritual fence around your heart, guarding it against the intrusion of the enemy. Let's go back to Proverbs 4:23, this time reading from the Amplified

Bible: "Keep and guard your heart with all vigilance and above all that you guard, for out of it flow the springs of life."

You must guard your love walk with Jesus at all costs. It must remain first place in your life. If you open the door to compromise, a toehold becomes a foothold, and then a foothold becomes a stronghold. Don't let your love for God grow cold. You never want to get so used to Jesus that you lose the awe and wonder of knowing Him. On a moment-by-moment basis, keep giving Jesus first place in your life. Make Him top priority, guarding your heart as if your life depended on it *because it does.*

God Has Much More in Store for You

Before we end our time together today, I have to finish Becca's story.

Becca's hunger for more of life ultimately led her to apply to a four-year Christian university in a nearby city. She auditioned for a music scholarship and was awarded enough money to pay for her entire college education. The university's music department gave her a position as a lead singer in a new Christian singing group they launched the fall of that year. She found new friends—other young people who loved God, who would build up, not tear down, her faith walk.

With God's help, Becca turned her life around. A year later she recorded her first Christian music project that included some of her very own original songs. Then the university sent Becca on the road as an ambassador to visit other schools and churches and tell them about the university and her faith in Jesus Christ.

I have to confess right here and now that the young lady's name is not Becca—*it's Babbie*. That's right. That young lady who had compromised her faith was me. But God is loving and gracious! I'm living proof that He uses people with a past.

God knows your story, yet He chooses to use you anyway! God will help you and give you not only a second chance, but a third or fourth, or as many as you need to get it right. My hope is that you have a deep desire to grow: that your heart's passion is being stirred in a greater way than you could ever imagine. Sometimes it takes a new perspective on an old subject—a new way of seeing things—to develop a deeper love and appreciation for what you've already been given. God has much more in store for you as you receive and return His embrace.

Your brand-new start is just a prayer away. Consider this twenty-one-day journey you have embarked upon as a new season in your life. In doing so, you will bear much fruit for the Lord as you return His embrace. Galatians 6:9 says: "Let's not get tired of doing what is good. At just the right time we will reap a harvest of blessing if we don't give up" (NLT).

Learning to live *loved* means embracing another opportunity to start over. At this moment, you are beginning a wonderful new day!

EMBRACE YOUR DAY

As you spend time thinking about our discussion today, thank God for not keeping track of the mistakes you have made in the past. Remember what the Lord says in Jeremiah 31:34b, "I will forgive their iniquity, and I will remember their sin no more." Growth is a process. It happens over time. Down the road a bit, you'll be able to see how God is working in this brand-new chapter of your love walk. It's going to take a little work, but the fruit of your labor will be rich and sweet.

I have been greatly blessed by spending this time with you. I'm singing a song of joy, knowing that you are growing closer to God. I trust there's a song in your heart as well.

Tomorrow we will find that everything about us matters to God. For now, let's take a moment to pause and thank God for His unfailing love:

Dear heavenly Father,

I am so grateful that You are the God of second chances. This new day is a gift from You, and I thank You for another opportunity to walk in your love—another opportunity to please You with my life. I give You permission to break up the fallow ground in my heart, Lord. Forgive me for trying to fix things on my own. I'm appealing to You, gracious Father. I desperately need You now. I always have needed You; I just didn't know much until now. I don't want You to be an outsider or a stranger in my life. Like the great

hymn writer said, *"Take my life and let it be, consecrated, Lord, to Thee."*[3] *I make You first priority in my life. Please take Your rightful place. Once again, Lord, thank You. In Jesus' name,*
Amen.

Think About His Love

Before you run to tend to the business of your day, pause for a few brief moments to ponder the love and forgiveness God has extended to you. Jesus paved the way for you to be forgiven, so avail yourself of it. Think about it like this: Jesus paid a debt He did not owe because you owed a debt you could not pay.

Read About His Love

Second Corinthians 5:17 says, "If any man be in Christ, he is a new creature: old things are passed away; behold, all things are become new." After reading this promise, I encourage you to keep meditating on it today. You might even begin to see the most routine parts of your daily experience in a new light.

Pray About His Love

As you talk to God throughout the day, ask the Lord to replace any stubbornness in you with a tender heart, "good soil" that gives room for His word to take root and grow. Old mind-sets can be one of the biggest roadblocks to the process of starting over. So, ask God to speak to you specifically about any preconceived ideas you may have concerning you and His love for you.

Be About His Love

In the same way God has extended the gift of a second chance to you, extend this same grace to someone today. Freely extend your forgiveness, letting that person know how much he or she means to you.

DAY 3

YOU MATTER TO GOD

There is no such thing in anyone's life as an unimportant day.
—Alexander Woollcott[1]

See then that ye walk circumspectly, not as fools, but as wise.
Redeeming the time, because the days are evil. Wherefore be ye not
unwise, but understanding what the will of the Lord is.
—Ephesians 5:15-17

You are of great significance to God.

You are not an accident or an afterthought. You are not illegitimate, a mistake, a slipup, or an "oops." Your parents may not have been expecting you, but God always has. In His eyes there are no illegitimate births. Everything that God made, He made for a reason *and* said it was "good." This includes you.

God can never, ever, make a mistake. And He will not begin making mistakes with you. It was God's divine plan that you would make your entrance on the planet exactly when you did. Long before your mother ever knew she was going to have a baby, you were fashioned in the heart of God. Jeremiah 1:5a says, "Before I formed you in the womb I knew you, / before you were born I set you apart." (NIV)

Ages before you took your first breath, God knew the time and date of your birth, the shape of your nose, and the texture of your hair. He knew the address of the house where you would grow up and how many years you would live on the earth. Psalm 139:15-16 confirms this truth:

> You saw my bones being formed
>> as I took shape in my mother's body.
> When I was put together there,
>> you saw my body as it was formed.
> All the days planned for me
>> were written in your book
>> before I was one day old. (NCV)

"You mean me?" you might ask with a hint of cynicism. Yes, *you.* Although you may not feel like it or even believe it, the truth is, your life is intentional. You matter to God.

God created you because He loves you, and He wants to express His great love for the world through you. Try to wrap your mind around that truth for a moment. *The God of the universe created you intentionally, with a purpose and destiny in mind, so that He could love you, be loved by you, and express His love through you.*

The power behind your very existence is the dynamic force of God's love. He wants to do extraordinary, unbelievable things both in and through your life. The color of your skin could be brown, white, or yellow; you could be rich or poor. It doesn't matter if you were born in the ghetto, in the suburbs, or in some remote part of the world. It makes no difference whether or not you have a college education. You could be the mom of preschoolers or the CEO of a high-powered corporation. You could work in a factory, wait tables in a restaurant, or be unemployed. You could live in a nice house or even be homeless. Your life is important to God, and your role in this world is significant.

You may never be a household name or have a street sign with your name on it, but your life has meaning and worth. You have a destiny to fulfill. No one could ever take your place.

Everything about you is important to God. He is interested in each intricate detail of your life. If something matters to you, then it matters to God. Your relationships, finances, and job situations are of utmost concern to Him. Your health problems, family concerns, and apprehensions for the future all matter to God. You may feel unimportant or even insignificant. But God says you have *always* been important and significant.

Read the truth of God's word in Ephesians 1:4-5:

> Even before he made the world, God loved us and chose us in Christ to be holy and without fault in his eyes. God decided in advance to adopt us into his own family by bringing us to himself through Jesus Christ. This is what he wanted to do, and it gave him great pleasure. (NLT)

Even before God made the world, He found pleasure in loving and choosing you! Western culture says in order for you to matter in life, you have to be famous—even if it's just for sixty seconds on the Internet. This curious mind-set drives people to stand out and make some noise. It screams to them, "Get noticed! Promote yourself. Get your name out there!" Not so in God's economy. Even people nobody else notices get recognition from God.

God Knows Your Name

As a child I used to love the show *Romper Room*. At the conclusion of each episode, the host would bring out her Magic Mirror. She'd hold that mirror up to the camera as if she could actually see every child who was sitting in front of the television. She would look into the mirror and greet all her friends who were watching in television land. Then she would begin to call them by name. In a very sweet and inviting way she'd say, "I see Lisa, and I see Joey . . . hello, Fran! Happy birthday to you, Susan. Have a great vacation, Laurie."

Every time I'd tune in to that wonderful program, I would make sure I leaned in and got closer to her at the end of the show. I listened very attentively in case that nice lady called my name. But she never did. As a child, I wondered for the longest time why I was never recognized. Didn't she know I was watching her show? Didn't she care that I was a dedicated fan? Wasn't she aware that I had had a birthday too? Why didn't she want to know about my family's vacation?

Then one day I had an epiphany. One day I made a connection. I figured out that sending in a postcard with my name, address, city, and state printed on it would probably increase the chances of getting my name called. But until I figured that out, I yearned just to have that sweet lady call my name. I longed for her to recognize me.

Have you ever felt this way? Have you ever just wanted to be noticed, but instead, you were overlooked? Being ignored and rejected hurts, doesn't it? I know how you feel. Even more than that, Jesus knows how you feel. Isaiah 53:3 says this:

> He was despised and rejected by men;
> a man of sorrows, and acquainted with grief;
> and as one from whom men hide their faces
> he was despised, and we esteemed him not. (RSV)

So, you see, although others may fail to recognize you, God sees you. He takes notice. He lovingly created you with a special purpose in mind and understands there will be times when you go unnoticed. The Lord understands, firsthand, how it feels to be disregarded. And He cares. You matter to God.

Keep reading about another kid who got overlooked—by some, but not by all.

In the book of John we read the story of a great miracle that Jesus performed:

> After these things Jesus went over the sea of Galilee, which is the sea of Tiberias. And a great multitude followed him, because they saw his miracles which he did on them that were diseased. And Jesus went up into a mountain, and there he sat with his disciples. And the passover, a feast of the Jews, was nigh. When Jesus then lifted up his eyes, and saw a great company come unto him, he saith unto Philip, Whence shall we buy bread, that

these may eat? And this he said to prove him: for he himself knew what he would do. Philip answered him, Two hundred pennyworth of bread is not sufficient for them, that every one of them may take a little. One of his disciples, Andrew, Simon Peter's brother, saith unto him, There is a lad here, which hath five barley loaves, and two small fishes: but what are they among so many? And Jesus said, Make the men sit down. Now there was much grass in the place. So the men sat down, in number about five thousand. And Jesus took the loaves; and when he had given thanks, he distributed to the disciples, and the disciples to them that were set down; and likewise of the fishes as much as they would. When they were filled, he said unto his disciples, Gather up the fragments that remain, that nothing be lost. Therefore they gathered them together, and filled twelve baskets with the fragments of the five barley loaves, which remained over and above unto them that had eaten. (6:1-13)

The story of that little lad's meal is a favorite to preachers, songwriters, and storytellers alike. It has become quite famous, in fact. This child's part in the miracle that Jesus performed played a significant role in the Lord's earthly ministry.

Many details are brought to light in this story. We read about the location and how many people were there. We read about the time of year that it was, and in the other Gospel accounts, the time of day that it happened (Matthew 14:15; Mark 6:35; Luke 9:12). But one detail is missing. We don't know the name of the little lad who brought his food—two fish and five loaves—to Jesus. His name is not mentioned anywhere in the Scriptures.

He was just a young boy on his way to who knows where, when he was asked to share everything he had to eat. *We don't know his name, but God does.* This nameless lad handed his fish and bread to Andrew, Simon Peter's brother, that day. And thousands of lives were changed forever. Even today, more than two millennia after the fact, we are still telling the story of this cooperative little boy, and God is still receiving the glory.

Little is much whenever God is involved. And I can just imagine Father God leaning over the balcony of heaven, smiling as only He could when that small, simple meal became a supernatural banquet for a multitude. I can just imagine God turning to His "great cloud of witnesses," saying, "That's my boy." And when Jesus lifted up the loaves and fish to give thanks, knowing how much children delighted Him, I'd like to think He included that young lad in his prayer of thanks.

Somewhere in the annals of time, God has recorded the name of that little fellow, just like He has recorded other people in the Bible who have gone nameless . . . like the woman at the well in Samaria (John 4:7), the woman with the issue of blood (Luke 8:43), and the woman caught in the act of adultery (John 8:4).

People may not always notice you. But *people* often miss seeing the bigger picture. *With God, everyone is important.* Every good deed is significant, and no one goes unnoticed. We are all part of His magnificent, eternal plan that was intricately conceived before the world began.

If there have been times when you responded in faith to God, and it seemed people around you didn't acknowledge or even appreciate it, know that God never takes you for granted. He is pleased when your life demonstrates His love, even when others don't seem to notice.

Just think about it. Here we are in the new millennium still talking about this young nameless boy. I cannot help but believe God wants you to know, even when people fail to recognize you, He's looking your way. And when Father God takes notice of an act of kindness, He always remembers. Each time you follow His lead in faith it is recorded in His heavenly archives. God will make sure you are rewarded for returning His embrace—either in this life or in the life to come.

Even though your boss may not pat you on the back for the good job that you are doing, God applauds you. No one may have noticed that you chose to stand during your bus ride home, so an older lady could take a seat. But God observed how you put the comforts and conveniences of another ahead of your own. Your kids might forget to say thank you for waiting in the long carpool lines, but your Father is pleased with your efforts. Your generosity pleases God and demonstrates His love to those around you.

Living to please God is the primary reason you were born. I really hope you get this. If you can truly understand this powerful principle, you will never again, not even for a moment, wonder whether your life makes a difference.

Take a few seconds to let the weight of this truth sink in. Right now, right where you are at this very moment, consider it deeply. Whether you are sitting in your kitchen, lying in a hospital room, or pacing in a prison cell, it doesn't matter. Why? You matter to God. Everything that pertains to *you*—your thoughts, words, and actions, your joys, challenges, and more—is of great importance to Him.

Your enemy and adversary, the devil, will tell you the complete opposite. He will tell you that you don't matter: that you are damaged goods and that no one loves you, let alone God. This, my friend, is a lie. And telling lies is one of satan's chief evil tactics; in fact, it's the oldest trick in his book.

God Loves You Without Measure

I once had a conversation with a young lady who told me that although she knows God loves her, she still struggles with feelings of insignificance. She shared with me that she was verbally abused growing up. She said, "I still hear those words over and over again in my mind, playing like a tape recorder on repeat":

> *You're hopeless.*
> *You're worthless.*
> *You're helpless.*
> *You're useless.*
> *You're weak and insignificant.*
> *You're damaged goods.*
> *You'll never amount to anything.*

I prayed with this young woman who had been emotionally damaged by careless words. After we prayed, the Lord prompted me to ask her a question. I said, "If you were sitting in your car and a tape was playing something that you just couldn't stand, to the point that you didn't want to hear it any longer, what would you do?" She replied, "I'd take the tape out and put in something else!" Immediately, I affirmed her answer and said, "Absolutely! And that's what you must do in this case. You must press the eject button. Remove the tape. Destroy it, so it can never be heard again. Then you must replace the tape."

Let me pause here to say that if you were ever told cruel and heartless lies like the ones this precious lady described to me, it was wrong. If there are people in your life who either are or have been mean and hard to please, hear me. Do not confuse what they have said about you with what God says about you. And do not confuse how they feel about you with how God sees you:

> *You are loved.*
> *You are treasured.*
> *You are accepted.*
> *You are redeemed.*
> *You are gifted.*
> *You are unequalled.*
> *You are preferred.*
> *You are blessed.*
> *You are favored.*

The only thing that can destroy the lies of satan is the truth of God's word. Rehearse it. Memorize it. Say it aloud. Hide it in your heart. Don't fall prey to the enemy's lies. Believe what God says about you, and you'll flourish in this life. Understanding the love of God is your secret to being more than a conqueror. The greatest weapon against satan's attacks is to be fully and absolutely convinced of God's great love for you.

You matter to God. He looks at you through the eyes of uncon-ditional love.

I'll close our time together with a story about the great hymn writer Sir Isaac Watts. When he was a small child, he was visiting an older Christian woman who asked him to read a framed Bible verse that was hanging on a wall in her home. The text was from Genesis 16:13 as it is found in the King James Version: "Thou God Seest Me."

After young Watts had read it, the dear, saintly woman said,

> When you are older, people will tell you that God is always watching you to see when you do wrong, in order to punish you. I don't want you to think of it that way. I want you to take the text home and remember all your life that God loves you so much He can't take His eyes off you.[2]

It is so important to understand that God sees you through His perfect eyes of love. Though at times He will correct you when and if you veer off track, He does so with loving restoration in mind. God sees you, my friend. He knows your name. I pray you understand, now more than ever, how His love for you is without measure—because you matter to Him more than you know.

EMBRACE YOUR DAY

Has it ever occurred to you that nothing ever occurs to God? Everything He made, including you, He made *on* purpose *for* a purpose. As you go about your day, remember that you exist because God loves you and finds great pleasure and delight in you. Everything about you, and all that concerns you, is important to God.

The first three days of our *Embraced by God* encounter lay the foundation for the rest of the time we'll spend together during our concerts of love. If you can begin to comprehend how much God loves you, then everything else will fall into place. Now, that's something to sing about! Pump up the volume and sing to His glory today!

Tomorrow we'll embrace another fundamental truth concerning you and the God who loves you. So, before we turn the page and move on to our next concert theme, let's thank God for opening our hearts and minds to His deep, sweet, unconditional love. Would you pray with me?

Dear Father God,

Thank You for helping me understand more clearly just how much You love me and that Your love is greater than all my faults. Knowing that I matter to You brings me a great deal of comfort, joy, and security. It boggles my mind to know that no matter how many mistakes I make, if I confess my sins accord-

ing to 1 John 1:9, *You are faithful and just to forgive me and
cleanse me from all unrighteousness. Lord, I want to bring You
glory in all that I say and do today. Help me to remember that
my main goal in life is to be pleasing to You—my audience of
One. In the name of Jesus I pray,
Amen.*

Think About His Love

Keep in mind today that God is concerned about every area
of your life. He is interested in your family, your work, your
marriage, and more: everything that brings you joy, as well
as those things that break your heart. His list concerning
you has no end. Everything that matters to you matters to
God.

Read About His Love

With God's deep love for you in mind, meditate on this passage: "See then that ye walk circumspectly, not as fools, but as
wise, redeeming the time, because the days are evil. Wherefore
be ye not unwise, but understanding what the will of the Lord
is" (Ephesians 5:15-17). As you memorize these words, consider your unique, God-given purpose. Let it lead you into
prayer.

Pray About His Love

It is wonderful to start each day with God, both meditating on His Word and seeking Him in prayer. Yet always remember that you can talk to God anywhere and at any time. You could be in the car during rush hour, at the dentist's office, at work, or at the grocery store after a long, productive day; you can always express your cares and concerns to Him. Wherever you may be at any given moment, you can speak words of love to Father God or sing a song of worship to Him in your heart. By doing so, you will keep your mind on the Lord all through the day. And by doing so, you will stay in step with His purpose, poised to see the bigger picture.

Be About His Love

Practice this one-a-day exercise. Speak *one* kind word or do *one* act of kindness toward the people you come in contact with today. Let them know they matter to you because you see them through the eyes of faith and love.

GOD'S PICTURE OF YOU IS BEAUTIFUL

I placed every star with the sun and the moon
And I painted each sunset with its colorful hue
I created the blue sky and the waves on the seas
But you are My masterpiece[1]
—*Babbie Mason*

When God created the heavens and the earth and everything they encompassed, He proclaimed it was all good—and this includes you. How so? Before you were conceived in your mother's womb, you were in the mind of God. To Him, you will always be beautiful. You are His masterpiece.

There is no television commercial, magazine ad, or human opinion that can change this fact. You don't need anyone's approval or validation. The only thing that matters is what God says about you. If God says you are beautiful, favored, chosen, blessed, and free, then it is so. Now, it's time for *you* to believe it *completely*. From the very beginning you have been a part of God's great big, beautiful love story.

You have a choice to make if you desire to experience the depth of relationship with God that He longs for you to enjoy. You can choose to live according to the world's system. This system demands that you live your life based entirely on your own efforts—striving for perfection that will always be just beyond your reach. Or you can choose to live your life God's way, which is based entirely on receiving the undeserved love and grace of Jesus Christ and embracing the work that He accomplished for you at Calvary.

You could never do enough to earn this kind of love. You couldn't ever be good enough to deserve it. This perfect love has *nothing* to do with you. But it has *everything* to do with Jesus! You can't work for it. You don't deserve it. It is a free gift of God.

Join me for our next orchestral movement in God's amazing symphony of love. Each daily concert experience will only get better, richer, deeper, and more meaningful as we linger in His embrace.

FOR THE NEXT THREE DAYS, THINK ON THIS PROMISE:
*Because God loves me, He wants me to know
that everything He made is beautiful—including me.*

DAY 4

YOU ARE VALIDATED

A baby is born with a need to be loved—and never outgrows it.[1]
—Frank A. Clark

*Jesus answered and said unto her, Whoever drinketh of this water
shall thirst again: But whosoever drinketh of the water that I shall
give him shall never thirst; but the water that I shall give him shall be
in him a well of water springing up into everlasting life.*
—John 4:13-14

God has placed His stamp of approval on your life.

Bear with me as I briefly reflect on something we touched on in Day 3, this time more deeply and from a slightly different perspective—because life is much this way. Let's ponder this together. Have you ever been told things like these:

> *You'll never amount to anything.*
> *You're ugly.*
> *You're a failure.*
> *You're a constant disappointment.*
> *You have absolutely no talent.*

You don't count.

You're not good enough.

These verbal assaults and a host of others cut deep, right to the soul. Maybe one or both of your parents verbally abused you. Perhaps someone you looked up to, someone you really trusted, wounded you with careless words. And if you were told any of these things as a child, no doubt, you remember specific and perhaps countless times and places when those verbal bombs were hurled at you.

Let me ask you a question in review. Who is the originator of these verbal assaults and the relentless, repetitive attacks you might be hearing over and over in your mind? You may say:

> My *dad.*
> My *mother.*
> My *grandparents.*
> My *teacher.*
> A *coach.*
> My *husband.*
> The *bully on the playground.*

No, my friend, these people may be most immediately responsible for insulting you, but they are not the *author* of these destructive words. Satan is the author of every attack, whether it is against your body, your mind, or your spirit. Remember, the devil is your adversary. He will do all he can to keep you from becoming everything God has destined you to be. Listen to what Jesus said in John 8:44 about the devil, our enemy and accuser. He not only lies; he is the originator of lies: "He was a murderer from the beginning, and abode not in the truth, because there is no truth in him. When he speaketh a lie, he speaketh of his own: for he is a liar, and the father of it."

The very first lie the Bible records took place in the Garden of Eden when satan, in the form of a subtle, deceptive serpent, lied to Eve (see Genesis 3:1-5). And he's been lying to us ever since! The only way to cancel the power of a lie is to replace it with the dynamic power of truth. If you have ever believed the lies of the devil, then make up your mind that you will start believing what God says about you, starting right now! Today, we will affirm the truth of God's word concerning you.

As I shared in the overture at the beginning of this book, our world is suffering from a love deficiency. Like the old song says, "Everybody needs love." Each and every soul needs love. We crave it. So many people today sense a void in their hearts, an acute emptiness that can only be satisfied by love.

How many of us have gotten off track, to use the proverbial saying, "looking for love in all the wrong places"? Maybe you have looked to others at times to satisfy that empty feeling. Maybe you have searched for approval from those you thought had "that certain something" you felt you were lacking. Perhaps you have sought affirmation for the duties you perform at work, but time and again, you have been disappointed and disillusioned when you didn't get it.

The culture we live in often tells women: "You must have a husband in order to gain the approval you need." It also says, "You need more money in order to feel more important." Added to this, our modern culture counsels us, "To find the love you need, look within yourself." Countless people have tried each of these things and more, only to come up empty. Some have gone beyond them, making tremendous sacrifices for others, inwardly trying to gain the love they think they need, but sadly, all too often they end up in the same place. Disappointed, disillusioned, and discouraged.

So, where can you find *real love?* Lean in and listen closely. Recall this with me as we continue exploring this eternal truth. Love is not a warm and fuzzy feeling. Love is not an emotional urge or even a deep desire. Love is not feeling good about yourself or someone else. Love is not a sexual drive. Always remember, dear friend, that love is a person. That person is Jesus.

You could look inside yourself all you want, trying to find love, but you will come up empty every time. You could look to others for the affirmation you crave. And on some days you might even get it—but don't be surprised when you don't.

Right now, in the seat where you are sitting, stop and think about the *truth*—not your feelings or the opinions of someone else wrapped in human flesh—but the unchanging, undeniable, absolute truth. *The love you crave and long for is embodied in one person, Jesus Christ.* He is the only one who is both qualified and able to bring real love, meaning, and purpose to your life.

The Woman Who Craved True Love

No one could realize the transforming power of the love of Christ more than the woman at the well. Interestingly, John, the writer of this Gospel account, does not give her name. But as you know, this doesn't take away from her compelling story. We don't need to know this woman's name in order to identify with her circumstances.

With a slew of failed marriages to her credit, this lonely lady had become all too familiar with the pain of emotional drought. Now living with a man who was not her husband, she had paid the high cost of lowering her expectations. Added to this, she was the talk of the town. So, you can imagine how keenly she felt the sting of social isolation. By the world's definition the woman who encountered Jesus at a well outside her town in Samaria was a total loser.

If your story is even remotely like hers, then you need to hear these words well. *In God's eyes there are no losers, and God's opinion of you is the only one that matters.* Let's take a closer look at a day in the life of this woman at the well—a lonely soul who was craving true love—a day that changed her life forever.

She went to draw water from the well at noon, the hottest part of the day. By doing this, she probably thought she wouldn't encounter anyone who knew about the past she kept repeating, the present pain she was enduring, or the future she was dreading. She wouldn't have to overhear the whispers and the gossip. She wouldn't have to endure the judgmental looks and the ridicule.

Truth be told, most, if not all, of the things people were saying about her were accurate. The gossip circulating around town about her was true. No doubt, she carried feelings of guilt in the depths of her soul that were almost more than she could bear. This woman's personal shame cut so deep it might as well have been carved across her forehead. She hadn't intentionally chosen to live this kind of life, giving her heart to man after man who had used her, abused her, and then discarded her like soiled garbage. Nevertheless, this was exactly where she had found herself when she met Jesus.

The sum of every past mistake and every poor choice she had made constantly beat down on her like the heat of the noonday sun. All the guilt and shame she had wrestled with over the years had whittled away her self-worth, until the only thing that remained of it was a small pile of rubble. She had such a thirst to experience real love, joy, and peace. Yet she had concluded that such a wonderful life could never become her reality. Good things just didn't happen for women who had done what she did.

Around noon, she headed for Jacob's well to complete the laborious task of drawing water. While most people were home taking a midday rest from the hot sun, she seized the opportunity to draw water without the scorn and disapproval of her neighbors. A back-breaking task, drawing water from the well was a job for a much younger woman. But she had no one to help her. No friends. No confidants. There was no one to assist with the duty of carrying water back to her house and certainly no one to share the burden of her lonely existence. She had a live-in lover, but surely there was no real satisfaction in that sordid affair.

As she approached the well that day, she met a stranger, a Jew named Jesus, who asked her for a drink of water (John 4:7). It was unheard of that a Jew would ask a Samaritan for anything. Jews did all they could to steer clear of Samaritans, including going the long way around their town to avoid coming in contact with them.

Let's walk through their encounter:

> Jesus answered and said to her, "If you knew the gift of God, and who it is who says to you, 'Give Me a drink,' you would have asked Him, and He would have given you living water." The woman said to Him, "Sir, You have nothing to draw with, and the well is deep. Where then do You get that living water? Are You greater than our father Jacob, who gave us the well, and drank from it himself, as well as his sons and his livestock?" Jesus answered and said to her, "Whoever drinks of this water will thirst again, but whoever drinks of the water that I shall give him will never thirst. But the water that I shall give him will become in him a fountain of water springing up into everlasting life." (John 4:10-14 NKJV)

This statement took her off guard. Could she believe what she had just heard: that there was a way to never thirst again, even for someone like her? With hopeful desperation the woman said to Him:

> "Sir, give me this water, that I may not thirst, nor come here to draw." Jesus said to her, "Go, call your husband, and come here." The woman answered and said, "I have no husband." Jesus said to her, "You have well said, 'I have no husband,' for you have had five husbands, and the one whom you now have

is not your husband; in that you spoke truly." The woman said to Him, "Sir, I perceive that You are a prophet. Our fathers worshiped on this mountain, and you Jews say that Jerusalem is the place where one ought to worship." (vv. 15-20 NKJV)

Jesus went on to tell her that she and her fellow Samaritans didn't comprehend what they worshiped. He continued by saying the time was coming, and in fact was at hand, for true worshipers to worship the Father in spirit and in truth. (See John 4:22-24.) Now, let's continue: "The woman said to Him, 'I know that Messiah is coming' (who is called Christ). 'When He comes, He will tell us all things.' Jesus said to her, 'I who speak to you am He' " (vv. 25-26 NKJV).

Coming face-to-face with Jesus, the Messiah—the One from whom flows true, *living water*—would be the defining moment of her life. Perhaps for the first time, she met a man who wasn't looking for her to meet His temporal needs. She encountered someone who addressed her deepest longings and validated her true worth.

After this encounter with Jesus, this once lonely woman would go home very different than when she came. She would return to her town—filled with people who had witnessed her failings and characterized her as a lost cause—changed, forgiven, clean, and whole.

That day, Jesus went out of His way to help this "thirsty" woman at Jacob's well. And He is still going out of His way today. Jesus' love reaches to the heights and depths of wherever you are in your journey of life. His amazing love is available to you right now.

What do you thirst for today? Do you thirst for peace amidst the greatest trial or challenge of your life? Do you thirst for joy that once overflowed, but now, it seems to have dried up like a parched desert?

How about hope? Do you long to have hope that your circumstances will change and things will get better? Do you hope that you can be forgiven of the mistakes and bad choices you have made? Do you struggle with sins, either past or present, that may haunt you all day and keep you up at night? Do you hope to be set free from these sins once and for all?

How about love? Real love. True love. Love that is deep, sure, pure, and honoring. Do you thirst for love from someone who will build you up and not tear you down? Do you want to experience a love that stays the course—no matter what may come?

Then, my dear sister, I encourage you to have a life-changing encounter with Jesus, the only person who is both qualified and able to address your deepest longings and quench your every "thirst" forever. No one can validate you like Jesus: the One who lived, died, and rose again, so that you could experience living *loved* and share this *real love* with others.

A Woman Who Labors in Love

I had a conversation recently with my sweet friend, Lisa. She is a gifted singer and pianist. Lisa has a deep burden and sensitivity to the needs of hurting women in her neighborhood. She knows all too well that these women, much like the woman at the well, need to have an encounter with Jesus. They need to know that He can and will satisfy their deep hunger and insatiable thirst for true love.

Lisa opens her home to the women in her community on a bi-monthly basis and invites them to brunch. She decorates her home with flowers and candles to make it feel warm and inviting. "It's not about trying to impress people," she says. Lisa makes a point to use real plates, glasses, and cloth napkins, remarking that women sense God's love through her warm hospitality. She asks each invited guest to bring a covered dish to share with the group.

Lisa says she wants her guests to feel loved, pampered, special, and comfortable. After they have eaten their meal, she leads the women in a time of singing and prayer and then shares a simple devotional message. She finds that women are hungry for fellowship and connection and will often open up and share concerning the issues they face.

In this warm and safe environment, Lisa is able to pray with them. Several ladies have received Christ as Savior as a result of these gatherings. Lisa said, "One dear lady, who came as a guest with a friend, sensed the love of Jesus the moment she walked through the front door. Overwhelmed by the love of Christ, she cried the whole time she was here."

So many women are broken inside over marital issues, family crises, financial challenges, and more. Lisa uses her home as a safe haven and a beacon of light in a very dark, troubled world. She describes this effort as her labor of love.

I was humbled to learn that a song I wrote a few years ago, "Each One, Reach One," inspired Lisa to open the doors of her home and her heart:

> . . . *The message is unchanging*
> *Go ye into all the world*

Winning families to Jesus
Far away and door to door
Just like somebody told you
That Jesus loves you so
You must tell someone
Who will tell someone
Until the whole world knows

. . . Each one, can reach one
As we follow after Christ
We all can lead one
We can lead one to the Savior
Then together we can tell the world
That Jesus is the way
If we each one, reach one[2]

Lisa knows all too well that women are starving for validation and approval. She also understands that women often look for approval in the wrong places—like the hurting woman who met Jesus at the well. I agree. Meeting the needs of hurting women is why the Lord has moved strongly upon my heart to share my story and His love at our "Embrace Celebrations for Women," as well as at other conferences and retreats. As I go, I thank God for using people like Lisa who not only tell hurting women about Jesus, but show them as well.

Lisa has a final word of advice for you. If God gives you a burden to help women, then do something about it. Don't be afraid of what Lisa calls the "I can'ts":

I can't because I don't have the money.
I can't because I don't have the right resources.

I can't because I don't have anyone to help me.
I can't because I don't know how or where to start.
I can't because I'm afraid I'll make a mistake.

She continues, "If God gives you a vision and a burden to help hurting women, He will provide the resources. God will help you carry it out. It's kind of like what happened in the movie *Field of Dreams*. If you build it, they will come."

That's what Jesus does. He builds wonderful things, and all are invited to come. He builds new expectations from dashed hopes and broken dreams. He builds a great future for ruined lives and wrecked families. He builds a strong faith for the weak, the wounded, and the outcast. He builds a fire for those who have been tossed out in the cold and a foundation of truth for those who have believed the lies of the enemy. Jesus builds trust for those who have been abused and shelters for those with no place to go. The list goes on and on. Tell me, what has Jesus built in your life?

Jesus—Love Personified—Is Everything You Need

How do you find the love, validation, and acceptance you long for? First, admit that you need these things. Then admit that Jesus is the only One who can provide them.

Of course, this doesn't mean you can't enjoy wonderful relationships with people who love you and share your faith. Quite the contrary. Enjoy your friends, your spouse, and your kids. Love them deeply and completely in Christ. Just don't consider *people* to be your *source* of real love. People cannot give what they do not have. *Come to Jesus for the love you need.* He is your only source of real love. And while you're at it, invite your friends and loved ones to come along with you. Remember, each one can reach one. Jesus has more than enough love to go around. Everyone has a standing invitation to come to Him.

Are you desperate for love? This is what the Lord says to you: "Yes, I have loved you with an everlasting love. Therefore, with loving-kindness have I drawn you and continued My faithfulness to you" (Jeremiah 31:3 AMP).

How about acceptance? This is what Jesus says to you: "He made us accepted in the Beloved" (Ephesians 1:6b NKJV).

Don't think you're beautiful? Think again. If God says you're beautiful, that settles the matter. Psalm 45:11 (NIV) says, "The king is enthralled by your beauty; honor him, for he is your lord."

Need a really good friend? You've found one in Jesus: "There is a friend who sticks closer than a brother" (Proverbs 18:24 NIV).

Hungry for something food can't satisfy? Scoot up to the table. Jesus said, "I am the bread of life. He who comes to me will never go hungry" (John 6:35a NIV).

Got an unquenchable thirst? Bottoms up! There's a lot more where that came from. Jesus said, "He who believes in me will never be thirsty" (John 6:35b NIV).

Been rejected? Not anymore! Our loving Lord also said, "Whoever comes to me I will never drive away" (John 6:37b, NIV).

Think you're too bad to be forgiven? Never in a million, trillion, gazillion years. First John 1:9 says, "If we confess our sins, he is faithful and just and will forgive us our sins and purify us from all unrighteousness" (NIV).

Now, can you relate to the woman at the well in any way? Like her, have you had numerous relationships and found that with each broken promise, a little bit more of your self-worth broke off with it? Jesus can fix whatever is broken in your life. Have you looked for answers in the news, in your horoscope, or in the most recent issue of a women's magazine? Stop looking where there are no eternal answers. *Your answer is Jesus.*

Do you have empty pockets, along with an empty gas tank or cupboard? Jesus will certainly supply your needs, but He won't supply your greed. Do you have an empty life, an empty heart, or an empty nest? If you are *hungry* and *thirsty* for something money can't buy, there's not enough food, drink, drugs, or sex to satisfy those longings.

Regardless of who you are and how far you may have fallen, no matter how dark your nights may be, or how loose your grip may seem to be on experiencing real love and true happiness, just remember: *your deepest longings can only be satisfied as you develop an intimate relationship with Jesus Christ.* I'll say it again. He is everything you need.

So, go ahead . . . go to Jesus. Take a long, cool drink from His fountain of love, for only He can give you living water that quenches your thirst and fully satisfies your soul. Like our dear sister, the woman at the well, you can drink His living water and be certain that you will never, ever thirst again.

EMBRACE YOUR DAY

Today can be the start of an exciting new season in your life, knowing that Christ liberally supplies all that you need and long for. Our variation on the theme of God's great and wonderful love for us today is a life-changing message. Let's tune our hearts to talk to Jesus now, thanking Him for all He is doing in our lives. Until we meet again tomorrow, may the Lord keep you in perfect peace because your mind is stayed on Him. For now, I've chosen the words of the great and classic hymn "Satisfied" to be our devotional prayer for today:

All my lifelong I had panted
For a drop from some clear spring,
That I hoped would quench the burning
Of the thirst I felt within.

Feeding on the husks around me,
Till my strength was almost gone,
Longed my soul for something better,
Only still to hunger on.

Poor I was, and sought for riches,
Something that would satisfy,
But the dust I gathered round me
Only mocked my soul's sad cry.

Well of water, ever springing,
Bread of life so rich and free,
Untold wealth that never faileth,
My Redeemer is to me.

Hallelujah! I have found Him
Whom my soul so long has craved!
Jesus satisfies my longings,
Thro' His blood I now am saved[3]

Amen.

Think About His Love

Today, think about how the power of Jesus' transforming love has validated you and changed your life. Praise God that you don't ever need to search for love in all the wrong places and come up empty again. Having come to Jesus and received *real love*, you have everything you need and more.

Read About His Love

Jesus answered and said unto her, Whoever drinketh of this water shall thirst again: But whosoever drinketh of the water that I shall give him shall never thirst; but the water that I shall give him shall be in him a well of water springing up into everlasting life. (John 4:13-14)

As you read, meditating on and committing this promise to memory, try a slight variation on the exercise you did with John 3:16

in Day 1. Say aloud, "Whoever drinks of **natural water** shall thirst again: But as **I drink** of the water **Jesus gives me, I shall never thirst;** but the water **Jesus gives me** is a well of water springing up into everlasting life." This powerful confession will bring dynamic results.

Pray About His Love

As we walked through the story of the woman at the well from John 4, did you see similarities between her life story and yours? If so, bring each area to the Lord in prayer and drink His "living water." Are there areas of unconfessed sin in your heart, things you know are displeasing to God? Ask Him to forgive you and help you turn each of these areas around for His glory. Are you carrying guilt from past relationships? Talk to God about every broken area, and ask Him to heal your brokenness. Are you suffering from isolation? Tell God why you feel isolated, and ask for His help to restore you, both to Himself and, if it applies, to others. Remember, Jesus is everything you need.

Be About His Love

Do you know anyone who is lonely, broken, or isolated? Perhaps a neighbor down the street needs a friend? Maybe someone who comes to church alone needs a little fellowship? Make it a point to reach out to a thirsty person today. Take a small gift, like a few vegetables from your garden or some home-baked goodies. Make eye contact. Offer a hug. Invite your friend who may need a little godly validation to come with you to a special church or neighborhood event. In Christ, the opportunities are endless for you to express His *real love*.

DAY 5

YOU ARE VINDICATED

Do more than belong: participate. Do more than care: help.
Do more than believe: practice. Do more than be fair: be kind.
Do more than forgive: forget.[1]
—William Arthur Ward

Jesus said unto her, Neither do I condemn thee:
go, and sin no more.
—John 8:11

You are free from all accusation, allegation, guilt, and blame.

I talk about my dear husband, Charles, all the time. When you have been married as long as we have, thirty-two years, it's hard not to. I've already told you about Charles's garden and have begun to express how supportive he is of my music endeavors. As I think of today's discussion I can't help but lean on him again.

Charles has this unique ability to fix things. I'm talking about those everyday items around the house like furniture, bicycles, basic plumbing, cars, toys, and machinery. Once, when a couple of rungs on the front porch's rocking chair worked themselves out of their grooves, I didn't get too concerned. Charles would fix it.

When the kitchen sink's garbage disposal malfunctioned, I didn't worry about it. Charles would have it under control.

I bought an old bicycle from a roadside yard sale not long ago. I had been looking for an antique bike with a little character about it to place on the front porch, so I could put a big, pretty bouquet of flowers in it. I thought it would make a nice accessory and a warm welcome to friends. The bike was hardly off the pickup truck before Charles had his pliers applied to its bolts and screws. Before I could turn around well, he had located the air hose and had the tires perfectly plumped up with air. I had to stop him before he ruined all of the bike's "character" I had just paid good money for.

But, oh, there's definitely a very positive side to Charles's handyman ways. The man is a born recycler. He says that he grew up poor—so poor that he "couldn't pay attention." He was taught as a boy, instead of throwing a broken item away, to find a way to fix it and use it again. Needless to say, Charles has carried that same philosophy into our marriage. Nothing ever gets thrown away, but waits in the garage until the moment it can be reused. The problem with this can be expressed exactly the same way. *Nothing* ever *gets thrown away, but* waits in the garage *until the moment it can be reused!*

If you ever come to our home for a visit, I'll do my best to keep you from entering the garage. If somehow you do end up out there among the tools, spare parts, compressors, and hoses, let me warn you now. You will be taking your safety into your own hands.

There is one special item that has been totally renewed under Charles's care: his prized possession, a 1951 Chevy Deluxe.

Charles bought the car from our friend John. The day Charles pulled the car into our driveway I was convinced that John had gotten the better end of the deal. Hoisted up on the back of a trailer, the old car was nothing more than a big heap of metal ready for the junkyard; it was an eyesore.

Charles couldn't have been more excited. However, I was skeptical, thinking that he had bitten off more than he could chew. I tried to convince him that restoring a car was a huge, expensive undertaking. But Charles was not about to change his mind. He flashed his wide, bright smile, and my hubby's eyes twinkled like a kid on Christmas morning as he watched the old, dilapidated car roll off the trailer and into its resting place at the front of the house.

I stood there in the yard and prayed under my breath, "Lord, the thing I feared has come upon me." Our pretty, brick ranch-style house and beautifully landscaped yard were, in an instant, transformed into the neighborhood junkyard: on display for the entire world to see.

Much to my delight, over time, the car has seen a total transformation. Charles's skillful abilities and careful devotion to this car have brought this once lifeless, colorless heap of metal back to life. The 1951 Chevy Deluxe is now a beautifully restored collector's item. From the inside out, the car is stunning.

With its shiny new paint job, power steering, V-8 engine, shock absorbers, automatic transmission, compact disc player, and air-conditioning, I can't help but have a brand-new appreciation for this car. Lovingly called "The '51," the car is no longer an "it." Rather, it is now referred to as "she." At my husband's skillful hands, *she* has been changed from being an ugly mess into a spectacular masterpiece.

Isn't this the story of redemption? Isn't this the story of anyone and everyone who has encountered the life-changing, skillful, careful touch of Jesus? I can tell you, without a doubt it is! He is a master at fixing ruined lives, repairing busted families, mending broken hearts, and shoring up dashed dreams. Like no one else can do, Jesus takes damaged goods headed for the trash heap and gives them a new lease on life.

The Woman Who Was Caught in the Act

This is precisely the story of the woman we will meet today. It is found in John 8:2-11:

> Early in the morning he came again into the temple, and all the people came unto him; and he sat down, and taught them. And the scribes and Pharisees brought unto him a woman taken in adultery; and when they had set her in the midst, they said unto him, Master, this woman was taken in adultery, in the very act. Now Moses in the law commanded us, that such should be stoned: but what sayest thou? This they said, tempting him, that they might have to accuse him. But Jesus stooped down, and with his finger wrote on the ground, as though he heard them not. So when they continued asking him, he lifted up himself, and said unto them, He that is without sin among you, let him first cast a stone at her. And again he stooped down, and wrote on the ground. And they which heard it, being convicted by their own conscience, went out one by one,

beginning at the eldest, even unto the last: and Jesus was left alone, and the woman standing in the midst. When Jesus had lifted up himself, and saw none but the woman, he said unto her, Woman, where are those thine accusers? hath no man condemned thee? She said, No man, Lord. And Jesus said unto her, Neither do I condemn thee: go, and sin no more.

What a beautiful story of love, genuine care, and concern Jesus exhibited for this woman who had been caught in the very act of adultery. Just think about it. A crowd of people had gathered in the temple courtyard during the early morning hours just after dawn to hear Jesus teach, when the religious leaders of the day dragged her into the courtyard. Use your imagination and place yourself among the crowd. Can you see her now, frightened, embarrassed, shocked, humiliated, and ashamed?

It was bad enough that she had stooped to a new low and gotten herself involved with a man who was not her husband. But to be dragged to the temple of all places, probably with nothing more than a bed sheet wrapped around her, was definitely worse. Where was her husband anyway? Was he out of town on business? Had he already left for work?

Even more questions come to mind. Was she in love with the man she had cheated with? Did she love her husband, whom she had cheated against? Had she been seeing this man over a long period of time, or was it a one-night stand? I don't know. But one thing was certain. She was about to meet someone who cared enough to make sense of all the shadowy questions concerning her life. Now, let's get back to the story.

"We caught her in the act of adultery," they said. "The law of Moses states that she should be stoned!" How is it this group of religious men would just happen to know precisely where to find a couple engaging in an illicit affair at that hour of the morning in the first place? Then, that they would grab *only* her and head straight to the *exact place* where they knew Jesus would be teaching smells of a premeditated plot. Perhaps her partner in the affair was part of the charade? This could explain why he was conveniently absent from the public interrogation.

If you lean in a little closer and observe how those religious leaders approached Jesus, you'll see they were trying to test Him. They wanted to find out if the way He handled that situation might give them a reason to accuse Him. If Jesus agreed to stone her, He would prove to be merciless. If He agreed to let her go free, He would prove to be lawless. The Pharisees thought they had Him. They were more interested in trapping Jesus than they were in trapping her.

Just then Jesus did a strange and wonderful thing. And this is a notice to all of us. *Never put Jesus in a box.* With Jesus, always expect the unexpected. Ignoring them, He bent down and started writing on the ground with His finger. I wonder what He wrote. Maybe He etched out one of the Ten Commandments that had been carved on tablets of stone. Maybe He wrote the name of her male companion, who was conveniently absent from this mock trial.

Because Jesus knows it all, maybe He wrote a long list of sins committed by each of the Pharisees, complete with names, places, and dates. Maybe He wrote the words of John 3:16, and in place of the words *the world*, perhaps He wrote this desperate woman's name. He could have written the words of Jeremiah 31:3: "I have loved you with an everlasting love; / I have drawn you with loving-kindness" (NIV).

When her accusers continued to press Jesus to grant the stoning and give her what she deserved, He stood up from the place where He had been writing and said to them, "He that is without sin among you, let him first cast a stone at her" (John 8:7b).

I can hear the thud of dropping rocks now. These upholders of the law were convicted by their own lawlessness, and they went away one by one, beginning with the oldest to the youngest. Then Jesus was left alone with the accused. When He saw no one but her, He said to her, "Woman, where are those thine accusers? hath no man condemned thee?"

She replied to Him, "No man, Lord."

Then Jesus said some of the most beautiful words ever heard by human ears: "Neither do I condemn thee: go, and sin no more" (vv. 10b-11).

I don't know about you, but to know that Jesus does not condemn me, even though I'm guilty, unlocks the door to freedom and throws away the key. This was definitely a *hallelujah* moment! I can just see relief and joy break out all over that woman's face. Although she was a victim, she was also guilty. There was no getting away from that fact. She knew she had committed a grievous offense. Jesus knew this, as well. But she learned something at that pivotal moment we must also come to understand.

Jesus is never on a search-and-destroy mission as it concerns the Father's most-prized creations. (See John 3:17.) He is much more interested in *saving people from their sins* than *punishing them for their sins.* To be clear, Jesus is always on a seek-to-save mission for lost and hurting souls. (See Luke 19:10.)

Though Jesus didn't condone the adulteress's sin, He didn't condemn her either. He not only impressed this humbled woman to change her lifestyle; He demonstrated that He could change her life from that moment on. Jesus cared enough to give her hope. This is the only way transformation is possible.

While Jesus had cause, by law, to have the woman stoned to death, He never used it against her. He shunned using the law to browbeat her, shame her, or reduce her into submission. Anybody can take a person down by throwing stones. It takes real love to build up and restore. Jesus was the only person who was qualified to throw stones that day, yet He refused to lift a condemning hand against her. He genuinely cared for her soul.

When Jesus stood in the gap for that hurting woman, He demonstrated the difference between what religion does and what relationship is:

Religion condemns. Relationship cleanses.

Religion cares less about people. Relationship always puts people first.

Religion heaps on humiliation. Relationship releases oceans of hope.

Religion sees to it that you get what you deserve. Relationship sees to it that you get what you don't deserve.

Religion heaps on shame, guilt, and accusations. Relationship brings acceptance, pardon, and freedom.

Religion cares about reputation. Relationship cares about reconciliation.

Religion says, "Quit sinning and I'll forgive your sins." Relationship says, "Your sins are forgiven. Go and sin no more."

Hone in and take one last look at the scene . . . see just how much Jesus cares for the hurting and broken. This woman represented a home, a marriage, and a family. Only the Lord knows what led her to consent to sleeping with a man who was not her husband. For whatever reason, Jesus knew that deep down beneath the surface was a woman crying out for love and acceptance. Like so many people, she longed for peace in the middle of one of the greatest trials of her life. Not only did Jesus know this, He did something about it. Jesus cared enough to vindicate her. He affirmed her and set her free.

Another Unexpected Encounter

I must make a confession here that this passage convicts me too. It reminds me of the time I was invited to meet with a group of songwriters in the Atlanta area to tell them about an annual conference for songwriters and singers that Charles and I host called "The Inner Circle." The gentleman heading up their gathering told me they would be meeting the following Monday night at a place called Brookshire's. He said to come on over and tell them about my weekend music conference.

I invited my girlfriend Ruth and her husband, Curtis, to join me. It was not until we pulled up into the parking lot that evening that I found out Brookshire's was not a restaurant, and it was not a hotel meeting room . . . it was Brookshire's Bar! I told you my story in Day 2 about my experiences with bars, so you can imagine I wasn't too keen on going inside. Besides, I was concerned about what people would think if they heard that I had been hanging out at the local bar. I was also concerned about being in a room full of people who would be drinking, (likely) smoking, and using foul language.

But I felt even more concerned about the integrity of my word. I told the man I would be there. I felt obligated to show up. So, we said a quick prayer in the car and went inside Brookshire's Bar.

After settling down at a table, I milled around, introducing myself to the host and the other writers who were there that night. As I met people, I told them about "The Inner Circle" music conference, gave them a flyer with all the information printed on it, and invited them to join me.

There was a nice bluegrass band up on the stage playing some of their original music. A few songs into their set, the bandleader stopped to say a few words. He said, "There's a sweet lady in the house tonight. She's a singer and a songwriter, and I want her to come up and sing a number with us." Then he called *my* name! Hey, at least he could have given me a warning! As I walked toward the stage, I sent up a quick three-word prayer, *Jesus, help me!* and stepped onto the platform.

They didn't have a piano, so I couldn't play a familiar melody. I would have to lean on the band's musical talents to back me up.

As I searched for a song in my mind that I thought they would know, I landed on "Amazing Grace."

I told the guys the key and went for it. The folks in the room joined in. When I was finished and ready to take my seat, someone from the back of the room shouted, "Sing another one!" Searching again for a tune I thought the band would know, I came up with "Just a Closer Walk with Thee." Again, people joined in. When I was finished with that song, someone else shouted, "Sing 'How Great Thou Art'!" We all sang together. Then another person chimed in, "How about 'Shout to the Lord'?" Everyone sang along.

It was obvious that most of the people at Brookshire's Bar were church folks! After singing for about thirty-five minutes, I took my seat again, rejoining my friends at our table.

Throughout the rest of the evening people came over to meet us. A few people told me their stories. One young man said that he had grown up in church, but as he got older, he had walked away from his faith in Christ. My friends and I encouraged him. He said that he was impressed by how we were so comfortable talking about Jesus. A few minutes later, we prayed with that young man as he rededicated his life to the Lord—right there in Brookshire's Bar.

Then a young lady came to our table. She had enjoyed the singing and was curious about why I sang Christian music. A few minutes later, that same young lady prayed to receive Christ. I have to say again, this wonderful event happened inside a bar. Then a few days later I started getting e-mails, asking me when I was coming back to sing at Brookshire's Bar again!

I was stunned at what had happened there. Never in a million years would I have arranged an appearance at a local bar—but Jesus did. We can always find Jesus among the lost, the hurting, the broken, the hopeless, the forgotten, and the wounded. This is the very reason He came to earth in human flesh. People just like you and me are the reason Jesus came.

Trust me; people aren't looking for religion with all its rules and regulations. They are running away from it! Instead, they are looking for an authentic, life-giving relationship with Jesus. And every once in a while, God surprises one of His children by letting us take part in drawing others to Him.

EMBRACE YOUR DAY

I read somewhere that women are so consumed by guilt, almost 90 percent of what we do is driven by it. Perhaps you've made some dreadful mistakes that have caused you pain and then ricocheted and affected those you love. Now you are wracked with guilt. My good friend, author, and speaker Thelma Wells has comforting words for you in her book *God Will Make a Way*. She says,

> Whatever may have happened in your past is over and done with. It's history. You can pack your guilt and shame away in a box, use duct tape around all the edges to seal it tightly, and put it in the trash where it belongs. It doesn't need to haunt you any longer. Why? Because Jesus cares about what happened in your past. And He cares even more about what you're doing today to recover from it.[2]

Thank you, sweet Thelma, for the truth in your words. The word of God says, "As far as the east is from the west, so far hath he removed our transgressions from us" (Psalm 103:12). Praise God! Because Jesus loves you more than you know, you never again have to be consumed or controlled by guilt.

I don't know if your marriage isn't what it could be. Jesus does. Maybe you've been a little too friendly with someone else's husband. Maybe you just thought about it. (And, by the way, before you try to let yourself off the hook, the Bible says that *thinking* about something is the same as *doing* it.) Jesus knows all about your sins, whatever they may be. And He still wants to wipe your slate clean.

Don't worry about disappointing Him. You can't let Jesus down because you can't hold Him up. In your own strength you will never be able to do enough to qualify for His love. It's free . . . yours for the taking through God's amazing grace. Just receive His love today. He cares too much for you to hold you hostage by using the law to condemn you. Let's receive the same invitation for freedom that Jesus extended to the adulteress, believing Him when He says, "Neither do I condemn thee: go, and sin no more" (John 8:11).

No doubt about it, Jesus is your defender. He is ready, willing, and able to vindicate you of any guilt and accusation. Romans 8:1 (NRSV) is a promise you can stand on: "There is therefore now no condemnation for those who are in Christ Jesus." Let's thank Jesus for just how much He really cares for us. Would you pray with me?

Sweet Father,

I am so grateful that Jesus is an advocate who has never lost a case. I am grateful that I can roll my guilt, shame, doubt, and every other dead weight I carry, over on Him, because He cares for me. When I can trust no one else, I can share my deepest secrets with Him, knowing I will not be condemned. I praise Your name, merciful Father, that I can receive Your grace and forgiveness for my sins and move on with my life. Hallelujah! Calvary covers it all. In Jesus' mighty name,
Amen.

Think About His Love

Today I ask you to ponder the power of the cross. Because of the shed blood of Jesus, your sin debt is paid and guilt has been absolved. You are free! Celebrate freedom today. Throughout the day, think about the joyful words of the gifted hymn writer Anne Steele:

> *Jesus demands this heart of mine,*
> *Demands my love, my joy, my care*
> *But, ah, how dead to things divine,*
> *How cold, my best affections are!*
>
> *'Tis sin, alas! with dreadful power,*
> *Divides my Savior from my sight;*
> *O for one happy, shining hour*
> *Of sacred freedom, sweet delight*
>
> *Come, gracious Lord; thy love can raise*
> *My captive powers from sin and death,*
> *And fill my heart and life with praise,*
> *And tune my last expiring breath.*[3]

Read About His Love

"Neither do I condemn thee: go, and sin no more" (John 8:11b). Commit this small, yet incredibly powerful verse to memory. When Jesus spoke these words to the woman who had been caught in the act of adultery, He set her—and countless women who have fallen prey to this subtle trap of the enemy—free for good. But regardless of whether we share her sin or are struggling with another, we must receive *and* embrace this promise, along with the exhortation it gives: receive forgiveness and sin no more. As you meditate on this verse, say, "Jesus does not condemn me: I will go and sin no more."

Pray About His Love

During the course of your day, as often as the Holy Spirit may remind you, thank God for your salvation. He paid a debt He did not owe because you owed a debt you could not pay. Today, don't take the precious gift of eternal life for granted. Once again, I counsel you to use your daily Bible portion as a springboard into prayer. If our wonderful Comforter quickened you about areas of sin in your life as we explored God's love today, bow your heart to the Lord in prayer and bring all your cares to Him according to 1 John 1:9. He cares for you and will take great joy in cleansing you of your sins.

Be About His Love

Who has met Jesus today because you cared? As the Holy Spirit gives you opportunity, share the story of how you came to know Christ with someone today. Don't worry about where you may be; God can use you in your home, in the supermarket, at the office, or someplace you never dreamed that you'd share about His love. Just trust God and step up to the "platform," like I did that night when I least expected it. He'll take care of the rest.

DAY 6

YOU ARE VALUED

Finish each day and be done with it.
You have done what you could.
Some blunders and absurdities no doubt crept in
Forget them as soon as you can.
Tomorrow is a new day, and you shall
begin it well and serenely and with too high a spirit
to be encumbered with your old nonsense.[1]
—*Ralph Waldo Emerson*

I will not leave you comfortless: I will come to you.
—*John 14:18*

Jesus makes your life worth living.

The human body is worth approximately five dollars. It is made up of inexpensive ingredients like water, oxygen, hydrogen, and carbon—but your soul is priceless! Shouldn't we care for our souls just as much as, if not more than, our bodies?

I met a woman who, after years of practicing drug abuse and a careless sex life, was diagnosed with HIV/AIDS. She said something I will long remember: "Identity theft is nothing new. The devil has been trying to steal my identity, kill my dreams and destroy my life for a long time. His only mission is to kill, steal, and destroy, and I almost let him do it. But, praise God, with Jesus it's never too late. Others may count you out, but Jesus didn't just give me back my old life—He gave me a brand-new life. I'm grateful for each and every day that I have been given since my diagnosis. And you know, I can really say that this has worked out for the best because this disease is what drove me to God. That was almost twenty years ago."

This transformed woman knows she should have been dead and gone, and her doctors are amazed how she has defied the odds. "It ain't nothin' but the grace of God that I'm still here," she says. "I'm a walking miracle." She's lost a few friends along the way because of her situation, but she's quick to say, "They weren't my friends to begin with. I've got too much living to do today to be worried about the past. The past is past, and that's where I intend to keep it."

She has discovered, with Christ, her life has real meaning and value.

In Christ, Your Value Is Much Greater than Your Issues

There is another woman in the Bible who had what the King James Version describes as an "issue of blood." When I read her story, I get a glimpse of a desperate, lonely woman who had lost all sense of her self-worth and value. While Jesus was on His way to take care of someone else, we meet the woman with the "issue of blood." Let's read a bit of her story from Luke 8:41-44:

> There came a man named Jairus, and he was a ruler of the synagogue: and he fell down at Jesus' feet, and besought him that he would come into his house: for he had one only daughter, about twelve years of age, and she lay a dying. But as he went the people thronged him. And a woman having an issue of blood twelve years, which had spent all her living upon physicians, neither could be healed of any, came behind him, and touched the border of his garment: and immediately her issue of blood stanched [stopped].

Hopelessly incurable and an outcast in her community, this woman had suffered with this affliction for twelve long years. She had depleted all of her money trying to find a solution for her sickness, and she was no better off twelve years after she began. As a matter of fact, she was worse. She had probably once been a person of financial means, but after twelve years of going from doctor to doctor, trying this potion and that notion, she found herself financially destitute. She was dead broke.

According to Mosaic law, this suffering woman was considered unclean. She was as much of an outcast as any person with leprosy. She likely lived outside the city walls, away from the general population, because she had to avoid coming into contact with other people. Anyone or anything she touched would immediately be considered unclean.

For certain, this meant she had no friends who would drop by for coffee and small talk. It meant no relatives would fill her house with laughter on holidays. She had long forgotten the joy of giving a birthday gift to a friend or loaning a cup of sugar to a neighbor. This woman's debilitating condition meant there was no possibility for her to have an intimate marital relationship. And because of this, there was no possibility she would ever bear children.

Finally, sadly, this certainly meant she could not go to the synagogue to worship God, and she so desperately needed Him. Surely, this weak and traumatized woman led an extremely lonesome, dreadful life.

So, it took a great deal of courage for her to leave home and navigate the streets to find Jesus. They were filled with people who had heard that He was passing through town. Word had spread that Jesus had healed the sick, raised the dead, and cast out evil spirits. While moving carefully among the massive crowd she saw Jesus, the object of her hope. Weak, anemic, and afraid, she dared reach out to touch the tassels on the hem of His garment, perhaps just brushing His cloak as He steered through the crowd.

She knew, technically, this risky move would also make Jesus unclean—but for her this was a now-or-never, do-or-die experience. So, she reached out and touched Him.

Immediately, she knew her body was healed. Feeling the healing virtue flow out of His body, Jesus insisted on knowing who had touched Him. Shaking and afraid, only after He had insisted, she came forward and confessed that she was the one. Admitting to making that desperate move, she told Jesus it was her last-ditch effort to end twelve years of misery.

Now, let's continue reading this story, beginning with verse 47:

> When the woman saw that she was not hid, she came trembling, and falling down before him, she declared unto him before all the people for what cause she had touched him, and how she was healed immediately. And he said unto her, Daughter, be of good comfort: thy faith hath made thee whole; go in peace. (Luke 8:47-48)

I love how Jesus responded to her situation. He did not reprimand her for touching Him or scold her for touching others. He did not embarrass, rebuke, or humiliate her for breaking religious rules or for going against the cultural norms of the day. Instead, with compassion in His voice and love in His eyes, He recognized her and called her *daughter*, a term of deep love and concern. Jesus knew her need all too well, just as surely as He had felt her desperate touch.

No longer was this once-lonely woman a victim *of* her circumstances; she had now become a victor *over* her circumstances. Jesus had made her whole.

In an instant, she was healed of the issue of blood that had plagued her for twelve long years. But she had other issues, as well. Her need for physical healing represented just one of those issues, which is the literal context of this passage. But beyond this, it's easy to conclude that she likely had many issues, all of which had stemmed from years of illness, desperation, and loneliness.

When Jesus recognized her faith, I believe He met all of her needs: physical, spiritual, social, and emotional. Just as Jesus had met her need for physical healing, He fulfilled her emotional need to be acknowledged. I could certainly understand that Jesus healed a void in her heart that had likely stemmed from a lack of love, validation, and human interaction. No doubt, Jesus filled the emptiness she had felt for so long. In its place, I am sure He must have quickened within her a renewed desire for fellowship, friendship, affection, and corporate worship.

I like to think that Jesus healed this brave woman of many issues that day. More than this, I believe He gave her something she desperately needed: something she hadn't had for a very long time . . . dignity.

Jesus is the absolute best at doing what He does: *restoring broken lives*. He masterfully heals wounded hearts, bruised bodies, and troubled minds. He perfectly restores dysfunctional families, broken fellowships, and dashed dreams. As I said at the beginning of this concert theme, Jesus takes damaged goods that are well on their way toward the trash heap and gives them a new lease on life. And now, as we bring this theme to a close, I'm so happy to say this again that I would shout it from the rooftops, God willing!

Jesus understands well how the issues of life can compile and compress, one upon the other, year after year, until it seems there is nothing left to restore. *Do you have issues that have made you retreat from the world?* Did a so-called friend betray you, leaving you unable to trust? Are you housebound because of age or illness? Do you long for friendship, fellowship, and the embrace of a close friend?

Even more important, do you long to experience God's embrace? Do you desire for His healing virtue to flow into your life, immediately healing the pain you've carried for years?

If you are battling against feelings of low self-esteem, you may be tempted to remain distant from God and others. But remember those destructive "arrows" of shame and insecurity come from the accuser, the enemy of your soul . . . the devil. Don't run from Jesus, my dear, sweet friend; *run to Him*. Resist the temptation to keep your issues to yourself. Things will only get worse if they are left untreated. Go to our faithful Counselor and Master Physician. Press through the crowd, beyond your fears, and touch the hem of His garment.

Now, listen to the words of 1 Peter 5:7 with me; listen with all of your heart: "Give all your worries and cares to God, for he cares about you" (NLT).

When You Need Him, He's There . . . No Appointment Required

I know personally that God relentlessly pursues us, making Himself available when life pulls the rug out from under our feet. I remember one of the most challenging times our family ever experienced. My husband, Charles, suffered a stroke from a blocked artery in his right eye on March 10, 2010. After the diagnosis came the grim prognosis that the stroke had damaged Charles's eye, and he would be totally blind in that eye for the rest of his life.

From the emergency room, Charles was admitted into the hospital and taken straight to the intensive care unit, where he spent an entire week recovering. During the day, our friends and family came by to visit and pray. But I refused to leave Charles's bedside. Each night, I catnapped in the chair alongside his bed, where Charles lay connected to wires and IVs.

I will never forget being on "night watch" in the hospital room. It seems that every dire situation has the potential to be magnified at night. As I sat in his room, reality set in and looked bleaker in the dark hours after midnight. Time just seemed to creep by like an older man out for a long walk, dragging his feet. But I can attest to the fact that during those hours I felt God's presence more than at any other time I can remember.

When all our visitors had gone home, my dear husband and I were kept company by Jesus—the Great Physician, the Great Company Keeper, and the Great Night Watchman—who never, ever left us.

Don't get me wrong. It was painful to see my husband lying there, hovering between life and death. During those moments, the long hours when I cried and prayed, prayed and cried, I found the Lord's presence to be the sweetest of all.

Oh, yes! And by the way, I am glad to report that the doctor's prognosis was wrong. Charles's eyesight began to return after twenty-four hours, and he has no side effects from the stroke in any other area of his body!

Like the woman with the issue of blood, Charles and I know that you don't need an appointment to see Jesus. *He is so good!* Sometimes, a tragedy that comes your way makes you realize just how fragile and priceless life, love, and family can be. They are of inestimable value to us and could never be bought or replaced.

God Is a Very Present Help for You

Sweet friend, it's quite possible that you have dealt with feelings of insignificance at one time or another. I know that, more than likely, you have cried many tears during your own long, dark nights. Perhaps you wondered if anyone cared; you might have even pondered if life was worth living. I know you can agree: friends are such a blessing, but they can go with you only so far, especially during times of deep trouble and distress. But praise the Lord, we do not ever have to go the distance alone.

Let Psalm 46:1 encourage you right now, especially if you feel that you are in your darkest hour. This precious promise reminds us: "God is our refuge and strength, a very present help in trouble."

God's grace is strongest when you are weak (2 Corinthians 12:9), and He is no respecter of persons (1 Peter 1:17). What Jesus gladly did for me, and what He did for our sister with many issues, He'll happily do for you.

You should find great comfort in knowing that Jesus understands exactly how you feel. He understands how the world can assault you right down to the core and leave you standing alone, feeling isolated and vulnerable. He knows what concerns you during the day and what keeps you up late at night. *Jesus understands you better than you understand yourself.*

So, if you have been struggling against the odds, coping with painful issues, don't let anything hold you back. Come to Jesus, just like that dear woman in the eighth chapter of the Gospel of

John. Take refuge in Him; He understands your pain. God is a very present help for you.

Hear this wonderful promise from Hebrews 4:15: "For we have not an high priest which cannot be touched with the feeling of our infirmities; but was in all points tempted like as we are, yet without sin." Whenever you feel down and out, busted and disgusted, let the following words bring this promise back to mind: *Jesus is touched by how you feel without being subject to sin, so He can touch you at your most vulnerable point and make you whole again.*

In Christ, You Are Never Alone

Jesus knows how it feels to be unappreciated by those you thought would cheer you on. You see, not only is Jesus the God-Man, the One who put on flesh and came down to earth. He is also the Man-God, the One who is acquainted with our sorrows and carries our grief.

The disciples didn't always fully understand Jesus' teachings. He was constantly standing in opposition to the religious elite. Jesus often found Himself on display when people came to see the miracles He performed instead of hearing His life-changing message. I find great comfort in the fact that Jesus knows how I feel when I'm tired, lonely, and depleted. In recent days I have heard it put like this, "He feels my pain."

Be assured, my friend. When you are hurting, Jesus is brokenhearted too. As a matter of fact, Jesus experienced the ultimate state of being abandoned and betrayed when He was in the

Garden of Gethsemane. On that fateful night when He was arrested and put on trial, just hours before His crucifixion, we find Jesus praying to His Father with great agony. It was one of the lowest moments of His life. Just hours before going to the cross, Jesus, the friend that sticks closer than a brother, found Himself deserted, betrayed, and victimized by those who claimed to love Him. Read with me:

> Then saith he unto them, My soul is exceeding sorrowful, even unto death: tarry ye here, and watch with me. And he went a little farther, and fell on his face, and prayed, saying, O my Father, if it be possible, let this cup pass from me: nevertheless, not as I will, but as thou wilt. (Matthew 26:38-39)

I've met so many of you who shared your hurts with me after concerts, conferences, and retreats. You stood in line, and when it was your turn, you whispered your painful story in my ear.

You told me about your lost job and your wayward teenager.

With tears in your eyes you shared your pain concerning a bad marriage and a bitter divorce.

You wore a cute pink ball cap adorned with Austrian crystals, but under it was a bald head that revealed your relentless fight with cancer.

You let me hug your sweet little baby boy who came a few months too soon.

You shared that you lost your home due to foreclosure.

You rested your head on my shoulder, exhausted from taking care of an elderly mother and two grandchildren who had moved in while their mom was in rehab.

I write songs so that the name of Jesus will be glorified, but He uses you and your circumstances as my inspiration. People say, "Wow, it's like you are telling my story." In a way, my dear friend, I am. I wrote a song recently, and the lyrics read like this:

> *Have you cried a pillow full of tears*
> *Do you pray and then you wonder if God hears*
> *Do you call on friends and loved ones*
> *But find that they're all gone*
> *Well, my friend*
> *You are not alone*
>
> *Do you question if it was God's will*
> *And your heart is in a struggle to be still*
> *Are you weak and heavy-laden*
> *On life's long and dusty road*
> *Well, my friend*
> *You are not alone*
>
> *God is there and nothing is too hard*
> *For His boundless love will meet you where you are*
> *Be of good cheer for He loves you more*
> *Than you could ever know*
> *And my friend*
> *You are not alone[2]*

If you feel that life has cheated you out of a relationship or robbed you of your dignity, you are not alone. Look to Jesus as the answer to your problem. If satan has tried to sell you a bill of goods and, in exchange, has tried to steal your joy, then you are not standing by yourself. *Run, don't walk, to Jesus.* He is your first choice, not your last resort. He is the One who brings real meaning and purpose to your life.

If you are experiencing a time of tremendous difficulties, let this challenging season motivate you to move closer to God. Let your crisis prompt you to spend intimate time with Jesus. Too often, we look to others to find our worth and value when we should be looking to Him. Nothing will build you up on the inside like being in the presence of God.

Some people seek the applause of others. Some are motivated by a big paycheck, while others are excited by first-class perks. Without Christ, all of these things are empty and meaningless. Jesus is the only One we really need to please. Serve Him as if you were onstage and He was your only audience.

Even at times when you don't seem to feel His presence, it's all right. Don't be led by what you feel. Be led by what you know is true. You are deeply loved by Jesus. Your life is worth more to Him than silver or gold. No matter what circumstances life may bring, look to Jesus to complete you and reveal your true identity.

EMBRACE YOUR DAY

I am so glad that we can spend this needed time together, getting to know Jesus on a deeper level. Let me commend you for setting aside a special part of each day to be alone in a quiet place with Jesus. Just as a close friendship or an intimate marriage relationship only grows better with time, getting to know Him takes time, effort, and commitment. Dear friend, as you draw near to Jesus over the coming days you are sure to reap great rewards. I know you will agree with Psalm 16:11: "Thou wilt shew me the path of life: in thy presence is fulness of joy; at thy right hand there are pleasures for evermore."

What we have been able to discover over the last three days moves us just that much closer to understanding how much God loves us. And we have only begun to scratch the surface. We'll continue tomorrow when we bring up the lights on a brand-new concert theme. For now, let's take time to spend a few moments talking to God, okay?

Dear sweet Father,

I am so grateful that You made me a relational person. But above all of my relationships, the one I treasure most is my loving friendship with You. I confess that I tend to forget You are my constant companion, intimate best friend, and closest confidant. I find myself looking to other people to validate me and give me their approval. I confess, I've been wrong for doing that and ask for Your forgiveness. I need only look to You to experience complete joy and peace in my life. Lord, You make life worth living. And during those moments when I am alone, help me to use them to steal away to be quiet: to move more closely to You. Lord, help me understand that I can be alone, but I never have to be lonely. And when I do feel lonesome or in need of company, help me not to feel sorry for myself, but to instead, give You permission to fill my emptiness. Thank You, Lord, for the way You build me up and for loving me the way You do. In the precious name above all names—Jesus.

Amen.

Think About His Love

Jesus makes life worth living. You must never look to others for approval, looking to them to place value on your life. Your worth is established in your relationship to God through His Son, Jesus. His loving presence began to dwell in you the moment you asked Him to come into your heart. He has all the time in the world, and then some, to spend with you. Never forget, you are His masterpiece. As you go about your day, keep these things in mind, and focus on one important truth. *The more time you spend with Jesus, the more you will get out of life.*

Read About His Love

Jesus said, "I will not leave you comfortless: I will come to you" (John 14:18). Meditating on God's word can be likened to a cow chewing on its cud. We take a bite, and then we chew, chew, and chew some more. We should chew on God's word so much that it builds strong muscles in our spirit man: muscles that help keep our soul grounded and balanced as we face the issues of life. Now, consider as you go about your day just how precious this promise is to you. Say it aloud. Personalize it. Chew, chew, chew. As you dine on this truth, you'll reap the beautiful results of committing it to memory, and you can call upon it again and again.

Pray About His Love

How do you call upon the word? Pray, pray, pray . . . whether you do it aloud or in your heart. There's something very powerful about praying the promises of God. Something dynamic happens when you remind God of His promises, personalizing them and calling to Him for help. There's no better prescription for deliverance, healing, and victory, especially when you find yourself in the midst of many pressing issues. Just remember as you pray, your love relationship with Jesus is the centerpiece of your life. Give the Lord His rightful place, and everything will fall into focus. Even when your life gets busy today, steal a few moments to talk with Him.

Be About His Love

Make a date with the Lord today. Sit outside in a park or at another scenic, quiet place. This time, fasting from words, sit completely alone; in solitude and silence, enjoy His presence. Don't speak. Just listen, enjoy, and be renewed in your self.

THEME THREE

GOD'S PRESENCE IN YOU IS PERPETUAL

Who in Heaven will hear
When my circumstances around me are changing
Who on Earth will be near
When my questions need answers and life overwhelms me
You are the One that I come to
The only One that I run to

Because I know that You are God
I know You're on Your throne
I know Your love embraces me
And I am not alone

I know that You are able
To keep what I've committed
Unto You against this day
I know
I know
I know[1]
—Babbie Mason

What do you do when facing a difficult situation? Do you share your concern with a family member? Do you talk to a friend or get information from the Internet? Though at times each of these "earthly" options can aid you in your time of need, the best place to find life's answers is from the pages of God's word. And the only place you can find real love, unexplainable peace, and complete deliverance is in the arms of our loving Lord, Jesus. My dear friend, *He is able.*

During the next three days, we'll continue to explore how Jesus is just as close to you as the mention of His name. Amid the deafening voices of today's culture, you can still hear the voice of God: either as a still, small voice or one that resounds as deeply and widely as the sea.

God is calling to you in an unmistakable way—through both His word and your everyday experiences—*so slow down.* Listen closely, or you might miss a real blessing.

With this in mind, let our next orchestral movement begin. I can just hear the clear, crisp sound of a perfectly tuned piano lifting praises as the Lord enters the room. I can hear violins sounding in, softly and worshipfully adding heavenly accents as He lingers in our midst. Then, as the glory of our loving Father descends upon us, I can sense the moment when every instrument stops, unable to play under the tangible weightiness of His holiness. Oh, yes, this movement in our symphony of love is definitely divine. I can already feel His embrace.

MAKE THIS CONFESSION DURING THE COURSE
OF THE NEXT THREE DAYS:
Because God loves me, He will never leave or abandon me.
He recognizes my voice, ever ready to attend
to my needs as only He can do.

GOD IS NEAR

*Walking with a friend in the dark is better than
walking alone in the light.*[1]
—Helen Keller

*Lo, I am with you alway,
even unto the end of the world.*
—Matthew 28:20

God created you to have sweet fellowship with Him.

At the dawn of time, Father God said of Adam, "It is not good that the man should be alone" (Genesis 2:18). God intended for this first man on earth to enjoy fellowship with Him and with those who would come after him. So, He put Adam to sleep and took Eve out of his side to be his life partner and companion. Then He blessed them together and, at the end of that sixth day of creation, declared that all He had made was "very good" indeed. (See Genesis 1:26-31; 2:18-25.)

There is no question about it. God created us to enjoy good relationships: first with Him and also with others.

Connecting with God and our fellow man builds us up; it has a very positive effect in our daily lives. I don't know about you, but being with others pours life into me and causes me to thrive.

Many people have a hunger for connection. This has made social media the power tools of the twenty-first century. Websites, e-mail, and instant and text messaging have allowed us to communicate with family, friends, and business associates all over the world at the click of a button. On Facebook, for example, more than ten million comments are made every twenty minutes.[2]

Yet and still, I have to admit: I have a lot of "old school" in me. When I want to do a quick song demo, I'll sit down at the piano, grab my trusted cassette recorder, and make a quick replication of my song. Keeping pace with technology is a challenge for me, but I'm doing my best to keep up with millions of people every day who are being connected by telephones and computers.

Without Real Fellowship, We Are Alone

In spite of all this progress, however, statistics show that people have never been lonelier and more isolated. Why? Computers can never take the place of enjoying intimate, one-on-one fellowship with God and our fellow man.

My life is richer because of great relationships. But it seems in my often hurried lifestyle that I seem to have less and less time to invest in them. I'll be the first to admit, when we run ourselves ragged, we sap our physical strength to the degree that it robs us of the joy and meaning Jesus intended for our lives.

You probably know like I do, finding time to develop and deepen relationships simply must be one of our greatest priorities in life.

Running at break-neck speed without slowing down to enjoy the relationships God has given you gives the enemy an opportunity to use your busyness against you. Here's a handy acronym, an old-school tool for your spiritual tool kit. As you go about your day, never get . . .

T oo tired
O verworked
I solated, or
L onely

When we toil, our work is hard and exhausting, and we make slow, difficult progress. I don't want TOIL in my life. Do you? This little acronym is full of meaning. It is a good reminder for all who are tirelessly trying to keep up in this rat race.

Now, I want us to revisit something that is a hidden aspect of this daily reminder: *loneliness*. When we toil, burning the candle at both ends, we aren't nearly as productive, and often we are very lonely indeed.

Have you ever been in that weary, emotional state of mind that is brought on by feeling isolated from others? The sense of separation is very real; it goes all the way to the depths of your being. People who are alone for long periods of time are extremely vulnerable. Void of real fellowship, they tend to relegate themselves to a lonely existence. When troubles come, they stay in a prolonged state of grief, sadness, and isolation. They may even fight emotional or physical illness longer than their more social counterparts, similar to the woman with the issue of blood in Day 6. It's been proved that loneliness can even elevate blood pressure.[3]

In recent years this sense of loneliness and isolation has grown. Most people admit to being lonely at one time or another. Many reveal they have no one with whom they can discuss important or intimate matters. So, more and more people are surfing the Internet these days to satisfy their longing for companionship. What's more, when people are alone and isolated they tend to abuse drugs and alcohol trying to dull the pangs of loneliness.

Being alone and *being lonely* are two distinctly different things. One can certainly be alone without experiencing loneliness. And one can be truly lonely in a crowded room. Have you ever sensed loneliness and desperation so deeply that you felt numb inside? Read the psalmist David's account as he cried out to God for help in Psalm 25:16-18, "Turn thee unto me, and have mercy upon me; for I am desolate and afflicted. The troubles of my heart are enlarged; O bring thou me out of my distresses. Look upon mine affliction and my pain; and forgive all my sins." If you've ever sensed this kind of loneliness, you know all too well these feelings of loss and sadness.

In the Old Testament, the Hebrew word for *desolate* is defined as "grow numb, devastate, be destitute, to lay or lie desolate . . . solitary, to lay waste."[4] If you've ever been lonely, then you know all too well the feeling it brings: a sense that you are alone in the world. There is no deeper hurt than the pain that comes with feeling that you are friendless or that no one cares. *Someone said that loneliness is like a toothache. It's a warning sign that something is wrong.* If left unattended, it usually gets worse.

Lots of people avoid becoming lonely by spending more of their time doing a lot of different things. Busyness is one way many well-meaning people try to take their minds off feeling lonely. They tell themselves if they just don't think about it, their loneliness will disappear. But busyness is only a temporary cure. It's like hoping that a toothache will be fixed by avoiding it. Have you ever had a toothache that went away just because you didn't think about it? Of course, not!

We all know such thinking is futile because a toothache always comes back, and it usually seems to get worse at night when you're lying awake trying to make it go away. Oh, yes. Loneliness is very much like this.

Spending money is another way we try to keep lonely feelings at bay. You know how it goes. You tell yourself that if you treat yourself to something new, then you'll feel better. You justify a trip to the shopping mall, having already determined that spending a little money will make things all right. And as it happens with most quick fixes, you actually do feel better for a while, but inevitably, the pain of loneliness comes back more intense than ever. Depending on how many impulse purchases you've made while shopping, these lonely pangs are now compounded by the pain of debt.

Spending *yourself*, that is, giving your heart away is yet another method we unconsciously use to cope with loneliness. Emotionally, one might determine that a relationship—with anyone who happens to cross one's path—is all that is needed. Often, these associations are short-lived. Many times, they involve developing unhealthy emotional connections that can lead to casual sex outside marriage.

Let me caution you against giving yourself away like this. When you invest your time, energy, and emotional resources in a relationship that doesn't contribute anything of value to your life, it will always bring you down: leaving you not only feeling lonely, but guilty, ashamed, and filled with regret. Think about the woman caught in the act of adultery we considered in Day 5. She is a sad, yet excellent, example of spending oneself unwisely.

God Wants to Have Intimate Fellowship with You

Just as God is the only source of *real love*, He is the *one cure* for the pervasive feeling of loneliness. Whenever you feel empty inside you can have sweet fellowship with Him, for He is "the God of all comfort" (2 Corinthians 1:3). Over and over again throughout the Bible, we find the Lord reaching out to express His love to His people: revealing Himself to them, pursuing them, longing to fellowship with them, and best of all, communicating intimately with them. First Samuel 12:22 tells us: "The LORD will not forsake his people, for his great name's sake: because it hath pleased the LORD to make you his people."

I collect coffee table books. My favorites are those filled with scenes of God's beautiful creation. I adore viewing peaceful landscapes of mountains, gorgeous deserts, and expansive prairies.

And I love pictures of beautiful beaches. I even enjoy gazing at the casual, bubbling stream that runs behind our house.

Every once in a while I go walking along our country road and bring along my digital camera. You see, my desire is to develop that "photographer's eye." I want to be able to recognize, at a moment's glance, the right subject, the perfect angle, and just the right light to capture one-of-a-kind Polaroid moments on film, much the way I capture them in a song.

In kind, I can readily admit that if I allow myself to become too busy, I'll miss some sweet moments with God. When an inspired thought comes along, that idea can just as quickly slip away from me if I don't immediately capture it on paper. Likewise, when I'm in songwriting mode, I've even been known to call the voicemail box on our home phone and sing my song ideas into the recorder. I have learned how to avoid letting inspiration get away from me. In the same way, I don't want to get so busy that I miss a beautiful sunrise or sunset, a dazzling shooting star, or a beautiful, fluttering redbird.

I was pondering thoughts like these once when I was on a cruise ship. So, one afternoon, I jotted some thoughts down in my journal while sitting on the deck with a cup of tea. I'd like to share this entry with you:

I am one of 1,432 passengers aboard the MS Zaandam, a luxury cruise liner in the Holland America fleet of ships. I have taken this cruise to the state of Alaska on a number of occasions, but I never, ever tire of it. I usually travel with my husband or my sweet friend, Ruthie, but I find myself alone on this trip. Yes, I am all alone on this excursion, but there is no way I could ever be lonely. God is making His presence known to me, wooing me, smiling at me around every bend. As our itinerary takes us from Seattle, Washington, up through the Canadian province of British Columbia, I marvel at God's creation here in the vast, beautiful land of the midnight sun.

On this particular balmy afternoon, everywhere I look, I see God on display. Everything in Alaska is big. The water, the sky, the mountains, the fish, the birds, and the animals are all massive in Alaska. And I have often described the state as a place where God is "showing off." As we sail through the crystal waters of the Pacific, I see an endless horizon where dark blue ocean meets light blue sky. The countless waves ripple and sparkle in the sun like diamonds. I am amazed that a ship weighing 61,000 gross tons and stretching 780 feet in length actually stays afloat.

I look among the trees now and spot a brown bear out for an afternoon stroll along the distant shore. The evergreen trees stand tall and stately, like a green blanket, for as far as the eye can see. The grand eagle is as plentiful as sparrows as she soars in and out of tree branches looking for food to feed her young eaglets. The landscape of tall trees eventually turns into snow-capped mountains that stand majestically in the distance, providing a picture-perfect backdrop, complete with a waterfall cascading from the precipice.

Then I see my favorite sight of all in the distance—the Hubbard Glacier. These impressive, mountainous fields of blue compressed ice command attention. I am in awe of them, speechless for many moments. I break my silence as the glaciers calve, break off, and crash into the sea below, creating a rumble that echoes through the valley like thunder. I recall and recite a favorite portion of Scripture from the book of Isaiah 55:12: "For ye shall go out with joy, and be led forth with peace: the mountains and the hills shall break forth before you into singing, and all the trees of the field shall clap their hands." I witness firsthand, God on display, God showing off . . . God, in all of His glory.

When my cowriter friend Donna I. Douglas and I wrote "In All of His Glory," we desired to compose a song that contained the complete message and story of the gospel. Within the standard length of a song we aimed to tell of the birth, life, death, burial, resurrection, and coming again of our Lord, Jesus Christ. This song, to our amazement, has proved to be one that has lasted long past its initial recording. The lyrics are descriptive and inspiring. The melody is memorable and easy to sing. But much more than anything else, the song is timeless, changeless, and compelling because it carries the message of the good news. After all, the gospel message remains the greatest story ever told. Let's share it together:

Awaiting the blessed event,
The whole earth lay in slumber
The heavens unveiled God's plan
With the birth of this wonder
A star would illuminate
What the angels made known
God's love was revealed to us
When a manger became a throne

. . . Very soon He will return again
We will spend eternity with Him
The trumpet sound will blast
As the eastern sky rolls back
And there He'll be, in all of His glory
The presence of God, in all of His glory
Beautifully arrayed in splendor and grace
Clothed in majesty,
There He'll be, in all of His glory . . . [5]

To see God in all of His glory, you don't have to look very far. *Just look around.* Savor the moment the next time you bite into a vine-ripened tomato, a sweet peach, or a slice of cool watermelon—so sweet that the juice runs down your arm. At that moment, remember to thank God, "who richly provides us with everything for our enjoyment" (1 Timothy 6:17 NIV).

Look beyond. Make an effort to rise early and watch the sun come up on a brand-new day and remember Psalm 118:24: "This is the day which the LORD hath made; we will rejoice and be glad in it."

Look upward. Sing a song of praise the next time you pause long enough to catch a glimpse of the Big Dipper or the tail of a shooting star trailing across a navy blue night sky. Then recall Psalm 19:1: "The heavens declare the glory of God."

Look inward and thank God for His Son, Jesus, our hope, for He is "Christ in you, the hope of glory" (Colossians 1:27). Then, *look in the mirror.* For God, in all of His glory, is pleased to dwell in you. Just like Alaska's vast, unforgettable landscape displays how big and beautiful God is—even more, He is pleased to reveal His glory in you.

Pay attention, my dear friend. Don't miss Him. Look for each opportunity to see our heavenly Father in this earthly realm. *God, in all of His glory, longs to show how great He is in you.*

Give Yourself Completely to the God of Glory

You and I were created and called to enjoy God—to know Him and to make Him known. The reason we exist is to bring attention to Him, pointing all people and nations His way. My sweet sister in faith, you were born to fellowship with God, bring Him pleasure with your life, and put His love on display. You must do so to such an extent that others will desire His love. When people see you, they should think of God and be absolutely convinced they cannot live another moment without Him.

It pleases God to call you His own. He desires your intimate companionship and friendship. A lot of people think they are a burden to God. Too many think they bother Him. Some believe that God is easily irritated and short-tempered. On the contrary, the Bible says that God is patient and longsuffering toward those He loves. Let's read 2 Peter 3:9: "The Lord is not slack concerning his promise, as some men count slackness; but is longsuffering to us-ward, not willing that any should perish, but that all should come to repentance."

Once you have trusted the Lord Jesus as your Savior, you never have to be lonely again. His loving presence began to dwell in you the moment you asked Him to come into your heart. Because God loves you, He wants you to return His embrace and accept this gift of friendship. He desires you to reciprocate by coming into intimate fellowship with Him.

You can be assured of this: God's presence will always be with you, even if your closest friends or loved ones abandon you.

I often think of how the Apostle Paul endured prison, how John the Revelator endured being exiled on the island of Patmos, or how Joseph kept his sanity in Pharaoh's prison. How did Jesus endure the Garden of Gethsemane? I believe—though they had been cut off from friends, betrayed, denied, abused, and accused—

each one was fully persuaded he wasn't alone. I am fully persuaded, as well.

Do you know *full well* that Jesus is always with you? Just pause a moment: look *around, beyond, upward, inward,* and finally *in the mirror.* Jesus is oh, so near. Christ, the hope of glory, is in you.

EMBRACE YOUR DAY

This is our hope today, dear one—that you realize wherever you are, God is with you. He's keeping you company, journeying with you, holding you in His loving embrace. You might be in a hospital bed or a nursing home. You might be working the night shift or be high above the clouds in an airplane. Like Paul, John, Joseph, and Jesus, you might even be in jail. You could be taking care of a sick loved one, or you could be enjoying a few quiet moments away from it all.

Wherever the quiet finds you, don't let it startle you. Because wherever you are, God is already there. Remember, when all goes silent in His symphony of love, the awesome weight of His glory is being revealed.

Tomorrow we will turn the spotlight on prayer. But right now, be reminded that God is occupying a seat right next to yours, gently urging you on. Now, let the words of this age-old hymn written by Elizabeth Scott in 1878 guide our hearts in prayer:

> *Serene I laid me down*
> *Beneath his guardian care;*
> *I slept, and I awoke and found*
> *My kind Preserver near*
>
> *Thus, does thine arm support*
> *This weak, defenceless frame:*
> *But whence these favors, Lord, to me*
> *All worthless as I am*

> . . . *My life I would anew*
> *Devote, O Lord, to thee;*
> *And in thy service I would spend*
> *A long eternity*[6]

Sovereign God, Abba Father, we dedicate this prayer to You in the precious name of Jesus,

Amen.

Think About His Love

When Jesus was walking on the earth, He was confined to being one place at a time. But now we have the Holy Spirit, our dear Comforter who is constantly with us. Now, our Lord is everywhere *all the time*. Most important, He lives inside you and me. Recognize God's presence today through the Holy Spirit. Think deeply about His love for you as you take time to look *around, beyond, upward,* and *inward.* When you look in the mirror, reflect on how wonderful it is to belong to Him. Everywhere you go, and with every breath you take, He is there.

Read About His Love

"Lo, I am with you alway, even unto the end of the world" (Matthew 28:20). It shouldn't take long to memorize this verse that says so much in so few words. So, take some time and let it sink deeply into your heart. You know the process. You may even want to insert your name in this eternal promise of our Lord, saying it again and again. Truly, as you read about His love this way, understanding you are never alone, you will see the situations in your life from a completely new perspective.

Pray About His Love

As you pray today, filled with faith and resting in God's presence, ask Him to quicken your ears to hear, your eyes to see, and your heart to understand far beyond your human limitations. Thank Him that He has promised to never, ever leave or forsake you and that you'll never be lonely again. Worship Him, acknowledging that whatever you encounter today, He is already there. Praise Him that you are a loving child in His kingdom and that His perfect will is being done, both in and through your life. Now be silent. Follow the Holy Spirit as He leads you on in prayer.

Be About His Love

Whether or not you are a photographer, take a moment to pay a little closer attention the scenes around you. Do you see a tall building? Are you gazing at sandy beaches? Perhaps you're standing in front of a majestic mountain range? Maybe you're viewing the glorious sight of little ones playing with colorful toys? Appreciate the world around you, my friend. Give the Lord thanks for making such a beautiful world, and most of all, be an active part of keeping it that way.

DAY 8

GOD HEARS

You can do more than pray after you have prayed,
but you cannot do more than pray until you have prayed.[1]
—Adoniram J. Gordon

Call to me and I will answer and reveal to you wondrous
secrets that you haven't known.
—Jeremiah 33:3 CEB

At this very moment, God desires to have an ongoing, loving, and life-giving conversation with you.

Imagine you knew that I had a secret to tell you. What would you do? How would you respond? I hope you would respond the way my grandchildren do when I share sweet secrets with them. I have two very precious, perfect grandchildren. When they visit, any work that I'm doing is quickly set aside. My personal plans are on hold for another day. I know from firsthand experience why these children are called *grand*—because that, my friend, is exactly what they are.

Just get me talking about them. I'll bend your ear so much until you're forced to politely excuse yourself from this grandmother's chokehold of storytelling. Your eyes will need a break after view-ing the endless display of their pictures on my mobile phone. So, before I lose you, let me get back on track.

Once when the grandchildren came for a visit, I caught my five-year-old grandson by the arm as he was galloping across the room on his imaginary horse. When I had his attention I said with excitement, "Hey, Punkin!" (That's the name I've given him. I call his big sister "Precious." She's nine and is as cute as a button.)

Now, bear with me . . . I'm about to digress again! When the grandchildren are at our house, as their Grammy (hey, I don't have one, but I can *be* one, right?), I reserve the right to call them "Punkin," "Precious," and all manner of sweet and syrupy, sugar-coated names. It tickles me as I hear words like "Honey," "Sugar," "Baby Cakes," "Sweetie Pie," "Honey Bun," and "Sugar Puddin" rolling off my tongue each time I see their angelic faces.

Ask any grandmother. When it comes to our grandkids, we just can't help it! I'll give my Precious and Punkin a few more years, though. When they hit their teens they'll probably run for cover when they see me coming. But for now . . . ahhh, I'm joyfully experiencing the bliss and blessings of being Grammy.

Okay, now that I've collected myself again let's get back to the story. After getting my grandson's attention, I scooped him up into my arms and held him close. At Grammy's house, casual hugs are not allowed . . . it's all about that lingering embrace: the kind you can feel all the way down to your bones.

I said to him, "Hey, Punkin, I've got a secret! Want to know what it is?" Wide-eyed and excited, he leaned in and placed his ear to my lips. Then he didn't move a muscle. He held his breath, raised his eyebrows, and waited for the "secret beans" I was about to spill. Ever so slowly, I cupped my hand around my mouth. Then with the kind of love, affection, and ridiculous excitement that only a grandmother could muster, I whispered, "You are my only Punkin! I love you."

In return, in that sweet, innocent manner of a five-year-old, Punkin cupped his small, dimpled hand around his mouth and whispered, for my ears only, "You're my Grammy! I love you too." Then he was off and running to slay giants and play with the puppies.

Okay. You can go ahead and stick a fork in me right now because I am done. This grandmother's heart is tenderized by sweet, unconditional love. It just doesn't get any better than that, my friend. Can I say it again? *It just doesn't get any better than that.*

Slow Down, Lean In . . . God Wants to Tell You His Secrets

Whenever I read God's wonderful promise in Jeremiah 33:3, I get a vision of the sweet moment I shared that day with my grandson. And it fills my heart with love for God. I sense Him calling to me (wooing me, even) to slow down and listen. He catches me in mid-stride while I'm hurriedly on my way to who knows where, and He compels me to stop, draw nearer, lean in closer. My precious Father God compels me to hold still and listen intently to what He has to say.

I hold my breath and, with great anticipation, pay close attention to His words. I surmise that if I, a grandmother, could desire to be so close to and to share anything I have on earth with my grandchildren—then how much more would God want to share the deepest secrets of His heart and the riches of heaven with me? What does Matthew 7:11 say? "If ye then, being evil, know how to give good gifts unto your children, how much more shall your Father which is in heaven give good things to them that ask him?"

As a songwriter, I know that one of the keys to good songwriting is being a good observer. I never know where or how that next song idea is going to reveal itself. The next great song idea, title, first line, or rhyme scheme could be on a billboard alongside the highway or in a magazine ad as I flip through the pages. It could present itself in a phone conversation or during my pastor's sermon. I have to keep my eyes and ears open so I will recognize that key phrase or melody line as it comes through my ear or eye gate, or as it dances through my mind in the form of a melody line.

I have to lean in and pay close attention, or I could miss it.

Oh, I've missed a few, and I was disappointed when I did. But even as I write this page, I won't miss it this time! While reading Matthew 7:11, I can now see how to remember this great promise. Let's see if this resonates with you.

When my kids were small, being a good mother, I would do everything within my power to supply what my children needed. In the neighborhood where we used to live, there were 7-11 convenience stores on just about every corner. They carried everything from bread and milk, to cough syrup and baby diapers, to ice cream. If I needed to dash to the store late at night to get something for one of my children, I could be certain that a 7-11 would be open. I didn't have to think twice about hopping in the car and going there.

How much more then does our Father in heaven bless His children from the storehouse of His abundance? I like that comparison. We can go to God, 24/7, and receive help in our time of need. He is always open when it concerns being there and providing for us.

Paying attention to that simple observation, as prompted by the sweet Holy Spirit, I will remember Matthew 7:11 a whole lot easier now. Pay attention, my friend, and be expectant. God is speaking to you *all the time*. I believe He's even speaking to you now.

A long time ago I heard someone refer to Jeremiah 33:3 as "J – e – r – e – 3 – 3 – 3" . . . *God's telephone number*. That simple analogy has really stuck with me over the years. Why don't you take a few moments and commit it to memory too? Guaranteed, you'll need it sooner than you realize. And guaranteed, you'll get through whenever you call.

God Wants You to Call on His Name

So, today I want us to turn a corner, head up the street, and take a closer look at Jeremiah 33:3. God says, "Call unto me, and I will answer thee, and shew thee great and mighty things, which thou knowest not." Let's see how we can apply this lesson on prayer to our daily lives.

When the Creator of the universe speaks to you through His word and says, "Call unto me . . . ," He's giving you an open invitation to call Him. Just think about it. You have a direct line to talk with the God of the ages! This is simply mind-boggling to me! *But that's what prayer is*—talking to God.

Through the miracle of prayer, you can communicate with God—the King and Master of the universe—who loves you deeply. He's never too busy. You don't need to make an appointment, and you won't find it necessary to go through the receptionist in the front lobby. You won't get a busy signal or get put on hold when you call. You won't get bounced to a voicemail box, and you won't have to wait while someone goes to bring Him to the phone. And you won't get that crazy menu business: "Please press '1' for a company directory; press '2' if you know your party's extension; press '0' for an operator . . ." Honestly, when I hear these recordings, it makes me want to scream with frustration and hang up!

You won't get any of that when you call on His name. The Lord promises in this incredible verse that when you call, *He will answer*. It's very easy to have an intimate conversation with someone who loves you unconditionally, when you know that person is attentive to you, even anticipating your call. *Isn't it wonderful this is God's heart toward us?* Now, let's read Psalm 17:6 (NKJV). It's a great promise too.

> I have called upon You, for You will hear me, O God;
> Incline Your ear to me, and hear my speech.

This psalmist understood what it means to be in the presence of God. *When we are in the "secret place" with Him, our Father hears.* There's no doubt about it. Take a few moments and read Psalm 91. If all the powerful promises this passage contains in the first thirteen verses weren't enough (and they definitely are!), it concludes even better:

> Because he [who dwells in the secret place] has set his love
> upon Me, therefore I will deliver him;
> I will set him on high, because he has known My name.
> He shall call upon Me, and I will answer him;
> I will be with him in trouble;
> I will deliver him and honor him.
> With long life I will satisfy him,
> And show him My salvation. (vv. 14-16 NKJV)

Wow! It just doesn't get any better than that, does it? When God whispers to you, and you cozy up to Him, speaking "sweet somethings" in His ear—His tender mercies begin to overflow in your life. Oh, yes, God definitely hears you when you call on His name.

The Four M's of Prayer

Now, let's take a little time to *lean in* and *look closely* at how prayer works. We'll cover four areas, each beginning with the letter *m*. This should help us to remember them well and call upon them when needed:

The **ministry** of prayer

The **maintenance** of prayer

The **methods** of prayer, and last, but certainly not least . . .

The **miracle** of prayer

The Ministry of Prayer

The great Methodist preacher Edward McKendree Bounds once said, "Prayer breaks all bars, dissolves all chains, opens all prisons and widens all straits by which all saints have been held."[2]

As a gospel singer and a speaker to women, I have the privilege of appearing before all kinds of audiences. Once, I was honored to be a guest at Arrendale State Prison in north Georgia. I am especially aware of and deeply sensitive to the needs of people under these circumstances. The moment we drove onto the prison grounds and I saw the barbed wire fence encircling the entire property, I began to pray.

When we gathered for prayer before the service that night, I asked God for a special grace to minister to the women. I called upon Him to handpick every inmate who would attend the meeting. I asked God to help me encourage hearts. I requested that He extend to me a special measure of grace to minister to the ladies, asking Him to meet the needs of those who would enter the meeting discouraged, depressed, and filled with doubt.

As we continued praying, I asked the Lord to give me a concise message to convey His love and hope for His daughters. Then I asked God to help me give a clear invitation for women to receive Christ.

God always gives us more than we ask. Almost eight hundred inmates attended the concert, as well as guards, the warden, and other guests. On that midsummer Sunday night in Georgia, in a gymnasium with no air-conditioning, the room was jam-packed and charged with anticipation. Inmates and guests were sitting in the bleachers, in the balcony, in chairs, and even on the floor.

As I ministered, I observed the singing was louder among those who were incarcerated; it was more joyful and intense. Their praises were more fervent. And as it usually goes during prison ministry, the entire audience was more attentive. There were more *amens* there than in many churches I've visited outside prison walls.

Maybe this is what Paul meant in Romans 5:20 when he said, "Where sin abounded, grace did much more abound." God's spirit moved powerfully in our hearts that night. When the invitation was given, hands went up all over the room to receive Christ as Savior and Lord. Many inmates, though locked in a cell, are freely experiencing God's love today because of the power of prayer.

Now, the words of E. M. Bounds ring out to me even more clearly than ever: "Prayer breaks all bars, dissolves all chains, opens all prisons and widens all straits. . . ." What a wonderful blessing it is to call unto God! Not only can we receive His love and give Him our love in return; we can cry out to the Lord for others and watch Him move: embracing them with His amazing, unconditional, all-encompassing love.

The Maintenance of Prayer

Just as best friends maintain their relationship by spending time with each other, we maintain intimacy with God through prayer and by reading His word. Here are some basic keys for you to enjoy a vibrant and productive prayer life. They are very simple. You can put them into practice, starting today.

Adoration. Tell God how wonderful He is. Before telling Him all that you need or want, tell God what He means to you. Tell Him how awesome He is. Recognize His lordship over everything, and esteem His greatness. Let Him know how good He has been to you. This is the perfect time to sing your favorite hymn of praise to God. It doesn't matter if you don't think you can sing well. Your praises are beautiful to Him. *As you come into His presence, remember Psalm 66:1-3:*

> Make a joyful noise unto God, all ye lands: Sing forth the honour of his name: make his praise glorious. Say unto God, How terrible art thou in thy works! through the greatness of thy power shall thine enemies submit themselves unto thee.

Confession. Just as keeping your body clean on a daily basis is important, you must routinely practice confessing your sins to the Lord; this is a necessary cleansing exercise for your soul. Just as we saw in both Day 4 and Day 5 of our devotions, nothing can make you feel more alone and isolated from God than unconfessed sin. So, if you fall into sin, run to Jesus with your confession. Your enemy, satan, will tell you to be consumed with guilt and run away from the Lord. But because the price for sin has already been met by Jesus, your sin debt has already been paid! With a grateful heart, you can be quick to run to Him for forgiveness of all your sins. Remember, it's not about what you did. It's about what Jesus did for you. Don't let your feelings get in the way. If you ask for forgiveness, God will hear you. You can be confident that He will grant your request. *Remember Proverbs 28:13 as you go deeper into the presence of the Lord:* "He that covereth his sin shall not prosper: but whoso confesseth and forsaketh them shall have mercy."

Appreciation. When small children forget those key words when their desire is granted or they are given a gift, right on cue, we prompt them, "Say *thank you*." This also applies to the children of God when we present our requests to the Lord. The principle of thanksgiving and appreciation is powerful. Thanksgiving is the access code into God's presence, so never forget to say "Thank You" to Him, especially if you have confessed your sins and received forgiveness and cleansing. Just as you need an access code to open your computer or e-mail files, the secret access code—the password, the way into the secret places of God's heart—is your heart and your words of thanksgiving. *Practicing the principle of Psalm 100:4 will bring you progressively closer to God in prayer:* "Enter into his gates with thanksgiving, and into his courts with praise: be thankful unto him, and bless his name."

Supplication. Tell God what you need. And there's no need for big, multisyllabic, superfluous *hithers* and *thithers*, *Thees* and *Thous* from the King's English: no need for vain repetitions and weighty phrases. Be yourself. Speak just as you would with a kind and trusted friend, whom you know well and respect deeply. Be honest and transparent as you bring your prayer requests to God. Remember, any good parent wants to bless his or her children, and the Father is pleased to give *you* the answers to your simplest request or your deepest need. Just ask. In the name of Jesus, present all your requests and offerings of prayers to God. As you believe, by faith, you will reap many blessings and avoid countless frustrations. *Let Psalm 4:1 be your guide as you submit your requests to the Lord:*

> Answer me when I call, O God of my righteousness!
> You have relieved me in my distress;
> Be gracious to me and hear my prayer. (NASB)

The Methods of Prayer

Now that you know how to come before God in prayer, how will you know His voice when you hear it? Basically, you learn God's voice much the same way you learn to recognize the voices of other significant people in your life. Because you spend endless hours with a parent, a sibling, or a teacher, you'd recognize their voices, even if they were calling you from another room. In the same way, as you spend intimate time with God, the easier it will be to recognize His voice. To help you understand more fully how to recognize the voice of God, consider these suggestions:

First, if you want to know God's voice, read the Bible. Every page from Genesis to Revelation contains God's wisdom: His precepts, counsel, and words that speak to the matters of your life. The more you talk to God and read His word, the more you will also recognize His desire to help you apply His wisdom. The Holy

Spirit has been sent to help you in this process. There are times, for example, when verses will jump off the page as you read them. Other times, you'll hear the Holy Spirit's still, small voice in your heart, bringing a promise to your remembrance. That's why Psalm 119:10-11 says, "With my whole heart have I sought thee: O let me not wander from thy commandments. Thy word have I hid in mine heart, that I might not sin against thee." You learn the *ways of God* and tune your ears to the *voice of God* by reading the word of God.

Second, if you want to know God's voice, look to the life of Jesus. Get to know God's only begotten Son. Learn all you can about the life He lived here on earth. Become intimately acquainted with His teachings *and* His ways. Jesus is the Word of God in flesh. John 1:14 says, "The Word was made flesh, and dwelt among us, (and we beheld his glory, the glory as of the only begotten of the Father,) full of grace and truth." The closer you get to Jesus, the better you hear God's voice.

Third, you will learn to recognize God's voice through your own experiences. During the daily course of natural events, God wants to teach you spiritual principles more than you want to learn them. As you draw near to God and follow the Holy Spirit, He will help you see beyond situations in the natural realm. God wants to relate to you right where you are on a very personal level. As you trust Him, walking in obedience to His word, He will alleviate all your doubts and lead you throughout the day.

I wrote a song with my friend Eddie Carswell called "Trust His Heart." Inspired by the great preacher and author Charles Haddon Spurgeon, we wrote this song quite a few years ago, but the words still ring true: *"When you don't understand, when you don't see His plan, when you can't trace His hand, trust His heart."*[3] This is the essence of walking by faith, my friend. As you follow the Lord, think of Psalm 119:33-34: "Teach me, O LORD, the way of thy statutes; and I shall keep it unto the end. Give me understanding, and I shall keep thy law; yea, I shall observe it with my whole heart." Then remember what Jesus promised in John 16:13a: "When He, the Spirit of truth, has come, He will guide you into all truth" (NKJV).

The Miracle of Prayer

Years ago I learned a very important lesson concerning what a privilege it is to hear God's voice. Let me tell you this great story. I was singing at a music conference, along with some other wonderful Christian artists, including a very talented young singer by the name of Jaci Velasquez. That day in her concert, she presented her beautiful song "When I'm on My Knees."

Just before the event concluded, having made our appearances onstage, Jaci and I slipped out into the huge lobby area to get ahead of the crowd and be at our assigned booths at the end of the program. We wanted to be ready to greet folks who might want to stop and talk to us, take a photo with us, or purchase our music.

Once the session dismissed, an enormous crowd, somewhere around ten thousand people, streamed into the long, wide halls of the arena. Jaci's booth was right next to mine. This is when I witnessed something I will never, ever forget. Masses of people were there that day. Some were in a hurry. Some were milling around and talking. Others were waiting on friends.

Just then, I heard Jaci raise her voice and yell to her father who was way down the corridor, about a hundred feet or so. I didn't see him. I didn't know him that well, plus he was in and among the huge crowd. Jaci called out, "Daddy! Daddy!" At that moment, I saw a man in the crowd stop, turn completely around, and look in the direction of her voice. She waved. He caught her eye and waved back to her, acknowledging that he had seen her. Then he shouted back, "There you are!"

I was stunned at what I had just witnessed. I couldn't believe, from so far way, she could recognize him by just seeing the back of his head. I was even more amazed that he could distinguish her voice above all the noises coming from that huge crowd of thousands. And when she called out to him, I saw a simply beautiful thing. She didn't call him some formal name like "Mr. Velasquez" or "Sir." She called him "Daddy." And when she did, no one, I repeat, *no one* else turned to answer her voice but him.

This is living proof that every good Daddy knows the voice of his child and delights in answering. It is also proof positive that every child can know his or her Daddy's voice, distinguishing it from any other. What a miracle this is! *Do you want to know God like that?* I'll tell you, sweet friend, I sure do!

More than anything, God wants to be with you and help you with your decisions. So take Him up on His invitation to bring all your requests before Him. Tell God the deepest secrets of your heart, and even more than this, take time to listen to Him. This is when He will reveal the deepest secrets of His heart to you. Evangelical Christian missionary Frank Laubach said this: "The trouble with nearly everybody who prays is that he says 'Amen' and runs away before God has a chance to reply. Listening to God is far more important than giving God our ideas."[4]

EMBRACE YOUR DAY

I hope as you read it's really settling in your heart that Jesus is right where you are. He is nearer to you than your next heartbeat. When you call on His name, whether you do it under your breath, by whispering in His ear, or shouting above a crowd, *God is there*. And He hears you more clearly than you'll ever know.

Now, listen closely again as we finish today's devotion because at times incorrect attitudes and intents of the heart can hinder our prayers. Take worry, for example. The Bible tells us not to worry about anything, but instead, to pray about everything. Choosing to worry instead of pray is like starting your car, but leaving it in park and then gunning the accelerator. This, my dear friend, is an exercise in futility and a tremendous waste of time. Much like that parked car, worry makes you expend an enormous amount of energy, all the while getting you nowhere.

A wise friend once told me, "If you worry, don't pray. And if you pray, don't worry." Philippians 4:6-7 puts this into perspective:

> Be anxious for nothing, but in everything by prayer and supplication, with thanksgiving, let your requests be made known to God; and the peace of God, which surpasses all understanding, will guard your hearts and minds through Christ Jesus. (NKJV)

We'll spend one more day talking about the nearness of God. I can't wait to get there, can you? For now, it's time to wrap things up and let you get on with your day. As you can see, not only can I talk and talk about my grandkids—I can go on and on about the goodness of the Lord.

Before you and I head out into this noisy world today, let's acknowledge Him. He's with us right now, you know. He's wherever you are and wherever I am. Though I don't understand how He can be everywhere at once, I'm so glad He is. *Do you sense His loving presence?* Pause with me for a moment, breathe out your cares, and let's talk to the Lord:

Abba, Father, Daddy-God,

You are such an awesome God. I give all the glory to Your matchless name. I am amazed how You can be everywhere at once, hear the prayers of all Your children, and answer each of us according to our own individual needs. No one can do this but You! There have even been times when You answered my prayer before I even knew I needed what You supplied. You are such a wonderful Father. Lord, I won't ever look at a 7-11 store the same way again! Help me to not be anxious, revving up my heart to a hurried fever, spending all my energy, yet getting nowhere. I don't want to lose my peace in the chaos of life. Lord, teach me to rest in the fact that when I call, You will answer—when You want, how You want, and any way You want. Father, I'll be satisfied because I believe You know what's best for this child of Yours. Thank You, sweet Father. There is nobody, I repeat, nobody like You! In the precious name of Your Son, Jesus, I pray,
Amen.

Think About His Love

Today, think about how awesome it is that Father God, the Creator of the universe, gives you an open invitation to call Him. Of the billions of souls living on earth, you have a direct line to talk to the God of the ages! He is never agitated, wrathful, or put off by you in prayer. On the contrary, God welcomes you completely, whether you come to Him with silent cries or shouts of joy. Just think about it. As you approach the Lord like a little child, wide-eyed, just waiting to hear His secrets, He is attentive to your voice. He responds to your needs. Now, that's really something to think about!

Read About His Love

"Call to me and I will answer and reveal to you wondrous secrets that you haven't known" (Jeremiah 33:3 CEB). Receive this promise today as you meditate on and memorize God's word. Better yet, embrace it. Respond to God's voice as He graciously invites you into His secret place. Let it lead you into prayer.

Pray About His Love

Be reminded that prayer is simply talking to God about everything and anything that concerns you. If something matters to you, then it matters to your heavenly Father. Remember the words of A. J. Gordon, the founder of Gordon-Conwell

Theological Seminary in Massachusetts: "You can do more than pray after you have prayed, but you cannot do more than pray until you have prayed."[5] Now, quickly recall "The Four M's of Prayer" we discussed today, giving thanks to God that by His word and spirit He is helping you to hear His voice more clearly.

Be About His Love

Is there something or someone on your heart today? Be about His love by practicing prayer. Present that concern or loved one to the Lord. Throughout the day mention that circumstance or special person by name. *Don't worry about it.* Instead, with thanksgiving, tell God all about it. In return, His peace will sustain you as you await the answer from Him.

DAY 9

GOD CARES

*To anyone in any kind of suffering, Jesus Christ has earned
the right to say, "Come unto Me—bring your pain here to Me.
Together we'll find a way to make use of it.
I am your Redeemer. We will not waste a single tear."*[1]
—Eugenia Price

Cast your cares on the LORD *and he will sustain you;
he will never let the righteous fall.*
—Psalm 55:22 NIV

God is near to you, and He hears you because He loves you
deeply.

The sweet older couple sat across the table from one another,
having just finished their dinner in a local cafeteria-style restaurant. Leaving a tip on the table, they situated themselves to
leave. With doggie bags wrapped and ready to go, the husband
gathered his jacket and ball cap while his dear wife stood to put
on her light, all-weather car coat. She struggled, though,
wrestling with one sleeve. Her husband came around to her side
of the table to assist her. The solution was simple. One of her

sleeves had gotten tangled and turned inside out, making it impossible for her to find the opening. In no time, the older gentlemen had figured out the problem, straightened the twisted fabric, and helped her into her wrap. Then they were happily on their way.

Isn't that an accurate picture of life? You're faced with a problem that twists and gnarls itself into a knot, so complex you hardly know where it begins and ends. Sometimes life's circumstances can turn everything inside out, leaving you holding a knotted mess of unanswered questions, depleted resources, and strained emotions.

You try this option over here. You wait and hope, hope and wait, only to find that it hasn't worked. So, you try that alternative over there, but after months of treatments and procedures, you find all your efforts futile. As much as you may try, the tangled messes of life are relentless and unforgiving.

Not long ago I visited a friend I hadn't seen in a while. She brought me up-to-date on her journey with pancreatic cancer. The treatments her doctor prescribed had worked temporarily, but the cancer was back with a vengeance and for reasons too numerous to name here, surgery wasn't in the picture. The doctor had told her there were no more options. *No more options.*

Some say those words are like a jail sentence, like drawing the "Go to Jail" card while playing Monopoly: "Go directly to jail. Do not pass go." Don't let the jail cell that seems to be erecting itself around you make you lose hope. God holds the key to your deliverance. With Him, there are always options. God shines best when your situation looks bleakest.

God Cares About Your Shattered Hopes

In Judges 13 we read about a woman who couldn't have children. Like other women we have already discussed, she is nameless, but her heartfelt devotion to God reveals her noble character. I love the stories of nameless women in the Bible. Sometimes we get too caught up with people and names. We are too easily impressed with titles and too obsessed with fame in our culture, so people name-drop to make themselves look good in the company of others. Once again, this woman's name is of little importance, but her faith and obedience to God make her stand out.

Wouldn't you rather your name be forgotten, so that only Jesus' name would be remembered? Think about it. If someone forgets your name, but remembers what you did, consider it a great compliment.

We catch a glimpse of her story in Judges 13:2-3:

> There was a certain man of Zorah, of the family of the Danites, whose name was Manoah; and his wife was barren, and bare not. And the angel of the LORD appeared unto the woman, and said unto her, Behold now, thou art barren, and bearest not: but thou shalt conceive, and bear a son.

In those days it was considered a shame for a woman not to bear children for her husband. It's interesting to note that the possibility of infertility back then was always assumed to be the wife's problem, not the husband's. Either way, when it came to barren women in the Bible, the situation usually wasn't some random occurrence. Rather, God's sovereign handprint can always be seen in the picture.

One thing we do see is that barrenness produces desperation. A womb doesn't produce a child. Seeds that were planted in spring for one reason or another don't yield a crop. An investment made, after years of waiting, doesn't generate a dividend. Barrenness can be very disheartening. But in God's due season, He reveals Himself.

One day when Manoah's wife least expected it, the Lord revealed Himself to her through "an angel of God," whom the New King James Version describes as "the Angel of the LORD." Some scholars believe this was Jesus, making an appearance here on earth before His actual birth. This divine visitor revealed to her that she would have a son named Samson, who would be set apart as a Nazarite from the day of his birth until the day he died. Although Samson had his challenges, he is remembered as the strongest man who ever lived and a great leader in the nation of Israel. Let this small part of the story about Samson's mother give you hope and remind you that God cares for you.

Things may look pretty bleak right now. Your options may seem slim to none, and your resources may have dried up. Listen, my good friend, never give up on God or count Him out. God never gives up on you. He cares so much for you that He will provide a haven, a safe place, for you to rest when challenges are wearing you down. The writer of Psalm 61:1-3 prayed:

> Hear my cry, O God; attend unto my prayer. From the end of the earth will I cry unto thee, when my heart is overwhelmed: lead me to the rock that is higher than I. For thou hast been a shelter for me, and a strong tower from the enemy.

God Cares About Your Every Need

It may seem that everything around you is falling apart and that life is tearing at the seams, but hold on. God cares, and He'll make a way where there seems to be no way. At first, the widow of Zarephath didn't know how much God cared for her. But she would soon discover God had already made a way for her and her family in their time of need.

Come with me to 1 Kings 17 as I continue her story. Help would come to her in the form of a stranger, the prophet Elijah, who had been on the run, fleeing the clutches of King Ahab's wife, Jezebel. These two misguided people were ruling Israel in wickedness. At that time, Ahab and Jezebel worshiped false gods and were leading Israel to do the same. Added to this, Jezebel was seeking to rid Israel of every godly prophet, wanting every last one of them dead.

Elijah had just declared there would be neither dew nor rain for three years, and as a result there would be a great famine in the land. This was enough to make any Baal worshiper hot around the collar, since this pagan deity was considered to be the god of the rain.[2]

Elijah had been dwelling by the Brook Cherith, sustained by ravens that brought him fish and bread, morning and evening. He lived by the brook until it dried up. Then God commanded Elijah to go to the city of Zarephath, which was way out of his way *and* in Jezebel's territory (vv. 8-9). After he spent many months by the brook and then trekked many days on foot through the dry desert, I can imagine that as Elijah approached Zarephath, he had visions of a warm and tasty home-cooked meal dancing in his head—but alas, God's provision would come in the form of a malnourished widow making plans to cook her last meal.

This fearful woman was probably just as surprised to meet him as he was to meet her. (Notice her name is also withheld from us. Not a coincidence, right?) Let's look at 1 Kings 17:8-14 and see exactly what happened.

> The word of the LORD came unto him, saying, Arise, get thee to Zarephath, which belongeth to Zidon, and dwell there: behold, I have commanded a widow woman there to sustain thee. So he arose and went to Zarephath. And when he came to the gate of the city, behold, the widow woman was there gathering of sticks: and he called to her, and said, Fetch me, I pray thee, a little water in a vessel, that I may drink. And as she was going to fetch it, he called to her, and said, Bring me, I pray thee, a morsel of bread in thine hand. And she said, As the LORD thy God liveth, I have not a cake, but an handful of meal in a barrel, and a little oil in a cruse: and, behold, I am gathering two sticks, that I may go in and dress it for me and my son, that we may eat it, and die. And Elijah said unto her, Fear not; go and do as thou hast said: but make me thereof a little cake first, and bring it unto me, and after make for thee and for thy son. For thus saith the LORD God of Israel, The barrel of meal shall not waste, neither shall the cruse of oil fail, until the day that the LORD sendeth rain upon the earth.

I admire this widow who encountered a scruffy, tired, thirsty, and hungry stranger at the city gate. Near starvation herself, she had enough compassion on this mysterious stranger to tend to his request. She could have easily left Elijah to fend for himself. She had plenty of reasons to offer any number of excuses, such as:

> *She had a son, another hungry mouth to feed.*
> *She was tired and lacked strength.*
> *Elijah was a man and a foreigner.*
> *She had very few resources.*
> *Water was scarce.*

As this nameless woman provided food and shelter for the prophet, God took notice of her good deeds. For the next three-and-a-half years, He miraculously cared for her and her son, just as the prophet had said (vv. 15-16).

This Gentile widow came to know firsthand that there was one true and living God of Israel, and that He knew and cared for her. Widows were more likely than anyone to run out of food during a time of famine, but the great God we serve uses "the foolish things of the world to confound the wise" (1 Corinthians 1:27): things like commanding flesh-eating ravens to feed a grown man; things such as ordaining a Gentile woman to meet the needs of a Hebrew prophet of God. And just as the Lord had said, this obedient woman's "barrel of meal" did not go empty; neither did her "cruse of oil" fail until the day that the Lord sent rain.

What promises has the Lord given you, my friend? Let me remind you of a few that we have discussed during our time together:

> I will not leave you comfortless. (John 14:18)

My God shall supply all your need according to His riches in glory by Christ Jesus. (Philippians 4:19 NKJV)

The LORD your God is with you,
    he is mighty to save. (Zephaniah 3:17 NIV)

The Lord is faithful, and he will strengthen and protect you from the evil one. (2 Thessalonians 3:3 NIV)

The LORD shall guide thee continually, and satisfy thy soul in drought, and make fat thy bones: and thou shalt be like a watered garden, and like a spring of water, whose waters fail not. (Isaiah 58:11)

Wait and hope for and expect the Lord; be brave and of good courage and let your heart be stout and enduring. Yes, wait for and hope for and expect the Lord. (Psalm 27:14 AMP)

My dear friend, God cares for you. He's near, He hears, and He'll always find a way for you as you respond in faith to His word. I heard one young woman testify to this as she shared her "God story" with me. She told me in her letter that one Friday night she'd had all she could take. Fed up, she had determined to take her life. She loaded her gun, got in her car, and headed for the riverbed just a few miles from her apartment.

On the way, she turned on the radio, hoping to hear some music that would drown out her sorrows. The automatic search button on the radio dial stopped on a station; the reception came in loud and clear. It was a station she didn't normally listen to, but she thought, *What difference does it make?* In a few moments, it would all be over anyway. But the music drew her in and arrested her attention. By the time she reached the riverbank the words to the song were sinking in:

> At times the load is heavy
> At times the road is long
> When circumstances come your way
> And you think you can't go on
> When you're feeling at your weakest
> Jesus will be strong
> He'll provide the answer
> When you've found all hope is gone
> He'll find a way
>
> . . . For I know that if He can paint a sunset
> And put the stars in place
> I know if He can raise up mountains
> And calm the storm-tossed waves
> And if He can conquer death forever
> To open Heaven's gates
> Then I know for you, I know for you
> He'll find a way[3]

The young woman just sat there in her car and listened to the entire song . . . those words were touching places in her soul that hadn't been touched in a very long time. For the first time since she was a child, the young woman stopped running long enough to receive the precious gift of God's care. Instead of taking her life, she rolled down the window and, with all her might, heaved the handgun into the river.

As it turned out, the song this young lady told me about in her letter was on a *live radio program* I was doing *in her city* on *that same evening.* I was a guest singer at the local Christian radio station that night, and these concerts were always broadcast live over the station's network. Isn't that powerful? God cares for us so much more than we know.

That song, "He'll Find a Way," written by my friend Donna I. Douglas, is a standard in my repertoire, and it contains a timeless message. Only God knew at the very moment I was singing on the other side of town, a young lady would be listening to my concert broadcast on the radio. Her life would be touched, and her mind would be changed, convincing her to give God *and* life another go.

When life doesn't seem to make sense to you or even seem to be worth living anymore, don't throw in the towel. Let God have the last word on the matter. Don't let satan trick you into thinking that no one cares. God cares for you, my dear friend. And just as He used Elijah, who went far out of his way to reach the starving widow and her family, He will orchestrate all manners of people, places, things, and circumstances just to get to you.

EMBRACE YOUR DAY

I trust that you now understand a little more clearly: God is not aloof or distant concerning you, but wherever you are, *He is there*. God is not building a case against you. He has not put up his hand against you. On the contrary, God has stretched forth His hand against your enemies for your sake! He is on your side! God cares about everything that concerns you.

This is the final day of this concert theme, "God's Presence in You Is Perpetual." Tomorrow, we'll move on to hear other refrains of this beautiful love symphony titled *Embraced by God*.

But before we come to the end of our devotion today, let me remind you once again that God really cares. He cared about the barren woman with empty arms who became the mother of the world's strongest man. He cared about a widow, who wasn't even a Jew, who was planning the last meal for her family during a long, severe famine. They never missed a meal.

God cares about you, just as much as He cared for them, my dear friend. As you trust God, He will fill your days with promise. He will establish a godly legacy for your loved ones. Our faithful Father can top off your gas tank, your bank account, your cupboards, *and* your broken heart, overflowing you with faith and favor.

Yes, God cares about you. He even cares when you've gotten wrapped up, tied up, and tangled up in the muddled messes of life. He's the only one who is able to rummage through it all and pull out a miracle with your name on it.

Let God fill you with a song of hope today. Humble your heart with me. Let's allow the words of the great hymn writer John Ryland to express the sentiments of our hearts:

O Lord, I would delight in thee,
And on thy care depend;
To thee in ev'ry trouble flee,
My best, my only Friend

When all created streams are dried,
Thy fullness is the same;
May I, with this be satisfied,
And glory in thy Name

No good in creatures can be found,
But may be found in thee;
I must have all things and abound,
While God is God to me

O Lord, I cast my care on thee;
I triumph and adore:
Henceforth my great concern shall be
To love and please thee more

Amen[4]

Think About His Love

God is not against you. He is for you! And if God is *for you*, what force in the heavens, what adversary on earth, and what demon from the depths below could come against you and prevail? Take a few moments to think about how mighty God is . . . *He is invincible!* Yet at the same time, He cares for you so warmly and gently, providing everything you and your loved ones need to joyfully fulfill His plan and purpose. Take some time to think about any barren areas in your life. What could God's purpose be as you trust Him in those areas? Imagine the outcome as you walk hand-in-hand with your invincible God.

Read About His Love

> Cast your cares on the LORD
> and he will sustain you;
> he will never let the righteous fall. (Psalm 55:22 NIV)

As you read this verse, do you believe it? If not, then it's time to go to the Lord in prayer.

Pray About His Love

I want you to participate in the following exercise, okay? Do this now, or wait until later today when you have time to give it your full consideration. Gather two pieces of clean paper. On the first piece, at the top, write this heading: *My Cares.* On this piece of paper, list your cares and concerns. Make the list as long as you deem necessary. After completing your list, set it aside. Now, at the top of the second piece of paper, write this heading: *God*

Cares. Make a list of all the things you wish to leave in the hands of the Lord. Are your two lists identical? It's okay if they aren't.

Now, read aloud your first list labeled *My Cares*. Submit it to God. Then as an act of your faith, discard or even shred it. Now, pick up the second list labeled *God Cares*. Read it aloud, and submit it to the Lord, placing all of your concerns in His hands. Then place the list in a location where you can easily refer to it, such as in your Bible.

Don't be anxious about the things you have listed. Remember, you've prayed about and discarded that first list of "anxious cares" before the Lord. I trust that over time, you will continually see His faithfulness. Finally, ask God to help you always remember He is near you, He hears you, and He definitely cares for you.

Be About His Love

Today, whenever anxious thoughts try to creep into your heart, be diligent. Guard your heart by declaring today's promise as often as you need it. Be about the Father's love throughout the day by casting your cares upon Him.

GOD'S PROVISION FOR YOU IS IMMEASURABLE

Quiet, Lord, my froward heart
Make me teachable and mild;
Upright, simple, free from art,
Make me as a weanèd child;
From distrust and envy free,
Pleased with all that pleases Thee

What Thou shalt to-day provide,
Let me as a child receive;
What to-morrow may betide,
Calmly to thy wisdom leave:
'Tis enough that Thou wilt care;
Why should I the burden bear?

As a little child relies
On a care beyond his own;
Knows he's neither strong nor wise;
Fears to stir a step alone;
Let me thus with Thee abide,
As my Father, Guard, and Guide[1]
—John Newton

One of the most reassuring promises God has ever given is that He would provide for us because He loves us. No one can provide for you like the Lord. He knows exactly *what you need* before you even know you need it. He knows exactly *how to provide for your need* because He owns all heavenly and earthly resources. And only the Lord knows *when you need it most*. I have heard the following saying ever since I was a child. The words still ring true today. "He may not come when you want Him, but He's always right on time!"

In His perfect knowledge, power, and love, God is able to supply all your needs "according to his riches in glory by Christ Jesus" (Philippians 4:19).

There will be times during your journey when you come face-to-face with very real, obvious needs. But when you know beyond the shadow of a doubt that you are loved by God, you learn from experience that worry is a waste of precious time and energy. You need not worry yourself silly, fretting about how He will provide for you. You must have the assurance, no matter what may come, that He always will.

God has already proved that He is a ready, willing, and able provider. You must decide if you will trust in His provision, even when the things you can see, hear, and feel may not appear to line up with His word.

Now, it's time to continue flowing with our Father as He directs this next movement in His symphony of love. Let us follow Him by faith, knowing He has provided every single note that weaves together His beautiful melody. God has carefully composed each element of the score, so we'll know in advance *everything is in place as we experience His embrace*—even when we cannot hear every instrument.

Over the next three days, we'll look at this theme in three different, advantageous scenes. From the first *hallelujah* to the last *amen*, we'll celebrate God as our provider.

NOW THINK ABOUT THIS TRUTH:
*Because God loves me, I have the assurance
that He will provide everything I need.*

DAY 10

THE NAME TO TRUST

Trust Him when dark doubts assail thee
Trust Him when thy strength is small
Trust Him when to simply trust Him
Seems the hardest thing of all
Trust Him, He is ever faithful
Trust Him, for His will is best
Trust Him, for the heart of Jesus
Is the only place of rest
—Anonymous

Trust in the LORD with all thine heart; and lean not
unto thine own understanding. In all thy ways
acknowledge him, and he shall direct thy paths.
—Proverbs 3:5-6

Father God, the Creator of both the heavenly and the earthly realms, wants you to trust Him with all of your being.

It was in early spring, and the warm sunshine in Florida was a welcome change from the rainy weather we had been experiencing in Georgia. I had arrived at the hotel shortly after noon, several hours before my host would pick me up for my sound check and evening concert. So, I decided to take advantage of this rare gift of a little downtime. I stepped out of my hotel room to catch a breath of fresh air.

I'd recently purchased a new book, and I was eager to find a quiet spot near the pool where I could get started. I love starting a new book. The anticipation, the expectation, of what I might learn or experience on this new journey always does my heart good. I headed out of the back of the hotel and down a beautifully landscaped path, lined with exotic ferns, colorful flowers, and tall, stately palm trees.

It didn't take long for the blue skies and the warm sunshine to put a smile on my face, causing me to breathe out all my concerns. I spotted a chaise lounge by the pool, shaded by an umbrella, and decided this would be the perfect spot for my short respite. I had hardly read the book's foreword when my eyes were drawn toward the swimming pool.

I laid my book aside to observe a young family of four enjoying some afternoon recreation at the pool. The dad and his child, a little girl of about preschool age, were already in the water. Mom, who appeared desperate to catch a nap, had stretched out on a chaise lounge and was already leaning back, her eyes closed. She urged a younger toddler, probably no more than two years of age, to join her dad. What happened next would remain fixed in my mind until this very day.

As the little toddler walked toward the pool, Dad waded over a few feet closer to the edge of the pool. He held up his arms, opened them wide, and invited his baby girl—who was standing up on the pool deck—to jump in. She hesitated a moment. Her father's gentle voice called to her again. He stretched out his arms and, once again, encouraged her to jump.

I could see the wheels turning in her little head and empathized with her as she processed the situation. Once again, her dad's reassuring voice called out to her. Then in a flash that little baby girl made up her mind.

Instantly, she ran the few steps to the edge of the pool and took a flying leap right into her daddy's open, welcoming arms. *Of course, Daddy was there to catch her.*

Then both dad and daughter laughed and laughed and laughed some more with great delight. Her delicate voice carried across the water, and with uncontrollable joy this little princess giggled with glee and said, "Again, Daddy! I want to jump in again!"

What I saw that day at the pool was more than a daddy and his daughter having a day of fun. *What I saw was a relationship that had grown to a new and beautiful place because a little girl developed a confident dependency on her father.* It didn't take her long to realize that she could jump into water that was way over her head, again and again, knowing that her father would catch her.

This relationship was not one-sided, by any means. Dad found great happiness in being there with his family, enjoying the kind of relationship that is strengthened through hard trials: the kind of bond that only grows sweeter with time. At that moment, savoring the company of those he loved was all that mattered.

You Can Put Full Confidence in God

We all have the deep need to confide in a friend, to lean on someone completely with no thought of betrayal or duplicity. No one wants to be burdened with worries that defeat our joys, robbing us of our peace and our purpose. However, you probably already know that even the people who are closest to you, who love you and have your best interest at heart, will disappoint you at one time or another.

The Lord Jesus is the only One who is truly worthy of complete trust. He provides full confidence for all of your uncertainties. He is sure, reliable, proved, consistent, and dependable. God watches over us in a very personal way, reassuring us time and again, He is on our side.

You may already know the powerful promise from God's word that we'll focus on today. If you don't, I encourage you to commit it to memory. It is one of the Bible's most classic passages about unwavering trust in God. In light of all that is going on in the world around us, I think this is the perfect time to reflect on this familiar truth from Proverbs 3:5-6. Now, relax and join me as we walk through it together: "Trust in the LORD with all thine heart; and lean not unto thine own understanding. In all thy ways acknowledge him, and he shall direct thy paths."

First of all, this passage teaches us that God's ways are true. I don't want to discourage you from placing your trust in earthly friends. I praise God for a trusted friend or two that I am blessed to have in my life. Oftentimes God uses them to reveal a promise that I haven't yet discovered. Sometimes they remind me of a promise I may have forgotten.

At times, though, I hesitate to burden them with my problems because I know they have their own stuff to deal with. At other times I find it's not convenient. I might be on an airplane or in another time zone. Then times come when I'm pondering something in the middle of the night. And beyond this, now and then I have shared something with my dear friends, knowing they didn't have the power to fix it.

But to trust in the Lord with all your heart means to set all your hopes upon Him: to possess a bold confidence and a sure security in God, fearing nothing. It is having complete and total confidence in the Lord, resting in Him instead of in our own thoughts, the opinions of others, or our circumstances.

It is in the Lord, and in Him alone, that we can fully trust. His ways are tried and true.

To trust Jesus the way the Father desires, it is essential for you to maintain an intimate, ongoing relationship with Him. As we discussed in our devotion on Day 8, you must get to know Him through His word and by spending daily time in prayer. Our twenty-one days together with the Lord will help you get started. It is my prayer that by the time we finish, my friend, Jesus will have become your most trusted confidant.

People don't usually trust strangers or casual acquaintances they don't know very well. And this is wise because trust is never established casually. It is earned over time, by spending countless moments together, sharing one's confidences and concerns. Like that little girl and her daddy, you can enjoy a deep relationship with the Lord by spending time in His presence. So much so that when challenges come, you'll let go of every fear and concern and jump right into His arms.

As you experience God's unfailing presence in your life, you will find that to know Him is to love and trust Him more and more and more.

When you really trust God, you can truly let go of any and all worry and concern. When everyone else drops the ball concerning your situation, the Lord proves He is worthy of your trust. He never changes. His very nature doesn't permit Him to fail. Our heavenly Father is not like shifting shadows, unstable winds, or changing tides. James 1:17 says, "Every good gift and every perfect gift is from above, and cometh down from the Father of lights, with whom there is no variableness, neither shadow of turning."

When I saw that family at the pool that day, I examined why the child could trust her father so completely. I was certain that long before they ever came to the swimming pool, the little girl's father must have demonstrated many times his deep love for her. Even at such a young age, that little one innately knew her daddy would be there for her. She understood her best interest would always be of primary importance to him. That memorable day, I saw a little girl holding fast to that hope as if her very life depended on it.

You can have the same trusting relationship, and much more, with Jesus. You can trust Him completely with all that you are and with everything you possess. As today's devotional passage says, you can trust God with all your heart. You can give yourself to Him fully, freely, and without hesitation.

When you lean on the Lord you don't have to think twice. You never have to wonder if God will be true to His word. After calling a young boy named Jeremiah to become His prophet to Israel and to the nations, Father God made him this promise: "I will hasten my word to perform it" (Jeremiah 1:12b). And He did. As a matter of fact, God is still performing His word today, and He'll keep performing it throughout eternity.

Jesus said, "Heaven and earth shall pass away, but my words shall not pass away" (Matthew 24:35).

You may have plenty of reasons to mistrust people. Some might have even betrayed or misled you. If you have ever shared the deepest secrets of your heart only to have that trust betrayed, it should bring you great comfort to know that God will never betray your trust.

Jesus has a perfect track record. He never misleads, and He never disappoints.

You Can Rely on His Perfect Wisdom

Second, this passage reveals that God's wisdom is perfect. Throughout all time, man has trusted in his own knowledge. He has leaned on his own understanding. He has even prided himself in all the knowledge God has given him or otherwise allowed him to gain. But man doesn't have the capacity to know everything about everything.

God, on the other hand, is all-knowing. He understands everything there is to know about time and space because He created them. He knows about the past, the present, and the future—because He lives in the eternal realm outside the sphere of time and seasons. Our heavenly Father has complete knowledge and understanding about people, as well as powers in the spiritual realm. He created it all. His understanding is perfect.

The Bible calls God omniscient. Simply defined: *He knows everything.* Man could study a subject for years, earn a degree, and even teach it for a period of time; still, his knowledge of that subject matter might be minimal at best. First Corinthians explains that "we know *in part,* and we prophesy *in part.* But when that which is perfect is come, then that which is *in part* shall be done away" (13:9-10, emphasis mine). As long as we are wrapped in human flesh, living in this world, we simply cannot know everything.

That little girl at the pool trusted the wisdom of her father, who she knew loved her without reservation. Innately, she understood he knew everything about her. Daddy knew she was afraid to jump, but he kept calling to her anyway. *Daddy won't let anything hurt me,* she must have reasoned in that young, tender mind. And finally, at the pivotal moment she must have thought: *I'm gonna jump! I'll be safe in Daddy's arms.*

Yes, God knows everything, and He especially knows about you. When God created the heavens and the earth, He said, "Let there be . . . ," and it was so. Then on the sixth day He created the first man: Adam. He didn't just say, "Let us make man in our image . . ." He stooped down, gathered up some dust, and then blew His very nature into him. (See Genesis 1:6-10, 26-27; 2:7).

So you see, innately, in the deepest part of your being, you have the capacity to have deep communion with God. You possess the ability to trust God without hesitation—because part of you comes from the earthly realm, and the other part is divine. God has a vast understanding of every intricate detail of your life. His wisdom concerning you is without limitation and beyond comparison because He made you. He knows you completely: inside and out. He also knows that as you spend time with Him, both in His word and in prayer, you will look at the circumstances of life—even those things that may appear to be harmful to you— and say, "I'm safe in my Father's arms." Proverbs 30:5 says, "Every word of God is pure: he is a shield unto them that put their trust in him."

Because He is all-knowing, God is already aware of any sinful thoughts or attitudes you may want to hide. He knows the earthly part of you that He formed from dust. He knows that your sin will make you want to run away from Him. That's why, when you're looking into the deep abyss of your sins, afraid of drowning because of your own inabilities, He has mercy on you. He keeps calling you to come to Him, again and again, to jump into His open arms.

Hear me now. If your relationship with God is breached for any reason, He didn't cause it. But if your relationship is to be restored, you must respond in faith to Him.

Not only is God all-knowing, He is all-wise. He will never misconstrue the intents of your heart. He is not like people who tend to misunderstand or confuse what you say with what you really mean. There are no secrets within you that can surprise God, causing Him to say, "Wow, I wish you hadn't told me *that*. If I had been aware of *that*, I would have had nothing to do with you!"

Rest assured, my friend. God already knows everything about you. He understands every detail about your strengths and weaknesses; He is intimately acquainted with your hopes, dreams, and desires. After all, He created you and placed them inside you. God already knows the end from the beginning in every area of your life. You can rely on His perfect wisdom. And as His word promises, "He will direct your path."

God's wisdom is inconceivable, unsearchable, and uncontainable. Psalm 111:7-8 says, "The works of his hands are verity and judgment; all of his commandments are sure. They stand fast for ever and ever, and are done in truth and uprightness."

Now, let's take a look at this verse in two other versions of the Bible to get more clarity. The Common English Bible says, "All God's rules are trustworthy." The Amplified Bible says His precepts are "sure (fixed, established, and trustworthy)."

Not so for humanity. Even when our motives and intentions are right, we cannot place our full trust in human flesh: not in other people, not even in ourselves. On our best day, our most profound ideas, agendas, and plans are limited. For example, many entrepreneurs and company CEOs have proved that man's ideas and systems, at one time or another, have failed. Even the most creative and insightful ideas have to go back to the drawing board at times.

It is said that around the year 1896, Henry Ford failed to put a reverse gear in his first automobile. He also failed to put a garage door in the shed where the automobile was built. The result? He had to demolish the shed in order to get the car out.[1]

In 1963, McDonald's produced the Hula burger, created for Catholics who didn't eat meat on Fridays. It featured a sliced ring of pineapple in place of the beef patty. The idea failed miserably, costing the company time, money, and resources.[2]

In recent years financial systems all over the world have failed millions of people, resulting in bank failures, the crashing of the stock market, the collapse of the real estate market, and a crumbling economy. Man's systems will always fail because they are temporal and earthly . . . man-made.

Anything you can see with your natural eyes is temporary. If you can see something, one day it will decay and fade away. Houses, cars, money, clothes, products—none of them will last. Each will ultimately crumble and fall.

God's systems are eternal. Like His word, they will stand forever. Because you can always trust in God's word, you can be stable, trusting His (not man's) economy and knowing His plans (not man's) will stand the test of time.

Think about it. Jesus' model prayer in Matthew 6:9-13 reveals it is God's design for *His will* to be done in earth, just like it is accomplished in heaven. Therefore, it is not His design that you would be broke, sick, depressed, beaten down, or fearful. Those things come from your enemy who wishes to destroy you. Like that trusting little girl, you can look at things—even those that could harm you—and confidently say, "This isn't God's will for my life. I'm going to keep stepping out in His word, trusting Him. God loves me and won't let me go under."

My dear friend, you can rely on God's pure, holy, and powerful word! It will never pass away. He knows everything there is to know about everything. God's wisdom is perfect, and because this is so, you can always trust that *His kingdom* (not the kingdoms of man) will last forever. *His will* (not the plans and purposes of man) will be accomplished in the earth for His glory. Let 2 Corinthians 4:18 encourage you: "We look not at the things which are seen, but at the things which are not seen: for the things which are seen are temporal; but the things which are not seen are eternal."

Your Heavenly Father Simply Cannot Tell a Lie

Finally, Proverbs 3:5-6 affirms that God's word is dependable. His ways are true because His word is truth. God always does *exactly* what He says. God's truth has endured until now and will endure forever. He is the only being who is incapable of lying. Numbers 23:19 tells us: "God is not a man that he should lie; neither the son of man, that he should repent: hath he said, and shall he not do it? or hath he spoken, and shall he not make it good?"

Since God knows everything: past, present, and future, His statements predicting events that are coming in the earth are absolutely true. Through the ages, biblical scholars, historians, and other learned or curious people have examined and proved the validity of the Bible. Its accuracy is stunning. Even ancient artifacts confirm stories the Bible contains. And just take some time, as I shared before, to relish God's wonderful creation. If you look closely enough—at nature, science, business principles, family dynamics, and more—you can see *God's principles* at work.

God's word is truth. Sometimes it serves as a stern warning to us in light of biblical prophecy and coming events. Other passages reveal His divine sovereignty. Yet other precious words in the Bible declare God's justice and holiness. And so much of His perfect, divine counsel is given in His mercy to encourage us. *All in all, God's perfect truth speaks of His infallible, great love for us and teaches us how to live.* Every word of God proves to be true, even though history has proved human wisdom fails time and time again.

Our heavenly Father has never taken back a promise, nor has ever He broken one. It is impossible to think that God could even be tempted to tell a little white lie. Not once has He ever made a mistake: not even an honest mistake. God has no need to stretch the truth and puff Himself up in order to impress others. Nor does He twist or manipulate the truth to put people down because He lacks confidence and self-esteem.

Oh, no! God is perfect in every way. Second Samuel 22:31-32 (NASB) says,

> As for God, His way is blameless;
> The word of the LORD is tested;
> He is a shield to all who take refuge in Him.
> For who is God, besides the LORD?
> And who is a rock, besides our God?

It's amazing how much this passage sounds like Proverbs 30:5 that I mentioned to you earlier today. Because, my friend, God's word is true. The more closely you look at His word, the more everything ties together and makes sense. The Bible confirms itself. Even everything in your life confirms what is written in the Bible. And, yes, all of history proclaims the His word is true.

Knowing this, we should acknowledge God in all our plans and decision making. We should consult Him on everything: from the smallest, most insignificant things to the most vital matters. Because with God on our side, our every word and deed can stand on solid ground if we trust and acknowledge Him in all our ways.

Sweet friend, as you worship God, acknowledging Him in all your ways, He will direct your path. As you trust in His name, God will help you to make the best decisions in every area of your life.

And unlike some "intellectual" people who tend to look down their noses at others who aren't "on their level," God will never do that to you. *He is for you,* not against you. Like that loving dad with his daughter at the pool, your heavenly Father is well aware of your limitations, yet He gently urges you to step out and strive for more. Father knows best. With each word of instruction, each challenge to do more, and with every loving correction, God is working all things together for your good.

As we've already discussed, God does *not* lie, and He is *not* out to get you. So, you can be comfortable being totally real and honest with Him. You can ask Him about anything, knowing you'll get the best answers for everything without ever having to wonder if you can really trust Him, without being afraid He's too high and mighty to help you. You never have to second-guess your Father's wisdom or His love for you.

Corrie Ten Boom was a Dutch Christian Holocaust survivor who helped many Jews escape from German concentration camps during World War II. In spite of tremendous difficulties, she trusted God to sustain her. She shared,

Often I have heard people say, "How good God is! We prayed that it would not rain for our church picnic, and look at the lovely weather!" Yes, God is good when He sends good weather. But God was also good when He allowed my sister, Betsie, to starve to death before my eyes in a German concentration camp. I remember one occasion when I was very discouraged there. Everything around us was dark and there was darkness in my heart. I remember telling Betsie that I thought God had forgotten us. "No Corrie," said Betsie. "He has not forgotten us. Remember His Word. . . . For as the Heavens are high above the earth, so great is His steadfast love toward those who fear Him."

Corrie concludes, *"There is an ocean of God's love available—there is plenty for everyone. May God grant you never to doubt that victorious love—whatever the circumstances."*[3]

Whenever You Need Help or Don't Understand . . . *Just Ask*

Because He loves you, God will make the crooked places straight and the rough places plain (see Isaiah 40:4; 45:2). You can avoid confusion and mistakes every time by asking for and following His direction.

Trusting God doesn't mean you don't ask questions. Sometimes life bombards you with things that just don't make sense. No doubt, Corrie Ten Boom knew this quite well. For some, it's easy to point a finger at God when they consider life's most difficult questions. Over the years, I have heard from many people who pour out their hearts in a card, letter, or e-mail that comes across my desk. My heart breaks as I consider what they ask:

"Why do bad things happen to good people?"

"Why would God allow over 2,966 victims to perish in the attacks on the Twin Towers on September 11, 2001?"

"Why would God allow innocent children to be sold into the sex trade?"

"Why did my friend's husband die of cancer, leaving her to put two children through college on a teacher's salary?"

"When will my grown children give their lives to the Lord?"

"When will my husband find a good job?"

What about you? Do too many questions and not enough answers leave you reeling and wondering most days? Do they cause you to lie awake many nights, staring at the ceiling, pondering about how things will ever work out? You can never be too young or old to ask the Lord these questions. As you wade through all the questions in your life, let me offer a word of hope.

Listen to a few more words from the song I mentioned in our devotion on Day 8, which I wrote with my good friend Eddie Carswell, one of the members of the popular group New Song. These words serve as a reminder to me every time I sing them: Even when I don't know the way, God can be trusted. I believe it will remind you of this great truth as well:

He sees the master plan
He holds our future in His hands
So don't live as those who have no hope
All our hope is found in Him
We see the present clearly
But He sees the first and the last
And like tapestry, He's weaving you and me
To someday be just like Him

God is too wise to be mistaken
God is too good to be unkind
When you don't understand
When you don't see His plan
When you can't trace His hand
Trust His heart[4]

No matter how tough your life may be—no matter how bleak things may look or how difficult your situation may get—you can always hold fast to the hope that God is perfectly reliable and dependable. He loves you without condition. Without fail, without exception, you can trust Him. So, come boldly before His throne of grace. Ask for His wisdom. The Bible promises He'll give it to you freely and liberally, without faulting you at all (James 1:5).

EMBRACE YOUR DAY

Within the past few days we have talked now and then about worry. But I want to mention one more thing concerning worry here. *To worry is to sin.* (See Romans 14:23b.) It doesn't take any faith in God to put faith in your reservations and fears. When you worry, it means you don't trust Him. You cannot worry and trust God at the same time. Think about it. If you fully trust God, why would you worry about anything?

Trusting God is an all-or-nothing endeavor. It's kind of like skydiving. When you jump, you'd better know for sure that your parachute will open. If you're not certain about that, then you'd be better off staying in the plane. To walk by faith in God, you must decide whether you will trust Him and be at peace or worry and stress over every situation. Without question, we are not to worry. Matthew 6:31-34 says,

> Don't worry and say, "What are we going to eat?" or "What are we going to drink?" or "What are we going to wear?" Gentiles long for all these things. Your heavenly Father knows that you need them. Instead, desire first and foremost God's kingdom and God's righteousness, and all these things will be given to you as well. Therefore, stop worrying about tomorrow, because tomorrow will worry about itself. Each day has enough trouble of its own. (CEB)

God has a name you can trust! His word is tried and true. He has been providing for you since the day you were born. Just relax; God is in control. His wisdom is perfect. Be at peace; God knows what is best for you: yesterday, today, and in the days to come. You can depend on Him completely. He has not, nor will He ever, fail you. God can be trusted, no matter what!

Whatever difficulties you may encounter, you can rest assured: *God permits nothing to touch your life that He hasn't already determined will work for your good, not for your destruction.* More than this, He has already determined that your challenges will work for the highest good—for His kingdom and glory.

Sweet friend, I don't know about you, but I have needed this word from the Lord today. Trusting God is not something you learn in a day. It is a moment-by-moment dependency on Him: your heavenly Father, who never lies, who will never leave you, and who absolutely cannot fail. As we talk about the many ways that God provides for us, trusting Him to do so is the first step. Let's talk to Him again, this time, thanking Him for being true and trustworthy:

My dear Father,

You are faithful and true. There is no compromise or shadow of turning in You. I praise You that when everything around me is shifting, You remain constant. When I am faced with questions I cannot answer, I thank You that I can look to Your wisdom. Lord, when I am challenged and find life extremely difficult, I will turn to You for strength and direction. Dearest Lord, I put all my trust in You. You have already proved that You will remain steadfast and trustworthy. Forgive me for withholding my trust from You when others betrayed me, for You are my refuge and my shelter, Lord. All my hope and trust are in You. When I encounter situations that seem to be over my head, I know You will not allow me to be overwhelmed. Instead, like the perfect Father You are, You will catch me, even if it feels like I'm going under the waves of trouble for the third and final time.

I love You, Lord. In Thee I place my trust.

In Jesus' name I pray,

Amen.

Think About His Love

After reading today's study, how would you define *trust?* Think about it, and then write a few thoughts in your journal.

Read About His Love

"Trust in the LORD with all thine heart; and lean not unto thine own understanding. In all thy ways acknowledge him, and he shall direct thy paths" (Proverbs 3:5-6). Certainly, you now understand this passage is a mouthful! No doubt, situations in your life came up in your heart as you read through today's devotion. Why don't you try your hand at making a list of these things? Then, go to your Bible, find a key word in the concordance, and look up God's promises for each area of concern. This will help you commit these passages to memory, along with our devotional verses, as you write them in your journal today.

Pray About His Love

As you go about your day, imagine you were with me at the pool that day when the little girl took the flying leap into her daddy's arms. Picture her hesitating, thinking about the situation. Now look back at your list. In which areas have you hesitated most in trusting God? Which ones have created negative cycles in your life that you'd like to overcome? Present these areas to God. Surrender them to Him completely. Then, close your eyes and picture that trusting little girl jumping into her father's arms with total abandon. Yes, the water was way over her head. But she trusted her father as if her very life depended on it. And you know what? It did! Let me encourage you to pray wholeheartedly about any area in your life that seems to be way over your head. God is at work today. He will give you wisdom and help you come back up to the surface in each area, completely safe—ready to take the plunge again.

Be About His Love

Today, we're focusing inward again as you bask in the deep end of His love. Reflecting on our conversation about trust today, do you think it is possible to love God without fully trusting in Him? Beginning right now, when God quickens you by His spirit that you are about to say or do something that could lead you to repeat one of those cycles, stop right then, thank God for helping you, and do what would be pleasing to Him. Each time, thank the Lord for a being your closest friend in whom you can confide. Return His embrace, my dear friend. Each time you do, you will discover an increased capacity to love Him more.

DAY 11

THE COURAGE TO STAND

*Courage is not limited to the battlefield or the Indianapolis 500 or
bravely catching a thief in your house. The real tests of courage are
much quieter. They are the inner tests, like remaining faithful when
nobody's looking, like enduring pain when the room is empty, like
standing alone when you are misunderstood.[1]*
—Charles Swindoll

*Have not I commanded thee? Be strong and of a good courage;
be not afraid, neither be thou dismayed: for the LORD thy
God is with thee whithersoever thou goest.*
—Joshua 1:9

God has given you courage to go to battle in His name, knowing
He has already provided everything you need for a sure victory.

When I think of what it takes to stand firm in the face of
tremendous adversity, my mind goes immediately to our nation's
military. The men and women who protect our country, both at
home and abroad, put their lives on the line every day. Without
hesitation, they position themselves to protect the freedoms all
United States citizens enjoy. The sacrifices our servicemen and

women make as they tirelessly serve our nation are becoming more apparent by the day.

My father, Rev. George Wade, as a young preacher's son from the cotton fields of Alabama, made such sacrifices. He served this country in the United States Army during World War II. I recall when he told the story of how he surrendered his life to Christ and, soon after, was called to preach the gospel.

Dad said while he was on active duty in Belgium, he served as an ammunitions truck driver. One Saturday, while trekking down a rural, dusty road headed for the front line, his company came under heavy enemy attack and was captured. They were taken as prisoners of war and held hostage in the enemy's camp. Dad and several of his company comrades managed to escape the prison that night, and during their flight they were separated.

Dad hid out in a potato farmer's barn until daylight. Unbeknownst to anyone and on guard for his very life, he concealed himself underneath a stack of hay in a corner of the barn. As he lay there, secretly planning his next move, he heard someone enter. Slowly, as the potential threat moved closer and closer to the lofty stack of hay where Dad was hiding, holding his breath, he knew this could very well be the last breath he would ever draw.

Then the unthinkable happened. He had been discovered! A pitchfork thrust through the stack of hay, barely missing his body. Dad flinched. Slowly and cautiously, the white Belgian farmer peered through the hay. He was just as shocked to see a black United States Army corporal staring back at him. Stunned, Dad lay perfectly still.

Then something miraculous took place. The farmer lifted his pitchfork full of hay and replaced the straw right back on top of my father and then quietly left his barn. My dad was able to get out of there without being discovered further. Later that morning, he reconnected with his troops.

Dad knew his life had been spared for a reason. Knowing he had been given another opportunity, he prayed an earnest prayer that morning and surrendered his life to the Lord.

When he heard church bells ringing in the distance, Dad suddenly remembered this was no ordinary Sunday morning. It was Easter. Though Dad had heard the word of God preached his entire life by his father, a Baptist pastor, that Resurrection Sunday he had a new appreciation for Psalm 27:1-4:

> The LORD is my light and my salvation; whom shall I fear? the LORD is the strength of my life; of whom shall I be afraid? When the wicked, even mine enemies and my foes, came upon me to eat up my flesh, they stumbled and fell. Though an host should encamp against me, my heart shall not fear: though war should rise against me, in this will I be confident. One thing have I desired of the LORD, that will I seek after; that I may dwell in the house of the LORD all the days of my life, to behold the beauty of the LORD, and to enquire in his temple.

After my father was discharged from the army, he, my mother, and my oldest brother headed north to Michigan. Not long after settling down in Jackson, Dad was called to serve as the pastor of a fledgling church work there. The Lily Missionary Baptist Church, where Dad served as pastor for nearly forty years, and where I served as church pianist and choir director for nearly twenty years, still stands as a landmark in my hometown. Dad is in heaven now, but his legacy of courage, conviction, and commitment lives on. We'll talk about just that today—courage, confidence, and commitment.

In God, You Can Be Fearlessly Courageous

God chose Joshua to be the leader of the Israelite nation after forty years of wandering in the desert just before Moses' death (Deuteronomy 31:7-8, 23). Under the Lord's direction, Joshua would take God's people into a great, new land—the promised land. To carry out God's plan, they would have to conquer the inhabitants of this land of promise: Canaan. That meant, first of all, overtaking the great and mighty city of Jericho. When Joshua received his instructions, God assured him of His protection and guidance. Read what the Lord told him in Joshua 1:6-9:

> Be strong and of a good courage: for unto this people shalt thou divide for an inheritance the land, which I sware unto their fathers to give them. Only be thou strong and very courageous, that thou mayest observe to do according to all the law, which Moses my servant commanded thee: turn not from it to the right hand or to the left, that thou mayest prosper whithersoever thou goest. This book of the law shall not depart out of thy mouth; but thou shalt meditate therein day and night, that thou mayest observe to do according to all that is written therein: for then thou shalt make thy way prosperous, and then thou shalt have good success. Have not I commanded thee? Be strong and of a good courage; be not afraid, neither be thou

dismayed: for the LORD thy God is with thee whithersoever thou goest.

What a powerful promise! Joshua needed to hear and embrace every word of it because the city of Jericho was a mighty fortress. Surrounded by massive walls, it had an insurmountable defensive structure encased on every side. At first glance, I'm sure it seemed impossible to penetrate. But Joshua knew that this walled fortress stood between the Israelites and God's will for the nation: to enter and possess Canaan, the promised land.

In this unforgettable story, God instructs Joshua and the Israelites to do nothing for the first six (of seven) days, except to march around the city of Jericho once a day. No talking back or complaining would be allowed. As a matter of fact, Joshua instructed them that no one could open his mouth. Along with this, he told them not to fear. He warned them not to fight. He specifically instructed them not to do anything except march, in the exact order and way he described.

I can see this scene unfolding in my mind's eye as the people of Israel walked and walked around the walls of Jericho. No doubt, on day one, their enemies laughed at them as they paced around the city. On day two, after the laughing came the mocking, but God's people kept on walking. On day three, I can just hear the Canaanites taunting the people of God, heckling at them from atop the city wall.

This was a true test of courage for the children of Israel. I can imagine they probably felt intimidated. But they continued to walk all the same. I'm sure they felt like complaining, but they kept on marching.

Has God ever held you in a holding pattern, waiting for His next command? I fly in airplanes a lot. Often, I travel many miles across this country, as well as in foreign lands, singing and speaking. I'm happiest when my flights are predictable. I want every flight to leave right on time. I want my pretzels and my spicy tomato juice with no ice and a wedge of lime right at the expected moment midflight. Then I want to read a couple of chapters from a good book and take a short nap just before landing.

But every once in a while, for one reason or another, the plane I'm traveling on has to go into a holding pattern. A holding pattern is a condition of inactivity when no progress is made and no change is realized. I don't like holding patterns. They tend to make me nervous. I feel as if my fellow passengers and I are in the middle of nowhere, going around and around in endless circles. Besides this, a holding pattern usually means a delay. I don't like delays either. I've missed flight connections because of delays. I've been late getting to a few concert engagements because of delays.

But I realize that when I'm in those situations I can't see the big picture. From my perspective, I can't see all the things that have caused the delay. As my flight waits in a holding pattern, air traffic control communicates with the pilots in every plane that is affected—not just the plane that I'm on, but all the air traffic coming into and leaving the airport. Though I know this, I still don't like the wait. Then at just the right time in the "big picture" schedule, the pilot of the aircraft I'm on receives instructions to come out of the holding pattern. Yeah! I heave a sigh of relief as we prepare to land.

People haven't changed. We don't like waiting today any more than the people of Israel did as they were walking continuously around the city of Jericho. We get impatient waiting for the popcorn to finish popping in the microwave oven. We grow weary waiting in line at the fast food drive-thru. And we certainly have a tendency to get impatient when we're waiting on God to fix our personal situations, don't we?

We want God to move speedily. We don't like it when He makes us wait.

But aren't you glad that God knows best? Doesn't it give you a great sense of peace in your heart, just knowing that God is in complete control . . . even while, on the surface, a situation appears to be exactly the opposite? At face value, there are many times you may feel that God is afar off, maybe even aloof and uncaring, about your situation.

Don't fall for that trick of the enemy, dear one. The devil will try to convince you every time that God doesn't care about you or your problems. The father of lies would have you believe that God is too busy to look your way. Your adversary keeps telling you all the time to throw up your hands and quit. But don't even go there, my friend!

The devil is a hater. But God loves you. The devil is a discourager, and he wants to bring you down. God is an encourager, and He will lift you up.

God *is* working. God *is* moving. There are moments in our lives where we just have to give Him time. Behind the scenes, God is taking what looks like chaos at first glance and sounds like absolute mayhem and turning it around. He is creating a beautifully orchestrated symphony, aligning all things in perfect harmony to work *for your good* and *for His glory.*

Until the right moment reveals itself, God expects you to be humbly obedient to His word. Don't talk back. Don't complain. Don't make a sound in defiance. Does this remind you of anything? No matter how high the wall may be; no matter how many times God tells you to encircle it; regardless of anything the enemy is screaming at you, *don't fear, don't struggle,* and definitely *don't fight.* Keep your heart fixed upon the Lord and obey Him. *Just keep marching.*

As you obey God's marching commands, keep trusting in His great love for you. It takes tremendous courage to keep marching on when you're uncertain how your situation is going to turn out. It takes bold, audacious faith in God to keep moving forward on His instructions, even when you feel He is keeping you in the dark.

My friend, if this is where you are right now, do what the Israelites did: keep marching, no matter what. In return for their faith and trust in Him, God granted them a sure victory. In fact, He has a great victory waiting for you! God will perform His word for *your good* and *His glory*—but He will do it in His own time.

In God, You Can Have Perfect Confidence

On the seventh day, the children of Israel marched around the city seven consecutive times. Joshua instructed the priests to blow their trumpets and told all the people to lift up a shout of victory at the appointed time. When the trumpets blew and the people shouted, the walls of Jericho came tumbling down (Joshua 6:20).

God's ways truly amaze me! Not only does He move *when He wants*; He moves *how He wants*. Maybe Joshua's way to tackle that situation would have been to scale the wall or sneak through a crack or crevice somehow. But Joshua knew God. He trusted God's wisdom, knowing the results would be better in the end. From walking many years alongside Moses, he knew all too well that God has His own way of doing things. In Isaiah 55:9, our heavenly Father declares: "For as the heavens are higher than the earth, so are my ways higher than your ways, and my thoughts than your thoughts."

Think about it. Against human wisdom, God ordered His people to march silently for six days and then on the seventh day to march around that massive, fortified city seven times before blowing their trumpets and releasing a mighty, unified shout—and the walls crumbled to the ground. Surely, God's thoughts are heavenly indeed!

To stay in step with God's plan, the people of Israel had to go through the repetitious exercise of circling the city once a day for six days. That way, on the seventh day, when they had to circle it seven times, they were warmed up for it: spiritually, physically, emotionally, and otherwise. Besides that, these two numbers are definitely interesting. The number six is often interpreted as being the number of man, and seven is generally understood as being the number of perfection and divine completion. I guess you could say God allowed the Israelites to come to the end of themselves before He stepped in to complete and perfect the process by doing what only He could do. Have you ever had a "Jericho experience"? I've had a few of them.

I often wonder why God does things the way He does them. For example, why would God permit the children of Israel to wander around in the desert for forty years when the journey to the promised land actually should have taken a fraction of the time?

On your journey through life, have you ever wondered why you sometimes have to go over rough mountains and through deep valleys? Have you ever gone through dry spells and tight spots? Do you know how it feels to be surprised by a speed bump or a pothole? Do you sometimes encounter delays and detours that seemingly take you forever, just trying to get where you're going? Take heart, my friend. *God is working.*

He worked in much the same way with the people of God in Exodus 13:17-18. Read with me:

> And it came to pass, when Pharaoh had let the people go, that God led them not through the way of the land of the Philistines, although that was near; for God said, Lest peradventure the people repent when they see war, and they return to Egypt. But God led the people about, through the way of the wilderness of the Red sea.

Did you see what I just saw in the text? *God decided to lead His children the long way around to Canaan.* It was God who caused them to go around and around in circles. God created this divine detour. He ordained their delay. Dr. Adrian Rogers was one of the greatest preachers I ever had the privilege to hear. He expounds on this subject: "Why didn't God just take the shortest route? We say that a straight line is the shortest distance between two points. Well, it may be the shortest distance, but it's not always the best distance. And God has a purpose in His detours."[2]

In His infinite wisdom, God always knows what is best for His people. Had He taken them to Canaan by the most direct route, they would have encountered the Philistines sooner than they were prepared to do so. The Philistines would have caused the first generation of Israelites that left Egypt to become paralyzed with fear. God knows when we are fearful, we run. The Israelites would have run right back to Egypt, back to captivity and the cruel yoke of slavery.

Running back to slavery would have meant going back into bondage. Going back into bondage would have meant going back to a life of *oppression*. And once living in oppression, the Israelites would have gone back into *suppression*. Then, suppression would have eventually landed them smack dab in the middle of living lives of *depression*—which is where their parents were when God sent Moses to deliver the nation out of the hands of the enemies.

Oh, no! God wasn't going to allow *that* to happen!

Listen, my friend. If you are experiencing one of life's delays or detours on your journey, it doesn't mean that God has forgotten about you. On the contrary, God loves you. You are constantly on His heart and mind. God could never forget about you. He is well aware of your situation.

If you are on a detour right now, it is the true test of your confidence in the Lord. From His vantage point of *knowing all* and *seeing all*, you must be confident that His thoughts are higher than yours and that He knows your end from your beginning.

Trust God with all your heart, and don't lean unto your own understanding. He is a faithful provider, every step of the way.

Charles and I have discovered that sometimes God takes us *through* a situation because He knows it will make us stronger and eventually better. But at other times He gently leads us on a detour *around* a situation. Remember this: what may appear to be a delay or a detour doesn't necessarily mean denial. God is on our side; He is preparing us for the future and protecting us from harm. Read Philippians 1:6 with me and take confidence in the word of God: "Being confident of this very thing, that he which hath begun a good work in you will perform it until the day of Jesus Christ."

In God, You Can Be Unwaveringly Committed

As the people of God walked around Jericho's wall for seven days straight, they were committed to one single cause—taking the city. In order to be victorious, they had no choice but to do everything God's way. Resorting to any other plan would have meant certain destruction.

It is important to note that God ordered the Israelites to march in formation in a certain fashion. The armed guards went first, and afterward, the priests who were blowing the trumpets. After that, four priests followed, carrying the ark on poles. The rear guard came in behind the priests, and then the entire Israelite army marched behind the guard in silence (Joshua 6:6-9).

For whatever reason, the Lord had given Joshua and the army of Israel very specific instructions. Focused on God to achieve their purpose, the people humbly obeyed the Lord, following His every command. They were unwaveringly committed to God's plan because they needed God's results.

When you are totally committed to an endeavor, success is certain. You will always come out a winner. Listen to the words of the Apostle Paul, writing to Timothy, his son in the faith and a firmly committed disciple of Jesus Christ:

> I am not ashamed [of suffering for Christ]: for I know whom I have believed, and am persuaded that he is able to keep that which I have committed unto him against that day. Hold fast the form of sound words, which thou hast heard of me, in faith and love which is in Christ Jesus. (2 Timothy 1:12b-13)

THE MESSAGE says it even more powerfully, using more common language for today:

> This is the Message I've been set apart to proclaim as preacher, emissary, and teacher. It's also the cause of all the trouble I'm in. But I have no regrets. I couldn't be more sure of my ground—the One I've trusted in can take care of what he's trusted me to do right to the end. So keep at your work, this faith and love rooted in Christ, exactly as I set it out for you. It's as sound as the day you first heard it from me. Guard this precious thing placed in your custody by the Holy Spirit who works in us. (vv. 11-14)

American race car driver Mario Andretti once said, "Desire is the key to motivation, but it is determination and commitment to an unrelenting pursuit of your goal—a commitment to excellence—that will enable you to attain the success you seek."[3] God demonstrated His eternal commitment to excellence during the

Battle of Jericho. Every element had to be perfectly in place, and timing was critical. You see, God had a supernaturally perfect result in mind—tons of stone broken down and crushed together around a once formidable enemy encampment—without His people raising one hand to make it happen.

So, never pull back when God requires strict compliance from you in any area of your life. Because it usually means He's setting you up for a perfect, highly uncommon result. In any and all of your endeavors, if you want to experience the level of success God desires for you, be unwaveringly committed: both to Him and to thoroughly executing each step of His plan. Remember, God has already given you the innate ability to rise to the occasion.

The famous battle at Jericho will always be the subject of Sunday school lessons around the world, complete with the robust singing of the Negro spiritual "Joshua Fought the Battle of Jericho." Oh, I can feel it now. Why don't you sing a line or two with me:

> Joshua fought the Battle of Jericho, Jericho, Jericho . . .
> Joshua fought the Battle of Jericho,
> and the walls came a-tumblin' down."

Yes, they did!

But to the seasoned believer who wishes to do God's will, this inspiring story is much, much more. For here we find a man who is totally sold out to God and His cause. We see someone who is completely willing to lay down his life and put the lives of an entire nation in jeopardy, all because he was unwaveringly committed to his God.

In light of this, let us learn from Joshua how to fight, and win, the battles in our lives. *By listening to God and obeying His commands, victory is sure to come.* As we walk with God, we must remain obedient to His direction, ever careful not to take matters into our own hands.

Let me quickly wrap up this section with a glimpse of another, similar battle plan. King Jehoshaphat, after unwisely getting yoked in battle with Ahab, the most wicked king ever to rule Israel, got news not long after that his kingdom, Judah, was coming under attack by two other kings and their allies. Facing imminent war against the Moabites, the Ammonites, and the Meunites, King Jehoshaphat immediately went to prayer and called a nationwide fast. Then he stood in front of the people of Judah and cried out to God. (You can read about this story starting in 2 Chronicles 18 and reading through the fourteenth verse in chapter 20.) During this national prayer meeting, a Levite named Jahaziel, moved by the spirit of God, stood up and declared,

> Don't be afraid; don't pay any mind to this vandal horde. This is God's war, not yours. Tomorrow you'll go after them; see, they're already on their way up the slopes of Ziz; you'll meet them at the end of the ravine near the wilderness of Jeruel. You won't have to lift a hand in this battle; just stand firm, Judah and Jerusalem, and watch GOD's saving work for you take shape. Don't be afraid, don't waver. March out boldly tomorrow—GOD is with you. (2 Chronicles 20:15-17 *THE MESSAGE*)

So, you see, even when you make a mistake, if you run back to God like Jehoshaphat did, God will hear when you cry out to Him. And He'll give you the victory, as you humbly obey His battle plan. A few verses later, Jehoshaphat appointed a choir for God and dressed them in holy robes to go before the army to battle. As the choir sang, "Praise the LORD, for His mercy endures forever" (2 Chronicles 20:21 NKJV), God set ambushes against Judah's enemies. All three tribes (all enemies of Judah) then turned on one another until all of them were dead. What a story!

No matter what you're facing, there is always hope in God. So, be courageous! Have confidence in Him. Stand firm in your faith, boldly committed to the Lord. He will faithfully provide for all of your needs as you obediently trust Him in every situation.

EMBRACE YOUR DAY

Over and over again, we're reminded that miracles can happen in our lives because God is with us. This is the secret to our success. You could have it all by the world's standards, but if the Lord isn't on your side, you are fighting a losing battle. However, when you are committed to the work of the Lord, your battles become His. He will fight for you. You don't have to worry about when the Lord will overcome the enemy. You don't need to concern yourself about how God goes about His battle plan. You just have to rest in the fact that He will.

God is looking for dedicated soldiers to stand for righteousness. Are you signed up, sold out, and ready for battle? Let's review. The formula for winning life's battles is threefold. You must possess *courage* to follow God's direction, obeying Him with your heart even when it doesn't make sense to your head. Then, by faith, go by what you know in God, not by what you feel. When you are in the heat of battle, there is no room for compromise. Determine that no matter what may come, you will listen to His voice and, with *confidence* and obedience, carry out His will.

Finally, on a moment-by-moment basis, make a *commitment* to do what God has called you to do with your whole heart. Commit your life, your gifts, your work, and all your ways to Him. You will see the walls of the enemy "come a-tumblin' down" in your life.

I know it is very possible there are walls standing between you and God's promises. So, this could be the perfect time to pray, thanking the Lord for making a way where there seems to be no way. Let's pray together, all right?

Almighty God,

Sometimes it seems that the odds are against me. Some days I feel as if I'm fighting a losing battle, taking three steps forward and four steps back. And when I look at things with my natural eyes, Lord, it seems that everything in my world is falling apart. Sometimes I feel the pressures of life on every side, and when I look out ahead of me, all I can see is a massive wall. My life is full of speed bumps, potholes, holding patterns, detours, and delays, Lord. Sometimes my bill box is nearly full and my gas tank is nearly empty. If I didn't know any better during these tests of my faith, I'd think the whole world was turning against me. But I praise You that I do know better! I know that if You are for me, You are much greater than whatever is coming against me. So today, sweet Father, I ask for courage to stand when my knees are weak. I ask for confidence to carry out Your instructions, even when my mind can't make sense of them. And, Lord, I ask for a heart that is singularly committed to Your cause. I realize this is a dangerous request because asking this of You potentially invites more drama into my life. But I know that when I am weak, You are strong. And depending on Your strength is where I want to be. I know it's just a matter of time until I cross over into Your promised land of victory in my life. I love You, Lord. In the name of Your Son, Jesus, I pray,
Amen.

Think About His Love

Can you submit to God's plan while staring into the face of impossibility? Can you envision your promised land while staring directly at the walls of *your* Jericho? As your life intersects with God's love today, ponder the battles that God has already won in your life. Now, see yourself victorious as you obey God's new and unique battle plan.

Read About His Love

"Have not I commanded thee? Be strong and of a good courage; be not afraid, neither be thou dismayed: for the LORD thy God is with thee whithersoever thou goest" (Joshua 1:9). As you meditate on this verse today, put yourself in Joshua's place. What has God commanded you to do? Say this verse aloud, letting each word sink deeply in your heart.

Pray About His Love

Now, pray about the things God has instructed you to do for His kingdom and glory. If personal struggles have kept you from fulfilling one, a few, or all of them, it's time to bring your burdens to the Lord. Like Jehoshaphat did when Judah was coming under attack, you can run to the Father and receive grace and mercy in your time of need. Remember, the presence of hardship in your life does not mean that God's love is absent or that He won't help you defeat the enemy. As you pray throughout the day, thank God and declare in song, "Praise the Lord, for His mercy endures forever!"

Be About His Love

Embrace the tangible presence of God's love in your life today. Some battles are fought and won with weapons. Others are fought and won with praise! *Be about His love* by obeying God and letting Him defeat the enemy on your behalf. Amen!

THE PLACE TO REST

How sweet to leave the world awhile
And seek the favor of the Lord
Dear Savior, on Thy servant smile
According to Thy faithful Word

From busy scenes I now retreat
That I may come away and hear
O Lord behold me at Thy feet
To bless me with Thy presence near[1]
—Thomas Kelly

Come unto me, all ye that labour and are heavy laden, and I will
give you rest. Take my yoke upon you, and learn of me; for I am
meek and lowly in heart: and ye shall find rest unto your souls.
For my yoke is easy, and my burden is light.
—Matthew 11:28-30

You are invited to step out of the fast lane and enjoy the sweet
company of the Lord Jesus.

I once heard a story about a biologist's experiment with processional caterpillars. On the rim of a red terra-cotta clay pot, he lined up enough caterpillars, head to tail, until they completely encircled the rim. Inside the pot was a beautiful green leafy plant. For an entire week the fuzzy worms circled around and around the rim of the pot. Not once did a single caterpillar break formation to crawl over and eat any part of the plant. Eventually every caterpillar died of starvation and exhaustion.[2]

To me, the story of the processional caterpillar is an eye-opening illustration of how driven our culture has become. We miss what we really need in an effort to keep up with society's maddening pace and our unending obsession for more.

Do you know someone who is constantly on the run? From the moment she puts her feet on the floor at the crack of "dark-thirty" to the moment she lays her head down well after midnight, she's on the run. She runs to work, to school, to the bank, to the cleaners, to the baseball field, and to church. And of course, she runs behind. She runs late. She runs out. She runs scared. The chaos hardly ever ceases.

Even when she should be asleep, she lies awake with a long list of things to do and places to go running through her head. Now, she's running short on sleep! There is no rest for the weary, is there?

Ah, but there is, my friend. Jesus extends a personal invitation for you to step out of the position you occupy in the fast lane. He invites you to get off the endless treadmill of life that's been driving you. He invites you to wipe the sweat from your brow, exhale the breath you've been holding, and sit down to rest. Take a breather. Take a break. You know you need it.

Rested people are healthier. They are refreshed. They look better and are more fun to be with.

Jesus knows how much you need to come away from the noisiness and pressures of life. He even needed a retreat every once in a while. So, He went away from the madding crowds to spend time in His Father's house (the synagogue), in the garden, or at the lake. Jesus knows that living on this planet can leave you spiritually bankrupt, emotionally drained, and physically exhausted. He knows that heavy, back-breaking load you are bearing is getting more and more cumbersome with every step. This sort of load makes you feel like the weight of the world is on your shoulders.

Do you feel your body getting wearier with every step? Take heart, my friend. Jesus knows how it feels to carry the weight of the whole world on His shoulders. He experienced this all too well when He carried the old rugged cross up Calvary's hill to be crucified for the sins of the world. Jesus conquered death, hell, and the grave so that you could live. He conquered sin so that you could have salvation and enjoy a new, abundant life through Him.

Jesus is your supply. Your job may give you a paycheck, but Jesus is your source. You might have a good health plan, but Jesus gives you well-being. *Stuff* and *things* may make you happy for a moment or two, but only Jesus can give you real joy. You might even have a nice house, but only Jesus can make it the special place you want to come home to. In Matthew 11:28-30 (our opening passage for today's devotion), Jesus invited those who struggled under the oppressive laws of religious tradition to lay their burdens down. He offered them, in exchange, a new life of freedom. Let's read that passage now. Jesus said,

> Come unto me, all ye that labour and are heavy laden, and I will give you rest. Take my yoke upon you, and learn of me; for I am meek and lowly in heart: and ye shall find rest for your souls. For my yoke is easy, and my burden is light.

This is the invitation the world longs to hear. The Savior of the world says, "Come one, come all. Come and dine. Come and eat. Come and drink. Come and stay. Come and receive. Come rest in Me." If you are overworked, overstressed, or just plain "over it," come to Jesus. I think sometimes we put our love relationship with Him on a diet. It seems as if we are afraid to come to His table and eat, as though we are afraid to get a second, third, or fourth helping of His love. Listen to Isaiah 55:1: "Ho, every one that thirsteth, come ye to the waters, and he that hath no money; come ye, buy, and eat; yea, come, buy wine and milk without money and without price."

In other words, whatever you need, you can come and receive it from Jesus right now—just like the thirsty woman at the well did in the days of old. Come, get as much as you need from Jesus. Get filled up and be completely satisfied in His presence. He is your ultimate source of everything you need in this life. There's no need to fear; there's always plenty to go around at the Master's table. You don't have to worry about how much anything will cost. Jesus has already paid the price.

I say to you again: you can receive everything you need from the Lord. And because your salvation and restoration cost Jesus everything, they cost you nothing. Every heavenly blessing Jesus died and rose again to provide for God's children comes to you free of charge.

Come to the Savior

Living in the South, I have learned that when one receives an invitation, it's customary and polite to respond. The person inviting you is making special preparations for you and all the other guests attending the event. In the same way, Jesus has made very special considerations for you. So, when He says, "Come unto Me," He really means it.

With His loving smile inviting you and His arms open wide, Jesus compels you to spend time with Him. And that's what so many of us have so little of . . . time.

My hubby, Charles, came home the other day with two little puppies, each just a few months old. They are absolutely the cutest puppies on the planet! I'm not sure, but I think they are from the same litter. Buster Brown is a roly-poly, rambunctious, and playful little fellow with a rusty brown coat. Whenever he sees Charles or me coming up the walk he can't wait to get to us. Unable to contain himself, he runs right to us, happily wagging his tail all the way. He loves spending every moment that he can with us. And we love spending time with Buster Brown.

Then there's Lil' Lady. She's black with a tan face and legs. Her paws and the tip of her tail all look as if they were dipped in a bucket of white paint, complete with specks of white atop her little head. So tiny and painfully shy, Lil' Lady must have been the runt of the litter. Whenever she sees us coming, or *anyone* coming toward her for that matter, she runs and hides. She's skittish, apprehensive, and tentative. I call her name, gently inviting her to come to me, but she rejects my invitations. She just won't answer my call.

I've tried to get close enough to pick Lil' Lady up. But, I admit, I'm not as agile as I used to be, and before I can reach her she takes off running in the opposite direction. I've even tried feeding her from my hand to gain her trust. That doesn't work either. She won't respond to my invitations to love her and be her friend.

Not so with Buster Brown. We enjoy each other's company. That little fellow runs and jumps and dances at my feet. Just being together, walking through the yard or down by the pond, is what we like best. He's learning how to fetch and how to sit. He's learning the sound of my voice and my commands. No doubt about it. This little puppy enjoys my company, and I enjoy his. There are no pretentious attitudes. No airs. No putting on. There is no need to wear makeup or nice clothes when I'm with Buster Brown. Being with him is a great lesson in what feels like to have my own girl's best friend.

Lil' Lady, on the other hand, saddens my heart. Oh, if she could only understand that I want to be her friend too! If only she could know that I would never hurt her; she'd be so much happier—and I would be too. Lil' Lady rarely knows the joy of human touch or what it's like to eat from my hand. I want her to know that she doesn't have to run away and hide anymore. Until I win her heart, I'll do all I can to help her trust me. I long for the day when Lil' Lady finally realizes what she's been missing. I'm determined to win her over.

These two little puppies are teaching me a great deal about intimate friendship and unconditional love. They are helping me to see what it looks like to accept or reject the kind invitation of a friend.

Now, I have a better understanding of how it must break the Father's heart when we run from Him, neglecting sweet fellowship with Him. Dear one, don't let anything keep you from receiving everything you need in the presence of the Lord.

Your accuser, the devil, will do all he can to keep you from enjoying God's presence. If he can, he'll keep you distracted. He'll lie to you, trying to make you feel like being in God's presence is boring or useless. Your adversary will keep you busy tending to things that don't really matter, or he'll bind you up, making you feel guilty and full of shame. These are all tools that satan uses to keep you from enjoying the peace that can only be found in God's presence. But in Psalm 16:11 the psalmist writes, "Thou wilt shew me the path of life: In thy presence is fulness of joy; at thy right hand there are pleasures for evermore."

Whatever is missing or broken in your life, run into the Lord's presence to receive everything you need. You will find that He faithfully provides for you.

Receive from the Master

For more than three hundred years, between the mid-1500s and the mid-1800s, slavery was practiced here in America. Black people by the millions were captured and brought from Africa to the United States to work on plantations where the soil was rich and harvests were plentiful. By the 1860 United States Census, the slave population had grown to more than four million people, and by 1865 the practice was abolished and the Emancipation Proclamation was enforced.[3] These slaves endured oppressive work conditions, harsh treatment from their masters, squalid living conditions, as well as separation from their children and family members. Knowing this, many slaves chose to jump ship in the middle of the Atlantic Ocean and drown rather than live a life of slavery in the Americas.

I'm telling you this because this is the history of my people. Personally, I believe we don't discuss this travesty against black people enough these days. I want to do all that I can to keep this story alive, or we will forget. I have been to the slave stockades in West Africa, in Savannah, Georgia, and in the Caribbean Islands where slaves were processed like cattle before boarding filthy slave ships. Chained together, not able to lie down, and denied every privacy and privilege, they were brought to the Americas against their will and auctioned off like livestock.

I'm only sharing this because I want us to get a real picture of what it must have been like to be treated so cruelly by heartless, careless, slave-driving masters: people who had little or no regard for the sanctity of human life.

In comparison, our good Master, Jesus, invites all who have been enslaved by our oppressor (satan). He opens His arms to all who have been burdened and beaten down by life, chained to addictions, and robbed of hope, bidding us to come to Him. With tender affection, He draws us into relationship with Him, wooing us to obey His commands with all our hearts as loving, submitted servants.

Those who have spent their lives captive to sin and satan are invited to take the Lord Jesus as their Master instead. He is not abusive or insensitive to our needs. He is not overbearing with no regard for life. Oh, no, my dear friend; just the opposite is true. The Lord has always had great compassion for the poor and downtrodden. When we come into His presence, we find that He is ready to exchange *what we have for what He has*. Let's read from the book of Isaiah to get clarity on this:

> The Spirit of the Lord GOD is upon me; because the LORD hath anointed me to preach good tidings unto the meek; he hath sent me to bind up the brokenhearted, to proclaim liberty to the captives, and the opening of the prison to them that are bound; to proclaim the acceptable year of the LORD, and the day of vengeance of our God; to comfort all that mourn; to appoint unto them that mourn in Zion, to give unto them beauty for ashes, the oil of joy for mourning, the garment of praise for the spirit of heaviness. (61:1-3)

The prophet Isaiah spoke these words about the coming Messiah. Then when Jesus came and was starting His earthly ministry, He went into the synagogue, opened this scroll, and read these same words aloud. My friend, this is still the mission of our Master, Jesus, today. He invites every soul that searches for Him to participate in a great exchange. What good news this is to me!

I don't know about you, dear one, but I have known some oppression in my life. I have experienced sorrow and loneliness, broken relationships, sickness and pain. And I've exchanged all these things for Jesus—and I'd do it again any day of the week! If you haven't done so already, why don't you do the same? Jesus wants to take every burden you bear and give you rest for your soul. Let us remember His kind words: "Take my yoke upon you, and learn of me; for I am meek and lowly in heart: and ye shall find rest unto your souls. For my yoke is easy, and my burden is light" (Matthew 11:29-30).

Learn from the Teacher

I wrote in the introduction of this book about how my life-changing experience of being *Embraced by God* began. On that Sunday morning a few years ago when the pastor instructed everyone in the congregation to say, "I am God's favorite," everything changed for me. Because at that precise moment, as those words came across my lips, I heard chains fall to the ground. Though my mind initially struggled to understand this truth, my spirit felt a heavy burden lift off my back.

From that day until now, I have been learning how to live a truly unencumbered life. I am taking advantage of Jesus' gifts of grace, mercy, and forgiveness. As it is typical with Jesus, whenever He wishes to teach me something new or take me to a new place in Him, He usually gives me a song. This time, He not only gave me one song, He gave me another and then another . . . *the songs just kept flowing.*

One by one, song after song, words and music about His unconditional love for me came flooding from deep inside my being. From these songs, the Lord inspired me to record a music project called *Embrace* and then to create a worship concert called "Embrace: A Worship Celebration for Women."

At this concert, where I serve as worship leader, I guide women in an experience where we sing the praises of God together, observe sessions of corporate prayer, hear the stories and testimonies of other women, and celebrate Christian sisterhood. I invite mothers, daughters, sisters, and friends to come away from the pressures of life and enter into God's rest.

During the presentation, there are opportunities to do all the things we women love to do. We laugh, we shed tears, and we shed the weights of the past. There's no need to leave our issues at the door. Jesus invites us to bring our stuff inside and lay them at His feet. At every concert we discover as women that God loves us unconditionally. We embrace that He has great plans for us, that we matter to Him, that we are forgiven and accepted, and yes, that *we are God's favorite.*

After one "Embrace" celebration we held at a church in the Midwest, I received the testimony of a woman we'll call Lori, who had attended the night before. I learned that she had been living with a boyfriend and had been in this dead-end relationship for almost twenty years. During the course of the relationship Lori had experienced emotional, verbal, and physical abuse at the hands of her boyfriend. He was a drug abuser, had had numerous run-ins with the law, and had spent many years going in and out of jail. He'd always come back, and she'd always take him in.

A friend invited Lori to the "Embrace" concert, where women from all over the state had come to worship. She heard the music and the life-giving scriptures from the word of God spoken over her life. She heard the accounts of the woman at the well and the woman caught in the act of adultery, and how their lives had been altered by an encounter with the Lord Jesus.

She heard the testimonies of other women and how they had experienced the love of Christ in a very real and personal way. After hearing the invitation to come to Jesus as her Savior, Lori gave her heart to Christ at the conclusion of the "Embrace" celebration.

Then Lori went home and did something that was very brave on her part. She told her live-in, abusive boyfriend what she had experienced at the concert that night. She shared with him that for the first time, she heard that not only did God love her, she was His favorite. She heard that she was cherished, forgiven, and accepted by God. She heard that she was valued and that she mattered to Him.

Lori knew the Lord was giving her the opportunity to begin again. Then she asked her boyfriend of almost twenty years to pack his things and move out.

You see, when you keep company with Jesus, you can't go back to the way things were. *Everything changes after you have been with Him.* When you accept Jesus' invitation to come away—not just for a vacation, a long weekend, a day, a moment, or even for a ninety-minute worship service—*you are invited to come away for life*. You are compelled by the Lord Himself to live your life differently forever.

Jesus encountered two rough and rugged fishermen one day by the Sea of Galilee. In Mark 1:17-18, Jesus said to them: "Come ye after me, and I will make you to become fishers of men. And straightway they forsook their nets, and followed him."

After that pivotal moment for Simon and Andrew, the word *home* would take on an entirely new meaning. From that day on they found their home with Jesus, following after Him.

When you come away with Jesus you learn the truth that you will never be rejected. In John 6:37, Jesus said, "Him that cometh to me I will in no wise cast out."

As you follow Him, you observe how Jesus lived and loved here on earth. And you learn that age, race, gender, status, income bracket, name, shape, size, looks—all of the things that concern human flesh—don't concern Jesus, not for a single second.

In the book of Revelation Jesus says this: "The Spirit and the bride say, Come. And let him that heareth say, Come. And let him that is athirst come. And whosoever will, let him take the water of life freely" (22:17).

Now, remember, if you think that "coming away" with Jesus means packing a bag and heading for the hills (although that is a wonderful proposition), it is not necessary, nor is it always expedient. Jesus invites you to come away *right where you are*: whether you are in the kitchen, in rush-hour traffic, or in the boardroom, bedroom, or bathroom. The Lord Jesus, by the presence of the sweet Holy Spirit, who is with you and alive in you, is calling to you—even in the middle of your workday. He's wooing you while you're at the ball game or running to catch a plane. Jesus is calling you to a new life . . . a lifestyle of complete peace and rest.

My dear friend, we've come to the close of another three-day theme. Our time together is hurrying by so quickly. Our "Embrace" encounter will be over before we know it. So, let us maximize every moment.

When we meet here tomorrow, we'll begin a brand-new concert theme and discover God's wonderful plan for you. But for now, starting today, ponder this loving, intimate invitation from Jesus with more care and sensitivity. Would you do this? Throughout today, this week, and for the rest of your life, you and I should live this way. Because Jesus so faithfully provides everything we need for life and godliness.

Matthew 11:28-30 from *THE MESSAGE* brings this timeless truth home to our hearts:

> Are you tired? Worn out? Burned out on religion? Come to me. Get away with me and you'll recover your life. I'll show you how to take a real rest. Walk with me and work with me— watch how I do it. Learn the unforced rhythms of grace. I won't lay anything heavy or ill-fitting on you. Keep company with me and you'll learn to live freely and lightly.

EMBRACE YOUR DAY

The Lord blessed me to write a song with my good friend Anita Renfroe called "Come Away, My Beloved." This loving request of the Lord has been reverberating in my heart for many years, ever since I read a book by that title, written by Frances Roberts. This wonderful book helped to inspire in me a deeper devotion to God. It fostered the yearnings I began to experience as a believer in my early adulthood. Many years later, the day that Anita and I wrote this song, the following words of love came like a flood:

> Come away, my beloved
> To a place that is blessed
> Where your soul can find refuge
> Your spirit find rest
> Leave your burdens behind you
> And enter My peace
> Take My yoke, it is easy
> You will find sweet release.
>
> Are you thirsty and tired
> So weary, so worn
> Is your heart heavy laden
> Your mind tossed and torn
> Streams of mercy are waiting
> Your hope to renew
> Come and drink from the fountain
> I am waiting for you

I Am Alpha, Omega,
Beginning and End
The God of the Ages
Your Redeemer and Friend
I Am all you desire
And all that you need
I fulfill every promise
I Am faithful indeed

The chorus creates a longing in my heart. Even now, as I revisit these words, I sense His sweet spirit singing it over me:

Come away, come away
My beloved, come away
Come away, come away
My beloved, come away[4]

All right friend, I hope you are as inspired as I am at this very moment. Let's talk to the Lord together, okay?

O gracious God and Father,

Grant me please, ears to hear You
A heart to draw close to You
Willingness to obey You
Wisdom to understand You
Courage to trust You
Faith to believe You
Patience to wait for You
A song to praise You
A life to glorify You

In the precious name of Jesus, I pray.

Amen.

Think About His Love

At the invitation of the King of kings, the Lord Jesus, you are summoned into His presence. Not to be shamed or belittled, but to love and be loved. With this in mind, pull out your journal and write a love letter to Jesus.

Read About His Love

> Come unto me, all ye that labour and are heavy laden, and I will give you rest. Take my yoke upon you, and learn of me; for I am meek and lowly in heart: and ye shall find rest unto your souls. For my yoke is easy and my burden is light. (Matthew 11:28-30)

As you read about His love today, write the above passage in your journal, immediately following your love letter to the Lord. Now, look up the word *yoke*, both in your dictionary and in a *Strong's Exhaustive Concordance*, if you have one. If you don't, just go online and Google it. Often, meditating on His word means to dig deeper. Now, write a few thoughts in your journal about what you have learned.

Pray About His Love

Let's keep it simple. As you pray today, exchange any heavy burdens you might bear for the light and easy love of Jesus. *Slow down. Take your time. Rest in His presence.*

Be About His Love

Surely, from lingering in the presence of God today, you have received some type of leading or direction concerning different areas of your life. As you go about your day, freed from worry, following Him, do something special and tangible that reminds you He is your ever-faithful provider.

GOD'S PLAN FOR YOU IS EXCEPTIONAL

I believe You're the Son of God
And You came from Heaven above
I believe You're the Son of man
And You rule the earth with love
I believe You gave your life
On a cross at Calvary
I believe You conquered death
And You reign in victory

. . . I believe You know me well
Your plan for me is great
I believe through Your mighty power
That I can do all things
I believe You were and are
The Ancient of All Days
I believe I'll lift You up
And give Your name the praise

Now every step I take is toward You
Every song I sing is for You

> *. . . And had it not been for Your grace*
> *I don't know where I'd be today*
> *I believe in You, Jesus*
> *I believe in You, Jesus*
> *I believe*[1]
> —Babbie Mason

You have been given only one opportunity to glorify God with your life. What are you doing with it? Some people drift like a boat without a sail, heading out to sea in deep, uncharted waters. But you must seize every moment, desiring to live each day to the fullest. It is God's will for you to enjoy a purposeful, satisfying life.

For the next three days, we will take a closer look at God's plan for you. I trust you will discover that, indeed, God has a wonderful plan that has touched every age and stage of your life. Jesus takes great delight in blessing you according to His plan.

Let me break this down. You'd never dream of starting a long trip without first choosing a destination, would you? And you wouldn't go on this trip without forming a plan and using a map to tell you how to get there? Without proper planning you would just wander around aimlessly, going in circles. And you would waste precious time, energy, and resources. Setting out on a journey without first having a plan would be setting yourself up for failure.

Dear one, you don't have to live that way. God has a specific plan for you to accomplish. As you seek and worship Him, you will be able to see His plan unfold. And as a result, you'll maximize your efforts. You'll discover what living the abundant life truly is all about. Oh, yes, as you walk out God's plan, you will experience His embrace, one that is just for you that goes all the way down to your bones.

So, let the curtains rise. Our next movement in the Father's symphony of love is about to begin.

MAKE THIS CONFESSION OVER THE COURSE
OF THE NEXT THREE DAYS:
*Because God loves me and has a great plan
for my life, I am a success.*

WHEN YOU KNOW
GOD'S PLAN

Until you make peace with who you are, you'll never be
content with what you have.[1]
—Doris Mortman

Commit your actions to the LORD,
and your plans will succeed.
—Proverbs 16:3 NLT

God has big plans for you.

As believers, we want to know how to find God's plan for our lives. Maybe you have been wondering, *Who will I marry?* or *Should I take the job?* Perhaps you're in a season where you are pondering, *Should I go away to college or attend the community college across town?* Maybe you are at a place in your life where you are deciding whether to buy or rent a home. Oh, yes, there are many questions in life.

The good news is God wants you to know His will and purpose for your life more than you do. He doesn't play hide-and-seek with you when it comes to discovering your unique purpose. Rather, God clearly says in Psalm 32:8-9:

> I [the Lord] will instruct you and teach you in the way you should go; I will counsel you with My eye upon you. Be not like the horse or the mule, which lack understanding, which must have their mouths held firm with bit and bridle, or else they will not come with you. (AMP)

You make plans to do this or that, or to go here or there. Parents make plans for their children. Kids make plans for the summer. Spouses make plans for a husband or wife. But the only plan that really matters is the one *made for you* by the God who loves you. His plan goes back—way back to before you were born. Listen to what God said to Jeremiah; I'm sure He is still saying this to us today:

> Before I formed you in the womb I knew you,
> before you were born I set you apart. (Jeremiah 1:5 NIV)

Because God loves you and wants you to enjoy every aspect of your life, He designed an intentional plan for you. Now remember back to Day 1 in our devotions: *you are God's favorite*. He has carried you in His heart from the beginning of time. Long before you took your first breath, God knew your name. He knew everything that would happen in your life, even before the day you were born. Psalm 139:15-16 says,

> My frame was not hidden from you
> when I was made in the secret place.
> When I was woven together in the depths of the earth,

your eyes saw my unformed body.
All the days ordained for me
were written in your book
before one of them came to be. (NIV)

Knowing God has always had a plan for you should bring you a great sense of security. And what a big plan it is! Your heavenly Father wants to show you how to maximize every moment He has given you. He wants you to get all you can out of life, all the days of your life. I like to call this, "squeezing all the juice out of life." You (yes, *you!*) can worship God and enjoy a prosperous, successful, and fulfilling lifestyle. And if you are anything like me, you relish the opportunity to do so!

I want to enjoy a life that allows me to maximize my relationships with people, my work, my times of recreation, and most of all my relationship with God. So, when challenges come, they don't intimidate me. I know that God loves me and that He causes even my challenges to work for me, not against me. No challenge is going to take me under. I am an overcomer in Christ!

God's plan for you is always the best plan. Remember: *Father knows best.* When you want to know anything about your life, *just ask Him.* God knows everything there is to know about you. There is no need for you to check your horoscope in the newspaper. If you have been tempted to call a psychic, I hope you hung up the phone. That little piece of paper inside a Chinese fortune cookie is just that—a piece of paper inside a hollow shell. *The God who created you has written your life story. He has a predetermined plan for you.*

Years ago I memorized another passage in the book of Jeremiah that has become a bedrock truth in my life. I suggest that you commit it to memory, as well. As you recall this powerful promise, it will remind you that God has great things in store for you: "'For I know the plans I have for you,' declares the LORD, 'plans to prosper you and not to harm you, plans to give you hope and a future'" (Jeremiah 29:11 NIV).

You Were Created for Relationship

First and foremost, God created you because He wanted to have a close, meaningful relationship with you. Your primary purpose is to give God first place in your life and make Him your main priority. So, if you have been focusing only on what will make you happy in this life, you have the wrong focus. Your priorities are backwards, and you will stumble and fall before you can get solidly up on your feet. Instead, ask yourself, *How can I demonstrate my love for God with my life?*

Remember Matthew 6:31-34 from our devotion on Day 10? God has a name you can trust. When you put Him first, everything else you need or could ever desire will be added in. I also love the way *THE MESSAGE* communicates this truth. It gives a good understanding of what living one's life fully aware of God's presence really is:

> So here's what I want you to do, God helping you: Take your everyday, ordinary life—your sleeping, eating, going-to-work, and walking-around life—and place it before God as an offering. Embracing what God does for you is the best thing you can do for him. Don't become so well-adjusted to your culture that you fit into it without even thinking. Instead, fix your attention on God. You'll be changed from the inside out.

Readily recognize what he wants from you, and quickly respond to it. Unlike the culture around you, always dragging you down to its level of immaturity, God brings the best out of you, develops well-formed maturity in you. (Romans 12:1-2 *THE MESSAGE*)

I love how this passage says, "Embracing what God does for you. . . ." Discovering God's plan for you begins with *returning His embrace:* finding Him and putting Him first. This goes against the grain of natural or earthly thinking and behavior. In fact, it is one of the great paradoxes of the Bible. Let's read what Jesus said in Matthew 10:39: "If your first concern is to look after yourself, you'll never find yourself. But if you forget about yourself and look to me, you'll find both yourself and me" (*THE MESSAGE*).

Take a car's navigation system, for example. Before the system can determine the route to an intended destination, it must first acclimate itself by finding true north. Then after the system's inner compass hones in on true north, it points the driver in the right direction as he or she journeys along. So, you must acclimate yourself to God's absolute truth that life is not merely about what makes you happy. You discover true happiness while doing what brings pleasure to God. Your inner spiritual compass points you straight to a loving, obedient relationship with your heavenly Father through His Son, Jesus Christ. This is true north for you and me, my friend. This is the spiritual compass point where discovering our true life's purpose begins.

You Have Been Made by Design

After living in Metropolitan Atlanta for twenty-two years, Charles and I decided after the children were grown and on their own, we'd find a nice, quiet piece of land in the country and then settle down and enjoy the peaceful life. We found a few acres in rural Georgia where Charles could raise vegetables and I could plant flowers. We wanted a piece of property where we could fish every once in a while. That way, when we weren't on the road, we could enjoy our rest at home.

We decided on what kind of house we'd build on our farmland. But long before one shovel of dirt was turned over or any cement was poured, we had to have a plan for our home. We scoured books and magazines looking for just the right home design to suit our needs and desires. We visited lots of beautiful homes, took lots of pictures, and made plenty of notes.

On the day we went to meet with the home designer, we took all of our notes, pictures, and ideas. We liked the kitchen layout from one picture and the family room design from another. We wanted plenty of windows to view the sunrises and sunsets. We wanted a great room with lots of space for family, friends, and of course, grandchildren. I wanted a room for my piano where I could write songs, and Charles desired a space where he could store seeds and farm tools.

After several visits we were excited when our designer presented us with the plans—the blueprint for our new country home. And the plans she presented to us weren't copies of any other home she had designed. They were unique to us: custom drawn with our needs and preferences in mind.

Once construction started I was amazed that our builder could determine how much cement, lumber, nails, and other building materials would be needed, just by studying the house plans. Soon, paint went up on the walls, and carpet went down on the floors. Then our hopes and dreams moved in with the furniture. By following the plan, our house grew from being a drawing on a piece of paper to a lovely home for our family to enjoy for years to come.

The same is true for you. You were born as a result of God's predetermined plan for your life. Your strengths and weaknesses, likes and dislikes, hopes and dreams were all placed in you by God's design.

If I wanted to know the reasoning behind a particular invention, I'd talk with the inventor, wouldn't you? I would learn the story behind the invention and find out why the inventor was compelled to make such an object. Great inventors and designers each have a vision, a purpose, and a plan for their creations. Think about it. Ground-breaking inventions like the automobile, the airplane, the light bulb, the microwave oven, the telephone, the bulldozer, and the Frisbee were invented with specific purposes in mind.

If you were to try using a light bulb to cook your food or drive a bulldozer from Georgia to Chicago, this would be a misuse (perhaps even an abuse) of each invention's intended purpose. In the same way, your heavenly Father conceptualized you in His mind, formed you with His own hands, and placed you here on earth to fulfill a specific purpose. Doing anything short of God's purpose would be a misuse (or even an abuse) of His intention for your life.

You are a unique treasure: a masterpiece of God's design. Just as Psalm 139 says, you are "fearfully and wonderfully" made (v. 14). Take a few moments now to read this wonderful psalm of David completely. It will fill your heart with a sense of awe and wonder concerning your heavenly Father and His purpose for your life.

You Are a One-of-a-Kind Creation

Every living thing God made is unique. Birds fly. Fish swim. Dogs bark. Cats meow. Snow is cold. Lava is burning hot. Ever noticed how God creates everything in such a unique way? That's right, everything—*including* you. That old saying is true: *when God made you, He broke the mold.* There is no one exactly like you! There never has been nor will there ever be anyone else with your unique design.

Truly, you are a distinctive expression of God's creativity in the earth. When God designed you, He placed within you certain gifts and abilities that are unique to who you are. He gave you desires and dreams that will help you to pursue His will and purpose throughout your life. When God empowers and equips you to accomplish His plan, you don't ever have to go it alone. Because where God guides He surely provides. As you follow Him, you can rest in the following promise from 1 Thessalonians 5:24: "The one who calls you is faithful and he will do it" (NIV).

We often question why people are the way they are: why they possess natural abilities or a particular bent toward a certain quality. Maybe you love cooking or chemistry, languages or art. I have a friend, Jill, who designs wonderful clothes. When I need a special outfit for a certain occasion, I pay her a visit. Whenever I arrive at Jill's warehouse, I pick from an array of beautiful fabrics she has to choose from. Within an hour or two, I walk out with a brand-new outfit, customized just for me.

I have to hand it to Jill. She's so gifted in this area. She creates her fashionable garments with unique style and flair. She pays attention to every detail. Her exceptional ability to make beautiful garments speaks for itself. Every time I wear one of her outfits, I get compliments from people wanting to know where these stunning, one-of-a-kind creations originated. I'm able to give credit to whom credit is due. There's no doubt, my friend Jill was born to sew.

Now, please don't ask me to sew anything. Darts and zippers, buttonholes, hems, and blind stitches . . . just the thought of it all overwhelms me. But sit me down in front of a piano, place a microphone on the stand, and you'll watch me come alive! I'll keep you entertained for hours. I'll sing and play the piano until my heart is content because that is what I was born to do.

This same creative principle applies to you. God has given you gifts and abilities that come alive when you are in your element. As you flow in your God-given gifts and abilities, your genius is put on display. When you do what you were born to do, you shine like a star.

More than this, when you are flowing in your purpose it doesn't feel like work at all. You can do that particular thing so well that you don't even break a sweat. Dear friend, that unique ability you possess didn't just happen. You are custom-designed: fearlessly and wonderfully created on purpose to fulfill a divine, God-given purpose.

God Created You to Worship Him

Along with your other productive abilities, you were created to praise and extol your Creator, Father God. As a matter of fact, all of creation has been designed with an inherent need to worship Him. The Bible tells us in Psalm 150:6, "Let every thing that hath breath praise the LORD." This means you were put here on earth to bring glory to God, both in and through your life. Everything you do that brings glory to God is an act of worship. Take a few moments and read Romans 12:1-2 (NIV). You are a *living sacrifice*. Your spiritual act of worship is to please God with all that is in you.

Oftentimes, we define worship as being confined to a place or a day of the week. Some people might even define worship as a style of music or the tempo of a song. But God defines worship as a lifestyle of commitment and obedience. This means in everything you do—in your conversations, your relationships, your work, and even your leisure—you should be focused *first and foremost* on pleasing God as an obedient daughter in His kingdom realm on earth.

Whatever you do as a result of your conscious love walk with God, desiring to please the Lord, He receives as an act of worship (Romans 12:1-2).

Johann Sebastian Bach is a great example of what it looks like to glorify God through one's work. He was one of the greatest composers in the history of Western music. A man of great faith, Bach believed that music was to be "a refreshment to the soul." He was persuaded that music was be used as a tool to proclaim the gospel. Bach believed music should bring glory to God, and to demonstrate this belief, he signed most of his scores with the statement "Soli Deo Gloria"—"To God alone be the glory."[2] What a beautiful display of worship!

It is too often the case that we worship our work, we work at our play, and we play at our worship. We have gotten things completely out of order from God's intended purpose. If we don't consciously become more mindful of this, we will worship created things instead of the Creator who made them.

On one occasion, the children of Israel made this terrible mistake. While Moses was up on Mount Sinai seeking God's best, the Israelites were down in the camp seeking what was convenient. Read what took place in Exodus 32:1-4 (NIV):

> When the people saw that Moses was so long in coming down from the mountain, they gathered around Aaron and said, "Come, make us gods who will go before us. As for this fellow Moses who brought us up out of Egypt, we don't know what has happened to him." Aaron answered them, "Take off the gold earrings that your wives, your sons and your daughters are wearing, and bring them to me." So all the people took off their earrings and brought them to Aaron. He took what they handed him and made it into an idol cast in the shape of a calf, fashioning it with a tool. Then they said, "These are your gods, O Israel, who brought you up out of Egypt."

This is a prime example of misguided worship. The Israelites were too impatient to wait for God's absolute best for their lives. And His best for them was to have His presence in their midst. God's intention was for them to discover His plan and purpose by loving and walking in obedience to Him. Instead, they settled for a counterfeit way of worship. They came together and persuaded Aaron, their leader in charge, to abandon the ways of God. Sadly, Aaron and a large group of God's people turned away from God's plan and decided to do their own thing.

When people make a decision to do their own thing, sin isn't too far behind it. Instead of obeying God's command to worship Him, the one and only true God, the Israelites were content to worship an idol that Aaron had made with materials from their own hands. Sadly, about three thousand men, their wives, and children were led into idol worship that day (Exodus 32:1-29). They carelessly created and gave honor to a false deity: honor that was due to God alone.

Sound familiar? This is what our culture is doing today. Instead of living a life of obedience by loving and worshiping the one, true God, people are content to worship houses, money, property, cars, entertainment . . . even other people. God is still saying the same thing about idols today that He said to His people back then. Read Exodus 20:4-5a with me:

> Thou shalt not make unto thee any graven image, or any like-ness of any thing that is in heaven above, or that is in the earth beneath, or that is in the water under the earth. Thou shalt not bow down thyself to them, nor serve them: for I the LORD thy God am a jealous God.

God desires and delights in our steadfast love and obedience as we live our lives before Him in worship. He would rather that we love and serve Him wholeheartedly every day than serve our own desires six days a week, and then, out of obligation, perform our "religious duty" to Him during a worship service one day a week. God desires our acts of worship—daily, hourly, each moment of our lives—given wholly to Him from loving, grateful hearts.

God didn't want the Israelites to bring sacrifices and offerings to Him unless their hearts were in it. He also doesn't want us to simply oblige Him by endlessly going through the motions. *God wants us to love and obey Him.* He doesn't want us to reduce our relationship with Him to mere religious form and ritual. (See 1 Samuel 15:22)

Dear one, God doesn't love you because of what you give Him; neither does He want you to love Him because of what He can do for you. The Father desires *true worship*—loving devotion that is offered to Him with all one's heart, mind, soul, and strength (John 4:23; Luke 10:27). This is where we find true joy. Psalm 112:1-3 also promises:

> Blessed is the man [or woman!] who fears the LORD,
>   who finds great delight in his commands.
> His children will be mighty in the land;
>   the generation of the upright will be blessed.
> Wealth and riches are in his house,
>   and his righteousness endures forever. (NIV)

EMBRACE YOUR DAY

Here's the bottom line. The Bible may not tell you specifically who to marry, what job to take, or whether to rent or buy your home. But the word of God will always tell you how to tune your heart and align your life, so you can recognize God's ultimate best when you see it.

Do you remember "The Four M's of Prayer" in Day 8? As we wrap up today's devotion, I'd like you to think about what I call "The Four W's of Walking in His Purpose." Try to keep them closely in mind, today and every day:

To know God's will, devote your time to reading His WORD.
God's will is found in His word. Just like a car's navigation system I described earlier today acclimates to true north, revealing turn-by-turn instructions that lead to its destination, reading the Bible is your spiritual compass. It is where you find God's instructions to live a life that is pleasing to Him (Romans 12:2).

To know God's will, develop an intimate WALK.
Knowing God's plan for your life means first getting to know Him: the Author of the plan. Putting first things first, you must know God personally through His Son, Jesus Christ, to begin walking in His plan. Look at it this way. *No God, no purpose. Know God, know purpose.*

To know God's will, delight in His WAYS.

If you want to know the ways of God, look at the life of Jesus. Do you want to please God? Live like Jesus. Do you want to develop lifelong relationships and influence people? Lead like Jesus. Do you want to be a blessing to people and serve well? Love like Jesus.

To know God's will, dedicate your life through WORSHIP.

Honor God by living a life of obedience. It doesn't matter how many times a week you go to church or how many Christian songs you know. God is concerned about one thing—your love and obedience to Him. Your daily life can be a wonderful act of worship if you live it to the glory of God (Romans 12:1 NIV).

I hope the time we've set aside together has been a blessing to you today. Knowing that God has a plan for me always leaves my heart at peace. Regardless of what happens during my day, I can rest assured that my life is securely in God's hands.

Life is busy and full of demands. As you leave your concert seat today, get up trusting that God's plan is at work in your life. Let's pause and talk to God for a few moments, all right?

Dear sovereign God,

Thank You for giving me peace in my soul concerning Your will for my life. The more closely I walk with You, the more I desire to do Your will. And the more I saturate my mind with

Your word, the more strength I find to accomplish Your pur-
pose. Please, Lord, keep my mind free of clutter and my heart
free of compromise. I want to live my life Your way. Guide me
by Your truth today and every day of my life. In Jesus' name I
pray.
Amen.

Think About His Love

Pause for a few moments and think about God's great plan for
your life. Consider the giftings and abilities He has given you . . .
just because He loves you. Now consider: Are you walking in
God's purpose, unto Him, as an act of true worship? Now, as the
spirit of God moves in your heart, write a few thoughts in your
journal.

Read About His Love

"Commit your actions to the LORD, and your plans will succeed"
(Proverbs 16:3 NLT). It shouldn't take long to commit this verse
to memory. It does, however, take some time to apply this practical promise to your life. Now, having both *thought* and *read* about
God's purposeful love today, write this verse, followed by a list of
plans you are currently pursuing or would like to pursue in
the future.

Pray About His Love

Present your list of plans to the Lord in prayer. Talk to Him throughout the day concerning His plans for you. As God unfolds and confirms His will, thank Him for doing so and obey. Keep moving forward. Finally, from this day on make it your goal to prayerfully consider everything you say and do—present it all to God as an act of true worship.

Be About His Love

Here's a simple assignment for today: go on a short walk with a friend. If you live in different cities, then connect by cell phone. As you walk, pray with one another. Talk about how much God loves you, what He's doing in your life, and how you are walking out His plan. Record any answers to prayer, insightful ideas, or confirmations of His will in your journal.

WHEN GOD IS WITH YOU

Let worldly minds the world pursue;
It has no charm for me;
Once I admired its trifles, too,
But grace has set me free

Its pleasures now no longer please,
No more content afford;
Far from my heart be joys like these,
Now I have seen the Lord.[1]
—John Newton

"For I know the plans I have for you," declares the LORD,
"plans to prosper you and not to harm you,
plans to give you hope and a future."
—Jeremiah 29:11 NIV

God wants you to be successful in every area of your life.

People all over the world have a passionate drive to succeed. It doesn't seem to matter whether they live in a tiny farm community or in a huge metropolis. People want to lead a successful life. Oftentimes when we think of success and prosperity, we think of owning things like houses, automobiles, money, or other tangible possessions. Of course, in and of themselves, there's nothing wrong with any of them; however, it's been proved time and again that things don't make people truly happy.

I'm persuaded that, deep down, people want more out of life—especially believers in the Lord, Jesus Christ. I'm sure you want your life to make a difference: you want it to be filled with real meaning and purpose. Ultimately, as a born-again, blood-bought believer with the breath of God stirring deeply in your self, you want to carry out His plan for your life. You want to be truly successful.

So, how can you be assured that you are a success?

Our culture measures success by accomplishments, awards, and applause. People are continually impressed by how many titles a person may have or by one's material possessions. However, there is a danger in pursuing the relentless, endless quest for fame, fortune, and notoriety.

Unfortunately, the headlines are filled with the sad stories of those who have chased after fame and fortune, only to find their pursuits empty and meaningless. Even some of the world's most widely recognized people have secured an infamous place in history, having lost their lives in the search of vain pursuits.

Your Success Is in God, and in Him Alone

The Bible gives us a completely different definition of success. According to God's word, success isn't wrapped up in possessions, fame, or recognition. When you get right down to it, my friend, success is not determined by *who you are*. Real success is determined by *who you are with*.

One of my favorite Bible stories is found in 1 Samuel 16:14-18. It details what took place when a young man named David was called upon to serve King Saul. Every time I read this passage, my heart is tremendously blessed by seeing God's mighty hand on David's life. Because I see how a great big God opened huge doors for a young shepherd who would become the king of Israel.

God's favor moved so mightily in David's life. The many psalms he wrote have found their way into countless songs and sermons. Even I have composed a number of songs that were inspired by the psalms of David. He was a man who possessed a number of great qualities. But of the many qualities David possessed, one was far more important than all the rest. Let's read 1 Samuel 16:14-18:

> "The Spirit of the LORD departed from Saul, and an evil spirit from the LORD troubled him. And Saul's servants said unto him, Behold now, an evil spirit from God troubleth thee. Let our lord now command thy servants, which are before thee, to seek out a man, who is a cunning player on an harp: and it shall come to pass, when the evil spirit from God is upon thee, that he shall play with his hand, and thou shalt be well. And Saul said unto his servants, Provide me now a man that can play well, and bring him to me. Then answered one of the servants, and said, Behold, I have seen a son of Jesse the Bethlehemite, that is cunning in playing, and a mighty valiant man, and a man of war, and prudent in matters, and a comely person, *and the LORD is with him.* (emphasis mine)

David was a great psalmist whose music soothed the soul of a tormented king. He was an able hunter who killed wild beasts with his bare hands. As a brave warrior, he slew a giant with a slingshot and a single stone. David was the envy of men and the desire of women. But David's greatest asset didn't have anything to do with his talent. His finest qualities were not found in his acts of bravery or his good looks. Nor was David's most positive feature his popularity or what others said about him.

The key to David's success was that God was with him.

You might be familiar with David's story. But let me give you a few details concerning his background. God had sent the prophet Samuel on a mission to Bethlehem to find and anoint Israel's next king. He had also told Samuel to offer a sacrifice there, inviting Jesse and his sons to attend. Unbeknownst to Jesse, the next king would come from among his sons. It was during this meeting that Samuel asked Jesse's sons to pass before him. Each son came and stood before the prophet. And each one was denied. I love what happened next:

> Samuel said unto Jesse, Are here all thy children? And he said, There remaineth yet the youngest, and, behold he keepeth the sheep. And Samuel said unto Jesse, Send and fetch him: for we will not sit down till he come hither. And he sent, and brought him in. Now he was ruddy, and withal of a beautiful countenance, and goodly to look to. And the LORD said, Arise, anoint him: for this is he. (1 Samuel 16:11-12)

For whatever reason, David did not initially attend the sacrifice. Maybe it was because he was the runt of his brothers, too young to hang with the big boys. Maybe it was because he was a shepherd who smelled of sheep.

David's father didn't seem to be concerned that his youngest son wasn't there. David's brothers probably thought he'd be in the way. But God doesn't think the way we think. While we think we are looking at the big picture, God is paying attention to the smallest details. God didn't just see David for who he was. He saw David for who he was destined to become. David's family saw him as the youngest child. God saw a great king, and a great king he was indeed.

David became the greatest king Israel had ever known. Thousands of years later, he remains an icon—a symbol of success and accomplishment—to Israel and to the world.

There is a powerful lesson to be learned through David's great and miraculous story. Can you picture this young shepherd in the hills minding his father's sheep? Can you envision him singing at the top of his lungs, strumming a groove on his harp for an audience of dumb sheep? You can know for sure that God saw him.

God considered David a huge success long before he ever became king. Even while David was performing the menial jobs of a shepherd, God took pleasure in him. He delighted in David's heart, causing him to be strengthened and his life to flourish. Even when David's family considered him a "nobody," God saw greatness in him.

Because of what Jesus did for you at the cross, that same favor is already yours. Remember, you can't earn God's wonderful favor in your life. You could never do anything to deserve it. It's God's free gift of love and grace to you, and the Giver finds great joy in presenting it to you. Your response should be to simply say *thank you*, open it up, and start enjoying it.

This, my friend, is amazing. Do you see how big God is? Never put a limit on His power and presence in your life. God is for you, not against you. He wants to help you, not harm you. There is nothing He can't do. There isn't a single adverse situation in your life that God can't use to bring about greatness in you.

As you assess your life today, don't define whether or not you are successful according to the world's standards. Don't determine you are or are not successful because of the things you either have or don't have. Don't compare yourself to others, gauging yourself against how they look or what they have accomplished.

Determine you are a success for one reason only—because the Lord Jesus is with you!

When you allow God's great love to influence who you are, there are no limits to what you can accomplish. Knowing God changes your life and destiny. It doesn't matter what your occupation may be. You could be in charge of a high-powered business. You could be responsible for a room full of elementary school students. You could be a college student, work in a cubicle, be a maid, or manage a family. It doesn't matter so much what you do *in* life, as much as it matters what you do *with* your life.

As you yield your gifts and talents to God, He breathes on them. He blesses and multiplies them so that people are blessed and He gets the glory.

Do Not Despise Small Beginnings

If you had asked me when I was a young girl what I wanted to be when I grew up, I would have told you that I wanted to be a singer and a teacher. I even had a short-lived aspiration to be a spy. But the vocation of a professional composer was never on my list of things to become.

I have always been a lover of words and even wrote songs as a hobby when I was in college. However, it wasn't until after I attended a workshop in the early 1980s that the songwriting gift God had planted in me really began to flow out of me. I now know that the Lord divinely placed me at that conference. He ignited my songwriting gift at just the right place and time.

After that experience, I began to work at writing on my own and collaborating with other writers. Pretty soon, I was recording my compositions, and other recording artists were too. I'm living proof that we all possess gifts and talents that are lying dormant inside us.

I firmly believe there is greatness within you, just waiting to be brought to the surface. You possess ideas, solutions, creations, designs, books, masterpieces, and inventions that God has divinely placed inside you. By God's great love and His amazing grace, He will place you right where He wants you to be, when He wants you to be there. Do you believe this?

Don't shy away from new opportunities. Seize them. Don't run from the challenge—run toward it. My father, the late Reverend George W. Wade, was a great preacher and pastor for forty years. He claimed some great words as his life's motto. I want to pass them on to you: "If God be your partner, make your plans larger." God is for you, so think big. Though it may seem at times you are small and insignificant, you can do great things for the Lord and the kingdom of God.

Don't think for one moment that God can't use you. That small-minded, defeatist attitude is just what your adversary wants. *Always remember, you are well able to accomplish any task that God calls you to complete.*

You Can Do All Things in Christ

I love the following passage from the book of Philippians. I call it the "Ten Finger Prayer." When I'm feeling overwhelmed or inadequate, I raise both hands, counting off each word as I recite it. Then I surrender my challenge to the Lord. Try this exercise as you read it. Now, lay the book down and rest something weighty across the top margins, so you can read this verse hands-free. Are your hands up?

> I can do all things through Christ which strengtheneth me. (Philippians 4:13)

Isn't this a great exercise? Can't you just feel God's truth sinking in as your fingers move in perfect rhythm with your words? It makes me want to recite this verse again and again.

Regardless of your faults and foibles, God can and will use you to accomplish His purposes. Over and over again, He used people with challenges and weaknesses to demonstrate His great strength. Take a look at a short list of some of God's most unlikely characters:

> *Moses stuttered.*
>
> *David was a murderer.*
>
> *Jacob was a trickster.*
>
> *Jeremiah was young.*
>
> *Peter was known to have a short temper.*
>
> *Matthew was said to occasionally dip into the treasury.*
>
> *Mary was a teenage mother.*
>
> *Abraham was old.*
>
> *Sarah was cynical.*
>
> *Naaman was a leper.*
>
> *Jehoshaphat was outnumbered.*
>
> *Thomas was a doubter.*
>
> *Mary and Martha were impatient.*
>
> *And Lazarus was dead.*

Never say that you consider yourself to be too old, too young, unqualified, uneducated, not the right size or color, financially challenged—or any other excuse you may come up with—to accomplish great things for God. When you think and speak negatively about yourself, you defeat God's purpose in your life.

You must allow God to demonstrate His strength through your weakness by placing your life in His capable hands. *Who you are with makes all the difference in the world.*

My friend Dr. Tony Evans is a great preacher and master illus-
trator. When he speaks, I listen. He also serves as the chaplain for
the Dallas Mavericks basketball team. In *Tony Evans' Book of
Illustrations*, Pastor Tony shares a story about when he invited his
family to join him at a Mavericks home game. The team was
playing at Dallas's Reunion Arena, and Pastor Tony was sched-
uled to deliver the pregame devotional message to the team.

He invited all of his family to join him for the big game and all
the pregame activities. Then he tells about how he instructed
them to caravan to the arena so they could all enter the arena as
a group. The story he tells goes something like this:

Be sure to park in the VIP parking lot. And should the gate-
keeper question why you're parking there, just tell him
you're with me. Enter the building through the VIP
entrance at the rear of the building where the team members enter. And if anyone should question why they should
let you in, just tell them you're with me.

Go on into the building and make your way to the dining
room. There you'll find a wonderful dinner prepared just for
you. Enjoy the meal. Eat all you want. Meet the team, their
spouses and families. And if anyone should question why
you're in there, just tell them you're with me. After dinner,
go on into the room where we will hold the chapel service
for the team, coaches, staff and their families. Enjoy the
service. And if anyone should question why you're there,
just tell them you're with me.

After the chapel service, make your way into the arena. There you'll find the VIP Executive Suite that has been reserved courtside for our family. You'll have the best seats in the arena. All your refreshments are on the house. And if anyone should question why you're in the suite, just tell them you're with me.[2]

And you see, you've been given every blessing, every privilege because of who you're with. And when you get to Glory and you stand before Almighty God, and He asks you why He should let you into His heaven, just stand real close to the Lord, the Author and Finisher of your faith and say, I'm with Jesus.

EMBRACE YOUR DAY

Here's something to think about. You can know a lot about people without actually knowing them. If you *know of* someone, you could name-drop and recite some easily known facts about him or her. You could even be in the same room a time or two—but unless that person *knows you*—there is no real relationship. If that person doesn't look your way, acknowledge your presence, and call you by name, you're just a face in the crowd.

Success is not in who you know, but in who knows you. *True success comes only from having a real, life-changing relationship with Jesus.* He knows the real you: your hopes, passions, and dreams. He loves your company and spending His time with you. Jesus has given you the wonderful gift of your life's plan, and He wants you to walk it out.

You have the choice to live your life in one of two ways. You can choose to go the way of culture, relying on your own strength, trusting in your own accomplishments, and chasing after the mirage of materialism. You can go through life comparing yourself to others and craving the affirmations of people.

But I encourage you to rely fully on the Lord and His presence in your life. In doing so, you will enjoy real love, incredible peace, and the security of His hope and favor in your life. God's ability in you, His relationship to you, and His hand upon you will allow you to accomplish your greatest dreams and aspirations. In God, there will be no limits to what you can accomplish.

As you abide in the Lord and follow His plan, nothing will be impossible to you.

Consider today another wonderful opportunity to please God with your life. You can live every moment confident of His love for you. Anyone can say, "God loves me." But does your life show it? It's easy to say, "God has a plan for my life." But do you believe this enough to diligently seek His will and His plan as you make your everyday decisions?

This is the true test of who you consider your source to be. Remember, people are not your source. On their best day, people will overlook you or even forget about you. Your source is not material wealth. Oh, it's okay to own material things—but it's not okay for material things to own you.

Your ultimate source for everything you need, want, and desire in this life is Jesus. He knows who you are, and He knows right where you are in the matters of life. You may not see Him, dear one, but He is there. Jesus is working on your behalf. His presence in your life is where *real success* begins.

Tomorrow we'll take another look at Jeremiah 29:11. We will examine the last part of this great promise—the future and the hope—closely. Jesus is the reason we can look forward to tomorrow. Our future is bright and our hope is great because of Him. But for now, let's pause together and pray. Let's give thanks to God for unfolding His plan and opening doors for you:

Awesome God,

    You are so amazing! You are concerned about every detail of my life. Nothing escapes You. With You, Lord, nothing ever slips between the cracks or falls off the radar. Forgive me for ever doubting Your love and concern for me. There have been times I didn't understand the ways You were at work in my life, but, Lord, I know Your ways are perfect. Help me to trust You in every way: with my family and friendships, in my work, in my service to You, and in every area of my life. From this day on, help me to depend fully on You to meet all my needs. More than this, Lord, stir up the gifts and talents You have given me. I thank You for each and every one—even those I am not yet aware of—and present them to You anew and afresh today. Jesus, I want to use all that I have and all that I am to promote the kingdom of God and make Your name famous in the earth. Help me to define success by Your standards from this day forward, and forgive me for ever looking to others for validation. I long for Your approval only, Lord. I understand now that real success is found in You and You alone. Receive my heartfelt devotion today and always. In the great name of Jesus I pray. Amen.

Think About His Love

As you go about your day, observe how people around you long for success. Pay a little more attention to our culture's lust for material possessions. Think about it. Do things like television, music, and the Internet feed these desires in you? A relentless drive to acquire more things is evidence of an empty life. Remember: *real success* is the reality of God's presence in your life—because when you know God's plan and you know He is with you, all things are possible. Now, humor me and do a little review. Go back and read the introduction for this fifth concert theme on pages 245–47. Say the confession at the bottom of page 247 again and again, as much as is needed for this truth to go down deep in your soul. Because, my dear friend, *God's plan for you is exceptional*, much more than you know.

Read About His Love

" 'For I know the plans I have for you,' declares the LORD, 'plans to prosper you and not to harm you, plans to give you hope and a future' " (Jeremiah 29:11 NIV). God has set a lavish banquet table for you. There are so many delicacies at His table you couldn't possibly eat all of them in one sitting . . . there's enough eternally fresh, nourishing food to eat for the rest of your life! So, take your time; meditate on this verse. You may even want to type it out, print it on a pretty piece of paper, and then put it up somewhere so you'll see it again and again. Then print another copy and put it inside the front cover of your Bible. You might even want to print and laminate a slightly smaller version of this promise and carry it in your pocket or purse. That way, each time life's distractions begin to draw you away from this truth you can immediately recall God's promise.

Pray About His Love

As you commune with God today, thanking Him for the great plans He has for you, remember to pray this promise for others, starting with your spouse, children, and/or extended family members, your pastor, church leadership, and so on. Then pray silently for those you pass along the way, like the postman, the grocery store clerk, and the day care worker. The opportunities to share from God's banquet table are endless, so be generous. Share this blessing by praying it over as many people as you can today, so they'll come to know success God's way.

Be About His Love

Now, let's take it a step further. Turn off the television, take a break from the computer, and put on some inspirational music. Include someone special in your plans today. Instead of sending that usual, quick text message or e-mail, send a brief handwritten note or card to remind your friend of God's love and His incredible plan for his or her life. *Be about His love* today by sharing this wonderful blessing!

DAY 15

WHEN LIFE IS THE PITS

When you say a situation or a person is hopeless,
you're slamming the door in the face of God.[1]
—Charles L. Allen

Why are you downcast, O my soul?
Why so disturbed within me?
Put your hope in God,
for I will yet praise him,
my Savior and my God.
—Psalm 42:11 NIV

No matter what your present situation may seem to be, God promises your future is filled with hope: hope that is as bright as His deep love for you.

As we ponder this concert theme just a little longer before moving on, let me encourage you again. *Never forget, beloved friend, you are God's favorite.* He wants to prosper you more than you know because He loves you. A great big God is on your side. He wants to "open you the windows of heaven, and pour you out a blessing, that there shall not be room enough to receive it"

(Malachi 3:10) as you follow His plan. In God, your future is brimming over with promise and pregnant with possibilities.

I am sure there have been times, however, when life has been the pits: when things around you have appeared to be anything but hopeful. During these times it can be difficult to stand and say there is hope. Hear me well, my dear friend; it's all too easy to slip into the miry quicksand of hopelessness and despair when circumstances seem to be just the opposite of God's best for you.

There is a pervasive feeling of hopelessness these days. But I want you to remember that as long as you have life, the very breath of God within you, there is always hope for you.

I don't know what your typical day may look like, but it may comfort you to know some things are common to us all. There are times when before we've hardly finished our morning cup of coffee, we've heard some sort of bad news. Almost every time we look up today we're hearing about economic despair, skyrocketing food and gas prices, joblessness, homelessness, marriage and family pressures, the AIDS epidemic, and more.

The long list of life's calamities can easily cause one's heart to sink. As far back as I can remember, the daily newspaper and the twenty-four-hour cable news channels have made it their business to tell us everything that's going wrong in the world. Yet I say to you: Have hope in God!

Thinking back, I can remember many times when my mother (the pastor's wife) hung up the phone and said, "Lord, if it ain't one thing, it's another." She had just finished a long conversation with yet another hurting soul going through life's challenges. Life isn't easy. Denise, a friend of mine, has a variation on that theme. She says, "If it ain't one thing, it's two."

My dear mother *and* my friend are both right! If it's not your kids, it's the car. If it's not your house, it's your health. And if it's not your money, it's your honey. Sometimes it seems one's list of woes never ends.

Even as I write this chapter, just this week we have experienced very unusual weather patterns in our area. We've barely seen rain all season long. For almost ninety days straight temperatures have hovered around the 100-degree mark. Here on the East Coast we have experienced drought, an earthquake, a hurricane, and flooding all within the same week.

It makes me wonder what in the world the world is coming to. Right about now, it would be easy to just curl up in a corner in the fetal position until the storm passes over and things cool down. *But God!*

God's Perfect Hope Is in You

Let me assure you, there is good news for us, the good news of the gospel! Because Jesus finished His perfect work at the cross, no matter what things may look like, we have a great hope and a bright future.

You may have a long list of challenges, my dear friend, but God loves you. He has already made a way for you. And He wants you to be assured by faith that hope is *not* just around the corner. *Hope is right where you are.* Hope is *not* just a wish away. *Hope is available to you right now.*

When hope makes its home in your heart, you discover that's exactly where Jesus is.

In Christ, you don't have to give up or give in to life's challenges. You can get filled up with His presence and believe for a turn-around, try again, start over . . . whatever the situation requires, you can do above and beyond that. Hope always rises above it all because God's grace is sufficient for your every need. His "power" is perfected in your weakness. (See 2 Corinthians 12:9 NIV.)

The devil knows this too. So, he works diligently to steal your hope. He tries to wear you down with constant attacks against your faith. He sends annoying distractions everywhere you turn. He shouts in your face about all the bad things that are happening both to you and around you. But you don't have to give in. Don't let the enemy steal your faith and hope in God. Run, don't walk, to the Master. Receive grace and help in your time of need.

Dear friend, as long as you focus your energies on your own needs and circumstances, *your problems* will always seem bigger than *your God*. It's time we quit shouting our problems while whispering our praises. Can I hear an *amen?*

Let's do a little faith exercise. Let's practice looking to God and remembering His hope-filled promises, so you can do it on your own when the need arises. Because when you rehearse His hope-filled truths, your problems diminish compared to the awesome greatness of almighty God. There is power in His word! Now, let's "Read about His Love" together. Psalm 27:14 (CEB) says,

> Hope in the LORD!
> Be strong! Let your heart take courage!
> Hope in the LORD!

I love God's word! My faith soars as I slow myself down and meditate on this promise. Yours will too! Now, let's personalize the promise. Notice how I've inserted my name below. Just look at what adding my name and arranging the words a little differently do. To me, this promise literally jumps off the page! I can almost hear the voice of young David the psalmist shouting out to me with passion:

> *Hope in the Lord, Babbie!*
> *Be strong, Babbie!*
> *Let your heart take courage, Babbie!*
> *Hope in the Lord, Babbie!*

He's shouting out to you, too, my friend. Now, take a moment and do the exercise, this time inserting your name at the end of each declaration. Write it down on a piece of paper, or type it on the computer if you'd prefer. That way, you can print out the promise and put it on display wherever you may like or need to see it. Now, declare *your* personal promise, thanking God for giving you hope and victory.

Each time hope comes under attack, *practice the promise.* Rise above the weakness of your flesh, and submit to the counsel of God's word. Then resist the devil, *and what will happen?* That lying, scheming, conniving adversary will have to flee, according to James 4:7. As a matter of fact, take a few moments right now to read James 4:1-7. No matter what you may be facing, *God gives more grace.* The spirit is willing and the flesh is weak, so when your flesh rises up, humble yourself before God. He'll take it from there, and the devil will have to get out of your way.

You'd better take God's promises and run with them, my friend. And while you're at it, share this good news with everybody you can. I'm sure they need to hear them too. When you share God's word and what Christ has done for you, it always spreads hope and encouragement. So, whenever you *receive* life and hope from Him, turn and *give* them to others. Hear this promise from God's word:

> Do not be deceived: God cannot be mocked. A man reaps what he sows. The one who sows to please his sinful nature, from that nature will reap destruction; the one who sows to please the Spirit, from the Spirit will reap eternal life. Let us not become weary in doing good, for at the proper time we will reap a harvest if we do not give up. Therefore, as we have opportunity, let us do good to all people, especially to those who belong to the family of believers. (Galatians 6:7-10 NIV)

Hope in God, my dear sister! Share your hope with others. I thank God for the psalmist David, who so often helps us sow the hope-filled word of God in our hearts. You see, David's hope was attacked, severely, repeatedly throughout his life. But as he received grace from God, he turned to others and gave it away. I'm so glad he did, aren't you?

We can do the same. God is faithful. We will reap a harvest of righteousness if we don't give up! Our hope is in the Lord, our *only* hope . . . our best hope . . . a hope that endures the test of time and will never be disappointed. I say to you: *Hope in God because God is in you.*

A lot of people think of *hope* as being wishful thinking, a waiting game, presumption, betting, wagering, or wishing upon a star.

They say things like, "I hope things will turn out okay," "I hope we get some rain soon," or "I have high hopes that we'll have a good team this year."

But the biblical definition of *hope* is much more than that. Hope in God is a confident expectation of good, based on our Father's perfect character and the integrity of His promises. Hope in God is a firm assurance concerning a situation or thing that is otherwise unclear or unknown. Hope is complete confidence in God, believing Him for a favorable outcome: "We know that all things work together for good to them that love God, to them who are the called according to his purpose" (Romans 8:28).

Need I say more? When you *hope in God* you can see yourself blessed. Because you hope in the Lord, you can envision yourself healthy. Because of godly hope, you can see every one of your needs being provided for according to His riches in glory by Christ Jesus (Philippians 4:19).

As believers in God and children of our loving heavenly Father, we don't place hope in some earthly thing or event. Our hope rests firmly and securely in the Lord, Jesus Christ, because of what He has done on our behalf. Hebrews 6:17-20 (*THE MESSAGE*) reminds us:

> When God wanted to guarantee his promises, he gave his word, a rock-solid guarantee—God can't break his word. And because his word cannot change, the promise is likewise unchangeable. We who have run for our very lives to God have every reason to grab the promised hope with both hands and never let go. It's an unbreakable spiritual lifeline, reaching past all appearances right to the very presence of God where

Jesus, running on ahead of us, has taken up his permanent post as high priest for us.

God's Hope Endures to the End

I receive so much encouragement when I read about men and women in the Bible whose lives were full of hope in God. One of those hope-filled people was Joseph. At the tender age of seventeen, Joseph was a "golden boy" who had everything going for him. His amazing story begins in Genesis 37. He was a favored son, an honest young man, full of integrity, and a worshiper of God. He lived faithfully for God, never knowing what the future held for him.

But Joseph's immediate family was another thing altogether. They had issues. If they were living today, they would certainly be fodder for prime-time television, perhaps even airing their dirty laundry on their own reality show. Joseph's family was the definitive dysfunctional family. It was filled with animosity, rivalry, and jealousy that existed among four wives—Leah, Rachel, Zilpah, and Bilhah—the mothers of a band of cutthroat sons. The resulting strife certainly affected every member of this blended family.

Jacob, the father of this tribe of twelve brothers, didn't help matters any. He made it very plain that Joseph was his favorite son (from Rachel, his favorite wife). To demonstrate the great love he had for Joseph, Jacob made his favored son a special "coat of many colours" (Genesis 37:3).

This show of favoritism made Joseph's brothers hate him all the more. Added to this, God spoke to Joseph in his dreams.

These dreams revealed details of how God would cause Joseph to rise to greatness as a leader and ruler over his brothers *and* their great nation. Perhaps seeking counsel, Joseph shared his dreams from God with his brothers, which made them seethe with envy (vv. 5-11).

The plot thickened as Joseph's brothers treated him the same way they had been treated. They felt rejected by their father, so they rejected Joseph. Weary of Joseph's bold display of his father's affection, they became spiteful, hateful, jealous, and vengeful, ultimately conspiring to kill him. Then when the opportunity arose, they chose once and for all to rid themselves of their younger brother. Deciding against killing him, they threw Joseph in a deep pit and later sold him into slavery for twenty pieces of silver (vv. 18-28).

The Pit

Has your soul ever been in a deep, dark, dank pit? Do you know anything about the pit of despair, a depth of misery that is so low it seems to never end? What about the pit of grief? Maybe something or someone very dear to you was taken. Maybe you lost your home, a marriage, or a job. It could be that you experienced the loss of a loved one. If you have ever traveled down this road, then you know that this kind of emptiness and grief is felt so deeply inside your heart it's almost tangible. If you have ever been there, you know that *this pit* is custom made for one. Friends don't usually go there with you. I'm pretty sure Joseph felt the range of human emotions that commonly rise up when hope is attacked. Sometimes life can really be the pits.

I can identify with Joseph on quite a few levels, having found myself "in the pits" a few times in my life. I know what it feels like to be on the receiving end of human cruelty. When I was a junior at Spring Arbor College, a Christian liberal arts college in southern Michigan (not far from home), I was the only black member of my college choir. In the late 1970s while we were on a choir tour, we performed one evening in a predominantly white church in Atlanta, Georgia.

After the concert we spent the night in the homes of church members who served as our hosts. My roommate, a sweet girl named Suzie, and I went to the home of our hosts, an older white couple. As we were getting ready for bed, Suzie came to me and revealed that she had just been asked if she minded sleeping in the same bed with a "[n-word] gal." In recent years, I recall being invited to churches to give a concert only to have them canceled when the deacons of those respective churches learned that I was black.

Each time, I found myself in a pit of hurt and confusion. How could people be like that? How could people say they love God, yet want nothing to do with me? Oh, yes, during times like these Jesus had to meet me in the pit. On these two occasions, I found myself stuck in a pit of despair. I was fighting mad in my pit. The Lord had to rescue me before my heart became bitter and filled with indifference.

Hurt and in desperation, I had to cry out for deliverance from the depths of my pit, or I could have become just like those who had wronged me. Of course, I have long since forgiven those people, but I have to be honest with you. I bear a deep scar from being on the receiving end of hatred and ignorance. Sometimes I even have to fight back tears. However, as I look back on those situations now, I can see the sovereign hand of God. These experiences have not made me bitter. They have made be better. I thank God for Lamentations 3:26-27, which reminds me:

> It is good that one should hope in and wait quietly for the salvation (the safety and ease) of the Lord. It is good for a man that he should bear the yoke [of divine disciplinary dealings] in his youth. (AMP)

I'm sure you have had your "pit experiences" too, just like Joseph did. His list goes on and on. Wronged by his brothers, abused by slave traders, carried away to a land of pagan worshipers, and sold again as a slave to Potiphar (an Egyptian official guard who worked for Pharaoh), Joseph knew all too well how pitiful pits can be.

Even the ugly sting of racism became a part of Joseph's experience. Potiphar's wife played the race card against Joseph after she had made sensual advances toward him, but he did not reciprocate. She was highly offended, and in order to cover her tracks, she accused Joseph of attempting to rape her. Read what happened in Genesis 39:11-12:

> It came to pass about this time, that Joseph went into the house to do his business; and there was none of the men of the house there within. And she caught him by his garment, saying, Lie with me: and he left his garment in her hand, and fled, and got him out.

Now, let's go to verse 17, when Potiphar's wife told her husband a heinous lie after he, no doubt, got back home from a strenuous day's work:

> She spake unto him according to these words, saying, The Hebrew servant, which thou hast brought unto us, came in unto me to mock me: and it came to pass, as I lifted up my voice and cried, that he left his garment with me, and fled out.

Her story may have been a cover-up, but her indignation was as plain as day. She was a woman scorned. I can read her heart like an open book. I can just see her stance now. Left hand on her hip and lips pursed tightly. Her forehead scowled. The other arm stretched out fully with index finger pointed firmly toward the servants' entrance. She set her voice in an unmistakable, unforgettable tone as she emphasized the words to her husband, "The *Hebrew* servant that *you* brought into this house. . . ."

Joseph, no doubt, knew all too well what it felt like to be on the other end of snide comments. A foreigner accused of a crime worthy of death, he got *picked out, picked on*, and it landed him in the dungeon.

Dear one, if you have been singled out this way in life and are in a spiritual pit—struggling in the wake of an offended, sinful attitude, the sting of rejection, or perhaps even an addiction—you are not by yourself. If you are wallowing deep in an emotional pit, fighting depression, fears, bitterness, or anxieties, you are not an isolated case. You may even be in a physical pit, dealing with an illness or disease for which the doctors say there is no hope. My friend, you are not alone.

Even when you are in your deepest, darkest, dankest pit, no matter how you got there, Jesus is there with you. But not to keep you company, though. He has come to deliver you!

My friend, Bible study teacher and confessed pit-dweller, Beth Moore wrote a great book, *Get Out of That Pit*. In this insightful book, she says in a very personal and profound manner that "God is driven by relationship. It takes two to tango, even out of a pit. His part is to lift you out. Your part is to hold on for dear life."[2] I firmly agree with Beth. You can get out of that pit. Raise your eyes. Raise your hands. And raise your hopes. As hope rises up in you, raise your voice to sing your victory song:

> Why are you downcast, O my soul?
> Why so disturbed within me?
> Put your hope in God,
>> for I will yet praise him,
>> my Savior and my God. (Psalm 43:5 NIV)

If you are in a pit right now, look up, if only for a moment! It's all the time you need to see that your Hero, Jesus, is right there to rescue you. It may look dark, but your redemption is at hand. You may have fallen into a pit, or you may have been thrown into it. You could have been pushed into the pit by others, or perhaps you slipped into it by accident. However you got there, Jesus is there to get you out.

The Process

Sometimes on life's journey we focus on the promises, but we don't want much to do with the process. We'd rather go back to the pain of the past or go with haste toward the future. But we have to remember that sometimes the only way out of a tough situation is not to back up or go around but to go through it.

While Jacob, Joseph's father, wept with grief back home thinking his beloved son was dead, Joseph, a young man of honesty and integrity, sat in prison and endured thirteen years as a slave there. Little did he know that before he would rise to become one of the most powerful leaders in the world, he would know firsthand what it means to be forsaken and forgotten by those who had promised to help his cause.

Joseph would learn the hard way what it means to be overlooked and underappreciated by others. He would pay a high price for choosing not to behave in the same dishonorable and shameful manner as his brothers did. This decision cost him his freedom, and for a while it seemed that his future would be in jeopardy as well. Let's go back briefly to Genesis 39:1-2 and recap his story from a different perspective. Let's see how hope appears on the scene for this young, favored son:

> Joseph was brought down to Egypt; and Potiphar, an officer of Pharaoh, captain of the guard, an Egyptian, bought him of the hands of the Ishmeelites, which had brought him down thither. *And the* LORD *was with Joseph,* and he was a prosperous man; and he was in the house of his master the Egyptian. (emphasis mine)

I want you to notice that the same words of hope we talked about in yesterday's devotion concerning David (taken from 1 Samuel 16:18) are used concerning Joseph. I italicized them for emphasis, but I'll say it again, "And the LORD was with Joseph." Potiphar might have been an Egyptian, but he saw it too. And because God was with Joseph, grace, favor, promotion, responsibility, and influence came right along with God's presence. Even while Joseph was in prison, God caused him to prosper (see Genesis 39:19-23).

My good friend and songwriting partner Tony Sutherland wrote a great book called GRACEWORKS. In it he says, "Because we move the heart of God, He moves the hand of man on our behalf."[3]

God's promises are from everlasting to everlasting. So, the same powerful promise is yours today! Even when you don't see any evidence of God in a situation, you can have the confident assurance that He's behind the scenes working all things together for your good. When everything seems to be going all wrong, God will cause your circumstances to work out all right.

I've always said, "God never does something for nothing. He always does something for something!" With God, even your pain has a purpose. What the enemy means to work against you, God causes to work for you as you stay in faith!

One Sunday morning while I was getting ready for church, I turned on the television just in time to catch the last few minutes of a sermon delivered by one of my favorite pastor friends and great Bible teacher Andy Stanley. I didn't hear the entire sermon, but I'll never forget the words I did hear. Andy's words filled my heart with hope and encouragement.

Let me encourage you as I paraphrase his words from memory. He said that it is imperative on life's journey to keep walking by faith. Just keep putting one foot in front of the other. Don't look to the left or to the right. Keep your eyes on your goal. Don't get discouraged by people who are wandering aimlessly on the road. Don't be distracted by meaningless signs and billboards that are on the roadside. If the road is rough, just keep plodding forward. If the way is steep, just keep moving methodically, putting one foot in front of the other.

You may or may not have an emotional experience with God during your journey. You may or may not have clear-cut directions. Just remain obedient. Wait for instructions, and then just keep walking by faith. One day, your faith and God's faithfulness will intersect, and you will finally see with your natural eyes what you only believed by faith beforehand.[4]

Later that week, I was working on some interviews with a friend at a local radio station in a downtown high-rise. We took a break for lunch and headed down to the café in the lobby area of the building. While we ate lunch, I shared with my friend how Andy Stanley's sermon had impacted me and had given me hope regarding my circumstances. When I finished sharing the details of the sermon with my friend, we noticed a woman seated in the corner of the café.

She was the only other person in the café besides us. Suddenly, she began to weep aloud at the table where she was sitting. Then her cries turned into sobs. Then from her sobs began to flow audible words of praise and thanksgiving to God.

Wanting to know what was going on, my friend and I got up and went over to her table to see if we could be of help. She shared with us that she had lost her job that day. And she was going to be evicted from her apartment. She had no money to feed her children. Then she said that for some reason she decided to come in to that café to escape the heat of the oppressive summer sun.

She didn't know what she was going to do about her situation. She prayed a prayer of desperation to God. She told us that if she didn't hear from Him soon that she was planning to just go home and find a way to end her life. This sweet woman said while she was crying out to God in her pit of despair, she heard words of hope coming from across the room. That's when she leaned in and eavesdropped on our conversation. Hope rose up inside her as she listened to our words of faith in God.

My friend and I were amazed! I wish you could have seen the three of us as we embraced. Then, together, the three of us applauded God, shouted praises to Him, and cried tears of joy.

Topping off this wonderful occasion, my friend and I thanked God for sending the word of hope our sister desperately needed to hear. We affirmed to her that God was on her side and that He had divinely directed her into that café. We bought her some lunch and blessed her with the cash that we had in our pockets. Then we gave her phone numbers and contacts to agencies and people we thought could help her employment and housing situations. Finally, we assured her that if God could arrange that meeting in the café, He definitely had an answer for every detail of her situation.

Yes, that sister needed money for rent and food, and she needed a good job to replace the one she had just lost. But more than anything, at that moment, that dear lady needed hope.

The Prize

It would have been easy for Joseph to give up after many years of being a prisoner in a foreign land. It would have been understandable, by human terms, for him to be angry with God. Joseph could have become bitter, angry, and resentful because of his condition. He had been given privileges while he was in prison, but he was still a slave, far away from his home in a foreign land, living among people who did not know his God.

It must have seemed that in spite of trying to do everything right, there were still a lot of things going wrong. But Joseph didn't give up. If he had, he would have forfeited the position God had designed him to fill. Of course, Joseph had been accused of attempted rape—against Potiphar's wife, no less. But I'm sure Potiphar could easily see over time that Joseph was still the young man of fine moral character he had put in charge of his household.

Under pressure, the gifts and abilities that God had placed in Joseph came out of him. In the midst of a stressful, unfair situation, Joseph's gifts began to flourish. Does this give you hope? God used this difficult, yet pivotal season in Joseph's life to develop all the skills he would need to become a great national leader. God even caused Pharaoh to have a dream as He worked out His will in Joseph's life. Let's read Genesis 41:15-16 to see how it played out:

> Pharaoh said into Joseph, I have dreamed a dream, and there is none that can interpret it: and I have heard say of thee, that thou canst understand a dream to interpret it. And Joseph answered Pharaoh, saying, It is not in me: God shall give Pharaoh an answer of peace.

Don't you love Joseph? Faithful to God, Joseph acknowledged that he could do nothing without the Lord's help. Faithful to Joseph, God acknowledged Joseph's dependence on Him and allowed the dream to be interpreted favorably.

From the dream came a word from the Lord. While in a time of surplus, Egypt was to prepare for a time of famine. Pharaoh was so pleased with Joseph's wisdom, integrity, and insight that he put him in charge of everything concerning his house—and over the entire nation—second only to himself. Ultimately, Joseph saved the entire nation of Egypt, as well as his own family, from a long, severe famine.

We've only covered the big picture of this great story about the faithfulness of God. Time or space won't permit me to expound any longer on all the wonderful details. I encourage you, though, to read all the way to the end of the book of Genesis. See for yourself how hope never loses, but always wins in the end.

EMBRACE YOUR DAY

There is so much we can glean from this three-day theme. My heart is full of hope! Is yours? To wrap things up for now, there are three things I want you to take with you before we turn the page. First of all, God always has a plan. Second, it's a plan to prosper you, not to harm you. Third, God's plan is always to give you hope and a future.

You should be well on your way to memorizing Jeremiah 29:11 by now. If you haven't, I trust you will start right now committing this great nugget of truth to memory.

Remember, good friend, that you are dearly loved by Father God today and always. Everything you need is available to you through His Son, Jesus. He is your source of hope. When you feel that life is the pits and you've been forgotten or overlooked, God has not forgotten you. Neither should you forget Him, my friend. Let the words of Psalm 103:1-5 encourage you:

> Bless the LORD, O my soul,
> And all that is within me, bless His holy name.
> Bless the LORD, O my soul,
> And forget none of His benefits;
> Who pardons all your iniquities,
> Who heals all your diseases;
> Who redeems your life from the pit,
> Who crowns you with lovingkindness and compassion;
> Who satisfies your years with good things,
> So that your youth is renewed like the eagle. (NASB)

Have you been challenged to pursue God's plan with more passion? I pray that your answer is an affirmative yes and amen.

We've come to the end of our fifth variation in God's powerful theme of love. Tomorrow, we'll strike the chord on a brand-new theme, activating God's power in our lives. You'll be reminded that the great God we serve has equipped you with power to carry out His plan and purpose for your life. I know you will be encouraged.

But for now, I want to talk to our sweet Father and ask Him to bless you in every way you stand in need. As you read this prayer, I ask for your participation. Would you set your book down and position it so your hands are free? On your table top, rest your hands on either side of the book, so your palms are facing upward toward heaven. Now, open them wide to convey that you are ready to receive from the Lord. Let me pray for you:

Dear sweet Father in heaven,

Thank You for always hearing our prayers and for being attentive to our outward cries of frustration or our silent requests from a heart of brokenness. You are aware of every single need that Your children have. Lord, You see my precious friend sitting here in Your presence, hands open and outstretched. Help my friend to release every care for Your simplicity, every burden for Your easy yoke, every broken dream for Your promise of a bright future, every hurt for Your healing, and every pit for Your pinnacle. In exchange, help my friend to receive Your help for her plans, Your grace for her weaknesses, Your love for her lack of charity, Your forgiveness for her sins, and Your acceptance for

every time she has been rejected. *Fill this heart with a buoyant hope and top it all off with a relentless joy that overflows into every area of her life. Bless my friend today and every day. This is my prayer. In Jesus' name,*
Amen.

Think About His Love

As we close the curtain on this fifth concert theme today, reflect on how God's plan has been active in your life. Whether you are standing firm on a mountaintop or have gone slip-sliding into a pit, God's plan is always at work. Take a little time today to think about how Joseph's story has impacted your life.

Read About His Love

> Why are you downcast, O my soul?
> Why so disturbed within me?
> Put your hope in God,
>   for I will yet praise him,
>   my Savior and my God. (Psalm 42:11 NIV)

So much has already been said about this pivotal verse in our devotion today. During your quiet time, start off reading, rehearsing, and personalizing this verse. Let it lead you into prayer.

Pray About His Love

Today, as the Holy Spirit guides you, instead of presenting your prayers as petitions, try singing some of your prayers by lifting up a hymn of praise, maybe something like,

> My hope is built on nothing less than Jesus' blood and
> righteousness.
> I dare not trust the sweetest frame, but wholly lean on
> Jesus' name.
> On Christ the solid rock I stand, all other ground is
> sinking sand.[5]

Be About His Love

Remember from our session today that when you receive a blessing from God, you should turn and give it to someone else. In the words you speak, with the people you meet, whether the news they bring is good or bad, practice hope today. Joyfully sow what you have received from God, and you will reap rich rewards.

THEME SIX

GOD'S POWER IN YOU IS ACCESSIBLE

Begone, unbelief, my Savior is near,
And for my relief will surely appear:
By prayer let me wrestle, and He will perform,
With Christ in the vessel, I smile at the storm.

Though dark be my way, since He is my Guide,
'Tis mine to obey, 'tis His to provide;
Though cisterns be broken, and creatures all fail,
The word He has spoken shall surely prevail.
—John Newton[1]

If you were given the choice to have a real diamond or a fake one, which would you choose? I don't know about you, but I would say, "Give me the real thing!" There's a popular saying going around that tells you to "fake it 'til you make it." I say with Jesus on your side, you are more than a conqueror, and there's no need to put up a front. Why fake it, only appearing to possess victory in Jesus, when you can have the bona fide, real deal?

For the next three days we'll celebrate God's great power that is available to you. This power—that equips you to make a difference, to do the right thing, or even to do the impossible—is *in Christ*, and He is *in you*.

We need the bona fide power of God in the world today. Because only His anointing equips us to complete the task to which He has called us. And only His mighty power can break every yoke of bondage. Only His love melody can penetrate a world gone crazy and bring light and life to hurting, wounded, wayward souls.

Every symphony has a crescendo, when the music intensifies to a dramatic peak. It is the same in God's symphony of love. He loved the world so intensely that it peaked and He gave His only begotten Son. Jesus came, continued flowing in love, and it peaked wherever He went. People who were blind could see, people who were deaf could hear, and people who could not speak could speak again. Broken lives and hearts were mended. Even the dead rose from the grave.

Now, my friend, it's our turn. The Father wants His children to keep flowing in His power, sharing His love in this lost and dying world.

The curtain is rising. We are about to enter a pivotal movement in this new concert theme. Are you prepared to receive, and then give to others, what only Christ can give? Are your ears tuned to our Conductor, so you'll be ready to hit the perfect note that is yours and yours alone? *I know you can do it!* Because, dear one, as the tempo builds you can truly discover all things are possible in Him. The greatest power of all flows in your self.

FOR THE NEXT THREE DAYS FOCUS YOUR
MIND AND HEART ON THIS:
Because God loves me,
He has given me the ability to accomplish
great things in His name.

DAY 16

TAKE A BIG LEAP OF FAITH

Give me the love that leads the way, the faith that
nothing can dismay, the hope no disappointments tire,
the passion that will burn like fire. Let me sink not to be a clod.
Make me Thy fuel, Flame of God.[1]
—Amy Carmichael

Lord, if it is You, command me to come to You on the water.
—Matthew 14:28b NKJV

God wants you to put your faith into practice.

The story of the disciples' faith adventure, which took place in a violent storm on the Sea of Galilee, is powerful. Sometime between 3:00 and 6:00 a.m., Jesus appeared to His followers, calmly walking on the high, menacing waves. Thinking they had seen a ghost, the disciples cried out in fear. Their boat was being dashed and battered by angry waves on every side when Jesus spoke to them, telling them not to fear.

Always the audacious one, Peter shouted out, "Lord, if it is You, command me to come to You on the water." (Matthew 14:28b NKJV).

That's when Jesus called out to Peter and said, "Come" (v. 29).

This small, yet powerful, word is such a beautiful invitation. It says so many things, like "Don't go. Don't leave. You are not a burden. I can help you. You are not a bother. You are a friend. You are welcome. Come on." Peter immediately responded to the Lord's invitation.

Let's read the rest of the account in Matthew 14:29-31a (NKJV):

> When Peter had come down out of the boat, he walked on the water to go to Jesus. But when he saw that the wind was boisterous, he was afraid; and beginning to sink he cried out, saying, "Lord, save me!" And immediately Jesus stretched out His hand and caught him.

Peter is often looked down upon because fear gripped his heart and he began to sink. But in my opinion, Peter deserves a standing ovation. While the other disciples cowered in fear, clinging to one another inside the boat, Peter was the only disciple who dared take a huge step of faith and get out of it. Peter will go down in history for defying gravity; he actually walked on water!

Stepping Out from the Crowd Isn't Easy . . . but Step On!

Peter is a shining example for us all. We should all pray to receive more of the ridiculous courage Peter had—courage to move beyond predictable boundaries and take a big faith step into deeper, seemingly troubled waters. It's easy to stay safe inside the boat. But I can hear Peter cheering us on to step out and trust Jesus to do more, even if the circumstances seem to be way over our heads. If for some reason we fall or even fail as we walk toward Him, Jesus will gladly rescue us with His strong, dependable arms.

It's interesting. None of the other disciples had enough faith in Jesus to get out of the boat, so Peter left them behind. Can you picture this scene in your mind? It's the middle of the night and completely dark. It's stormy. The disciples see Jesus and think they are hallucinating. But Peter doesn't run from the storm. He faces it. Peter did what he had to do completely on his own, alone.

If you are going to follow Jesus, at some point you will have to leave familiar surroundings and the comfort of the crowd. Your decision to take a risk may not always be popular. Others may try to discourage you and suggest that you take an easier way, but hear me, you will never grow in faith listening to the naysayers—and naysayers there will always be! As you step out in faith toward God there will be people in your life who say, "You're crazy to think you can walk on water. It's way too risky. The timing isn't right. Hurry! Get back in the boat!"

But don't be swayed by their discouraging words. Don't allow yourself to be so distracted by people that you miss the faith adventure of a lifetime. Don't be anxious to do what everybody else is doing, or you will miss the joy of journeying with Jesus to intimate places where few people choose to go. No, my friend; you must choose to be different.

Being different isn't always popular. It means you will stand out from the rest. But when groundbreaking people are asked why they chose to do the seemingly scary thing, instead of playing it safe, they usually respond, "I made that decision because I wanted to be different."

Many times, it is neither popular nor easy to step out into unfamiliar territory. When you take that big leap of faith, you don't always know how or where you will land. I know this by personal experience.

By 1984, after eight years of teaching middle high school music and English, I retired early to enter the music ministry as a full-time vocation. I was being invited more and more to sing in church meetings, at Billy Graham Crusades, and at women's events. These invitations to minister began to compete with my day job as a schoolteacher. Finally, I was forced to choose between the classroom and music ministry.

I had always dreamed of being a professional singer. Still, the decision wasn't easy. I prayed about it. I talked it over with my husband, Charles. I talked to my pastor about this potential life change. I shared my dream with my close friends. But ultimately, the decision was mine alone. Stepping out on faith felt a lot like stepping out onto thin air, but after much prayer and consideration, I left the classroom.

Being afforded the opportunity to share my faith in Christ through music was a dream come true. I was also very grateful to be in charge of my own schedule because it allowed me to be at home with my family. At the same time, Charles had started a business that he was trying to get up on its legs. We learned to sacrifice financially, but we were excited about the many possibilities the future would hold.

A Big Step Up in the Rockies

That summer I learned of a music seminar that was to be held in the Colorado Rocky Mountains. It would feature all kinds of classes taught by music industry professionals. Nightly concerts would feature the best there was to offer in the music industry. There would also be competitions, where record executives would serve as adjudicators. The brochure advertising the seminar featured beautiful mountain scenery and sported quotations from the industry's most popular artists, all endorsing the event.

Charles and I talked about attending, but we had no money for plane tickets and had very little in our cash reserves. So, when a Shell gas credit card arrived in the mail a few days later, we believed this was not only a great idea; we believed God had provided a way for us to go to Colorado. A few days later we packed Charles's truck, and we were on our way, headed west. We drove all day and well into the night, finally pulling into a low-budget motel.

The next day we ran into a big problem. We soon learned that there were *no Shell gas stations west of St Louis!* By the time we reached the conference grounds high in the Rocky Mountains, we had put a huge dent in our cash reserves. We ate bologna and cheese sandwiches one day and peanut butter and jelly sandwiches the next in the small cottage we had rented for the week.

But what happened up in those mountains changed our lives forever. For the first time, I attended songwriting classes taught by some of the nation's best Christian songwriters. I soaked it all up like a sponge. Then I entered a song in the seminar's songwriting competition, but I wasn't prepared for the judges' brutally honest assessment of my effort.

"The idea is nothing new," they said. "The lyric is trite, and the melody is a bit stale and familiar. Don't quit your day job."

Well, it was way too late for that piece of advice. That was not at all what I wanted to hear. I had made the decision to go into the music ministry, and there was no turning back.

I thought I would do better in the vocal competition, and by week's end I had won the third place trophy. Although placing third was quite an accomplishment (since several hundred singers had competed), I was especially hard on myself. I felt I hadn't done my best.

About three weeks after the conference, I got an inspiration to compose a new song. It had occurred to me that one day we will all stand before God and our earthly performances will not matter. Earthly trophies will pale in comparison to the beauty of His glory and holiness. I sat down at the piano in our living room to pen the words and the melody:

> *All rise. All rise!*
> *To stand before the throne*
> *In the presence of the Holy One*
> *All rise. All rise!*
> *As we worship the Messiah*
> *All rise!*[2]

After the song was fully composed, I began to sing it in my concerts all that year and returned the following year to the same seminar in the Rocky Mountains. Again, I entered in the vocal and songwriting competitions. God allowed me to win first place in both categories.

"All Rise" was the prize-winning song at the 1985 conference. One of the judges of that songwriting competition is a great singer/songwriter by the name of Scott Wesley Brown. He would actually record the song a couple years later. By the early 1990s "All Rise" had gained the title of one of the most-recorded songs of the decade.

I am not telling you this story to pat myself on the back. I am telling you this story to encourage you. I sometimes wonder what I might have been doing today if Charles and I hadn't risked time, effort, money, and pride to do what we believed to be God's will for us.

The Dynamic Power of Faith

Greatness lies deep within you. God has given you an assignment, and it's up to you to gain a clear understanding from Him of just what that assignment is. Once you have an understanding, pray for the faith, vision, wisdom, strength, and obedience to go and do it. Years ago, I learned an acronym for the word *faith*. I still remember it today:

> **F** orsaking
> **A** ll
> **I**
> **T** rust
> **H** im

To embrace your God-given assignment, you must *forsake* all other options and trust Christ alone. Put your faith into practice. When you look at your situation "from the boat" and all you see are angry waves, fear can easily set in. But remember, if something is over your head, it's under His feet. I'd rather be in the storm with Jesus than to be sailing on peaceful waters without Him.

When you step out in faith, some people will try to talk you out of obeying God. But listen to the One who calls your name above the noise of the crowd. The crowd will always try to convince you that you don't have adequate faith. Remind yourself that little is much when God is in it.

The naysayers will even remind you of past failures. And they may be right! While you don't have to have the greatest *ability* to follow the Lord, you must have *availability*. And if you fail along the way, remember Jesus has your back, and He turns every setback into a comeback.

It's highly possible that you will experience disappointment and discouragement. But Jesus will cause it all to work *for you*, not against you. You may have entered a contest and come in last place or not even have placed at all. But where you are is not where you have to stay.

Determine that you will rise up out of your comfort zone. Listen long enough to hear the voice of Jesus calling for you to peer into your future and *come to Him*. If you look up long enough, you will begin to see in yourself what God saw in you all along. When you can see with spiritual eyes what you could never see in your flesh, you'll find enough faith to launch your dream. You'll move into the next level of your destiny.

Be encouraged. No matter how much you want the godly dream in the depths of your heart, God always wants it more. He knows what is best for you. And His plan is always "exceeding abundantly above all that we ask or think, according to the power" that is at work in you. (See Ephesians 3:20.)

If you make the decision to step out into the unfamiliar, God promises you that His grace is sufficient—just like it was for His own Son, Jesus. He will meet you right where you are to equip you for the task that is uniquely yours.

Start out by making up in your mind to do God's will *God's way*. Surrender all that you are to all that He is. You'll know in your heart when you are ready to take the next step.

A few years ago, I wrote a song on this subject, "Steppin' Out on the Water." These are the words to the chorus:

> *You gotta go steppin' out on the water*
> *You gotta get out of the boat*
> *You gotta come leave the shore and come out of*
> *The safety of your comfort zone*
> *You'll never learn how to swim if you never get wet*
> *So launch into the deep and put your faith to the test*
> *You gotta go steppin' out, steppin' out on the water*
> *And trust the Lord*[3]

I encourage you to keep looking out in front of you, just as Peter did when he got out of the boat. God is already there, and so is Jesus. The Holy Spirit is in you, and angels are watching over you. Remember: many people see, but not everyone has vision. Keep your head, and don't let what is around you distract you. Dear one, as you step out on faith in Christ, keep Hebrews 12:2 (NIV) in mind: "Let us fix our eyes on Jesus, the author and perfecter of our faith."

As your confidence in Christ grows day by day, you'll become more confident in your vision and direction. Don't get it wrong here. Your confidence is not in *who you are*, but in *whose you are*. When you focus on *whose you are*, you will find yourself moving from where you are right now to where you are called to be.

Now, lean in a little more closely and listen more intently. Do you sense Jesus calling you to take a leap of faith? If so, what are you waiting for? *Step out!*

EMBRACE YOUR DAY

As you focus on our time together today, think about those areas in your life where you may be hesitating to make a move. Examine why you are hesitating. Is it due to the fear of failure or a lack of preparation? Do you not have enough finances or moral support from the people around you? The challenges you are experiencing may seem to be pretty big—like angry, menacing waves tossing you to and fro. But, my friend, God is bigger than any challenge you may face.

Because God loves you, He will equip and strengthen you to meet your challenges head-on. The Lord wants to remind you that He loves you too much to leave you stranded.

Do you remember what the Lord has said to you about your assignment? Do you believe Him? If you do, then take Him at His word. Just like Jesus called Peter to get out of the boat, He is calling you to take a step toward Him. He knows the hesitation you may be feeling right now. But remember: *don't be moved by how you feel. Stand fast on what you know to be true in God.*

God's love is sure, and He always has the answer. As a matter of fact, let's pause and talk to God about the challenges you are facing and the "deep water" that is out in front of you:

Dear faithful Father,
Thank You so much for loving me. I am so grateful that Your love for me is bigger than the challenges I am facing now or may

face today. *I confess that sometimes I am overwhelmed by my circumstances and that they cause my heart to feel anxious and uncertain. Please forgive me for not trusting You, Lord. I thank You that I don't have to be anxious about a single thing, but I can bring all my requests to You. You will exchange my doubts for faith and replace my fears with courage. Thank You for the confidence I have in You, regardless of what I face today. I love You, Lord. In the sweet name of Jesus I pray. Amen.*

Think About His Love

It's easy to stay safe inside the boat. But Jesus loves you and wants you to trust Him with every storm in your life. Take a step of faith, and trust Him with more, even if the circumstances seem to be over your head. Now consider: What does getting out of the boat look like in your situation? Record your answer in your journal.

Read About His Love

"Lord, if it is You, command me to come to You on the water" (Matthew 14:28b NKJV). Take some time and read the entire story in Matthew 14:22-33. Meditate on the lessons this powerful passage teaches. As the Holy Spirit quickens your heart while you read, jot it down in your journal. If you feel led to do so, stop and pray. Let the word of God open up your conversation with God today.

Pray About His Love

In your own words, thank God for loving you enough to call you out of your comfort zone into deeper water. In this solitary place, you will get to know Jesus like you have never known Him before. Ask Him to forgive you concerning situations where you have fallen short of trusting Him completely, but instead, took the easy way out. Ask Him to guard you from this day forward from taking matters into your own hands. Thank Him for giving you the courage to step out of the crowd and into the destiny He has for you. Throughout the day, surrender all that you are to all that He is, and praise Him for being in complete control of your life.

Be About His Love

Put God's love on the line today by relaxing and releasing the tight grip you have on your circumstances. Even if it's a small one, take a step of faith. Throughout the day, remember what "Forsaking All, I Trust Him" really means.

DAY 17

STAGE A BIG COMEBACK

Fall seven times and stand up eight.[1]
—An ancient proverb

*There came thither certain Jews from Antioch and Iconium, who
persuaded the people and, having stoned Paul, drew him
out of the city, supposing he had been dead. Howbeit, as the
disciples stood round about him, he rose up, and came into the city:
and the next day he departed with Barnabus to Derbe.*
—Acts 14:19-20

God's mighty power equips you to get back up as often as life's challenges knock you down.

On one memorable occasion, I had been invited to sing at a leadership conference before a large audience of several thousand people. As instructed, I stepped up to sing my song right after the speaker, who had delivered a message on resilience: bouncing back after difficult challenges. The soundtrack for my song began to roll, and I launched into the first verse. I was headed for the chorus when the soundtrack that accompanied me stopped cold. A singer's worst nightmare had become my reality. Dead silence.

I tried to stretch the time a bit, making a few awkward comments while I waited for the soundtrack to start again. Nothing. I looked to the back of the large room for a cue from my husband, who was running the player that contained my soundtracks. He and the sound guy were standing in the back of the room manning the soundboard. I didn't like what I saw. Dumbfounded, they were looking at each other with their hands up in the air.

I know how it feels, as they say, to be "thrown under the bus." I said to the audience, "Well, praise God, I'll just go over to the piano and play the song from there." What I didn't tell them was that I hadn't played that song at the piano since the day I recorded it several years before. So, not only was I being thrown under the bus, I was being thrown over the cliff with no one to catch me . . . *but Jesus!*

The audience waited quietly as I situated myself at the piano. I remembered the old adage, "Never let 'em see you sweat," so I prayed a silent prayer for divine intervention. I composed a simple introduction on the fly and started into the first verse. As I headed for the first chorus, the audience erupted into applause, as if to say, "She made it!" Then I sang the second verse. As I turned the corner to the second chorus, the crowd applauded again, cheering me on. I sang the song's bridge, threw in a modulation, and headed for the big finish. I held out the last note as the audience rushed to their feet to give me a standing ovation.

I had just become the object lesson for the speaker's sermon and the poster child for all overcomers.

Trust me, dear friend; it was by no means funny then. But we can look back on it now and get a good belly laugh out of it. And my sweet Charles? There are so many lessons, both spiritual and practical, that I could share from this fiasco turned fantastic, but I'll spare you for now.

You Can Rise Up and Get Going Again

Life can pull the plug on you without so much as a moment's notice. My experience onstage, however, doesn't compare to the Apostle Paul's situation in Lystra by any means—for his very life was at stake. But the Lord came to the rescue for Paul, just as He has for me and so many others on countless occasions. Now, let's take a closer look at Acts 14:19-20:

> There came thither certain Jews from Antioch and Iconium, who persuaded the people and, having stoned Paul, drew him out of the city, supposing he had been dead. Howbeit, as the disciples stood round about him, he rose up, and came into the city: and the next day he departed with Barnabus to Derbe.

The book of Acts progresses like an adventurous, fast-paced motion picture. The main characters—Peter, John, and Paul, all of them empowered, inspired, and directed by the Holy Spirit—relentlessly carry the gospel of the risen Christ throughout "Jerusalem, and in all Judea and Samaria, and to the end of the earth" (Acts 1:8b NKJV).

Through these apostles, the Holy Spirit healed the sick, quickened the dead, caused the lame to walk and the blind to see, cast out demons, and performed many other miracles, demonstrating

God's mighty power on their lives. Jesus had confirmed His authority in them to perform these mighty acts before He ascended to heaven (v. 8).

The account we just read about Paul and Barnabas's first missionary journey tells of their experience in Lystra, where Paul was stoned, presumed dead, and dragged from the city to be left out as buzzard bait. Notice the Bible says that when the disciples gathered around him, "he rose up" and went back into the city (Acts 14:20).

In a very real sense, when the circumstances of life knock us down, God *empowers* and *expects* us to get up and get going.

Let me emphasize, dear friend, that when the enemy we call satan can't kill you, he would like to leave you wounded and broken on the battlefield of life as an example to the world. Interestingly, I have heard that in military combat the land mine was primarily designed to cause injuries because it takes two able-bodied soldiers to transport one disabled trooper. So, three are incapacitated and removed from combat. But when a soldier is killed in battle, another soldier simply removes his dog tag and keeps on fighting.

Satan will try to take us down when he cannot take us out. But in Christ, our strength is renewed.

Everybody experiences failure and setbacks, defeats, disasters, and catastrophic occurrences. At times it can feel as though they have left us flattened like the cartoon character Wile E. Coyote in pursuit of the Road Runner. A lot of humor is found in the outrageous antics of the exasperated Wile E., but I have to give him credit. He always picks himself up and gives it another go.

Just like that day on stage, trouble can arise unexpectedly when things are going well. Paul and Barnabas, on their first missionary journey, were preaching Christ at Iconium and being quite successful. In fact, "they spoke so effectively that a great number of Jews and Gentiles believed" (Acts 14:1 NIV). That must have been a terrific experience.

The next verse, however, begins with that little word *But*. The buts of life are like temporary power failures. They can stop the music and bring any great performance to a screeching halt. We are immediately aware that trouble is at hand.

Often, it seems that when we are riding the crest of success, happiness, and well-being, the earth shifts, and we find ourselves standing on the stage alone, vulnerable, while the whole world watches. We build that dream home and a year after we move in, the real estate bubble bursts, property values plummet, and the mortgage we owe is greater than the value of the home. We finally reach retirement age and are poised to enjoy the golden years when the doctor tells us that the test results from lab work say a tumor is malignant.

The woes of life can suddenly appear in any area. After successfully completing training for a better-paying position at work, we are notified that the company is downsizing, and we will be facing an indefinite layoff. For some, it seems their marriage couldn't be better when they discover their spouse is having an affair. Life is filled with situations that can knock you down and leave you feeling mortally wounded.

But when you have been stretched to the breaking point, God always has a way of propelling you to even greater possibilities.

A Lesson in "Rubber Bandology"

Once while doing some housekeeping, I spotted a rubber band lying on the floor. When I picked it up, the kid in me emerged, so I pulled back on the elastic band and shot it. Just then, the Holy Spirit prompted me to engage in an exercise I now call "rubber bandology," or the study of the rubber band. When I pulled back gently on the band and released it to the air, it didn't go very far. I picked it up again. Only this time, I pulled back a little harder, applying more pressure on the band. When I released it, it flew out in front of me a little farther. Once more, I picked it up. This time I pulled back as far as I could, stretching it to the limit, without breaking it. When I released the rubber band, it lofted high into the air and went sailing across the room.

The Lord reminded me that to the degree that life's situations pull on my patience, put pressure on my finances, push against my marriage, stress my health, and stretch my faith to the limit—to that same degree and more—I will be launched into the next season of greatness in my life. The process may be uncomfortable. It may even be painful. But God is faithful.

I've said it before and I'll say it again. God loves us so much that He always causes our challenges to work for us, not against us. In Christ, what may appear to be a setback is not a setback at all. *It is a setup for a comeback!* Every challenge is a launching pad for success. It's another opportunity to experience God's power in your life!

So, what's the process? How do we come back strong after a setback? How do we stage the big comeback? *The first step in the process, after being knocked down, is simply to get up.* Don't wallow in the mire and throw a pity party. No one will come to join you anyway. People just don't want to come to pity parties. Don't put on the cloak of guilt. That's one little black dress you don't even need to try on. Don't become paralyzed by fear. Realize what's happening, and look it square in the face. Self-pity, guilt, and fear are arrows that the enemy uses to wound your spirit and render you ineffective.

Self-pity, guilt, and fear can disable you. Remember that satan is the great accuser. In our devotion on Day 5, when we discussed the woman caught in the act of adultery, we remembered that the Pharisees had brought her to Christ. He dismissed her accusers with a challenge for the one who was without sin to "first cast a stone at her" (John 8:7b). Then He turned to the woman and reaffirmed her. Jesus did not condemn this woman, pronouncing her guilty or inflicting severe punishment on her. He simply said, "Neither do I condemn thee: go, and sin no more" (v. 11). Jesus exhorted her to get on with her life and stop the destructive behavior.

Many times, God's loving forgiveness allows us to forgive ourselves.

There are times when our suffering is self-inflicted by sin in our lives. We develop a pattern of disobedience, and the consequences of our behavior cause anguish, leaving us with a tremendous burden of guilt. You can't make a big comeback dragging a load of guilt behind you.

Once after an outpatient surgical procedure, when the local anesthesia had worn off, I found myself in excruciating pain. If I could have ranked the pain on a scale from 1 to 10, it would have registered 101. The pain was so great I envisioned the very face of death peering over the foot of my bed. To top it off, I heard a hideous, heckling voice say, "You can trust God with your family, and you can trust God with your finances, but you can't trust Him with *this*, can you?"

I had maxed out on pain medication. My gown and bed sheets were soaked with pain-induced perspiration. I literally thought I would die. I had no place to go but to my knees, so I rolled out of bed and called on the Lord. And He heard my cry. The pain subsided, and I drifted off into a peaceful sleep.

Some folks would say the pain medication finally took effect. But I say I called on the Lord, and He heard my cry. My suffering had become an occasion for God to be glorified. For every believer, there will be times God entrusts us with suffering so that we will be found faithful to Him. In our faithfulness, God is glorified.

Say No to Self-Pity

Self-pity is a highly poisonous dart in satan's quiver. It robs us of our dignity and self-worth. In the Gospel of John, chapter five, we find the account of a man who had been sick for thirty-eight years and was lying by the pool of Bethesda. As the story goes, at a certain season an angel went down into the pool and stirred up the water; whoever stepped in first after the stirring of the water was healed of whatever disease he had (vv. 2-6).

Often, Bible readers assume this man had been lame because Jesus told him to *pick up his bed and walk.* The text, however, does not say that had been his condition. It says that he was sick or, in the King James Version, "impotent" (vv. 7-8). Jesus knew the man had been in that condition a long time, so He said to him: "Wilt thou be made whole?" The sick man answered, "Sir, I have no man, when the water is troubled, to put me into the pool: but while I am coming, another steppeth down before me." Jesus told him, "Rise, take up thy bed, and walk."

If we look closely at this passage, we discover some interesting insights into this man's personality. Jesus asked him a direct question. The man gave a lame excuse. His response was not the expected unequivocal yes! He gave Jesus an excuse that placed blame outside himself and declared his own helplessness and inability to compete. In effect, he said, "I am worse off than the others who are blind, lame, and paralyzed, and furthermore, I've been facing this challenge all by myself. I have no one *to put me in the water.*"

Not only was this docile man waiting for the miraculous "stirring of the water," he was also awaiting an unexplained appearance of an unidentified benefactor. This able rescuer would overlook all the other needy individuals, select him out of the crowd, pick him up, rush him into the pool (ahead of everyone), and place him safely in the healing waters.

Once I was approached by a young man addicted to crack cocaine. He asked me for money and quickly followed his request with an explanation. He said, "I've got a drug habit, so don't preach to me about how I need to change. I enjoy getting high, and when I get tired of being an addict, then I'll quit. But right now all I need is a little help. Could you spare two dollars?" There are many in our society today who are comfortable in their sickness. For them, healing could require getting a job, becoming a responsible person, perhaps raising a family, and taking control of their own lives.

People become addicted to many substances and behaviors, including food, sex, and impulsive spending. Although they overtly claim to want deliverance, they are quietly satisfied with their condition. We see Jesus not inquiring, but confronting the man at the pool. He saw a passive man who had brought a bed and found relative comfort in joining a community of incapacitated individuals. So He asked him, "Do you [really] want to be made well?"

Jesus is asking you the same question today: "Do you want to be healed?" If you are standing passively by while healing and wholeness keep bubbling up in front of you, Jesus would challenge you to rise up out of self-pity. He would tell you that if you really want to bounce back after a setback, if you really want to rebound from a guilty past, if you really want to overcome fear—*then you must choose to get up.* Jesus would challenge you to assume a measure of responsibility and exercise self-control, so you could master the circumstances that once mastered you.

When life has knocked you down, you must let your desire for healing be the driving force that propels you far away from an attitude of helplessness and codependency.

Though your strength may be limited, you must use this measure of strength to lift yourself up from that position of self-pity, guilt, fear, complacency, and comfortable despair. Jesus wants you to rise up and walk! Take up that bed you may have been dragging around for years—which has identified you as an invalid and has been your source of security—and move on!

Fear Not . . . Pursue God's Promises

Then there is fear, which comes in many flavors. There is the fear of pain—physical or emotional—fear of failure, fear for the future, and fear of rejection. Luke 12:32 (NKJV) says, "Do not fear, little flock, for it is your Father's good pleasure to give you the kingdom."

Someone once said there are 366 mentions of the words *fear not* in the Bible. That's one for each day of the year, including a leap year. I haven't found all of them yet, but the passages I have found hit a high note in my heart. I've discovered a common thread. Right behind every command to *fear not* comes a promise from the Lord. Read the following proclamations with me, and then read the promises:

In Genesis 46:3, after telling Jacob to "fear not," the Lord continued with a promise: "Go down into Egypt; for I will there make of thee a great nation."

In Joshua 8:1, read this command: "The LORD said unto Joshua, Fear not, neither be thou dismayed: take all the people of war with thee, and arise, go up to Ai." Now, here's the promise: "See, I have given into thy hand the king of Ai, and his people, and his city, and his land."

In Isaiah 41:10 the Lord says, "Fear thou not." Then comes the promise: "For I am with thee: be not dismayed; for I am thy God."

In Luke 1:13 the angel said to Zacharias, "Fear not." Now, here's the promise: "For thy prayer is heard; and thy wife Elisabeth shall bear thee a son."

And again, in Luke 2:10 the angel delivers the command, "Fear not." The promise is this: "For, behold, I bring you good tidings of great joy, which shall be to all people."

Now, go back and read Luke 12:32, and you'll see the same powerful pattern. There are many more of these proclamations and promises in God's word just waiting for you to discover and apply them to your life.

Dear friend, considering the days in which we are living, this is no time to be passive. Aggressively pursue and diligently trust God's promises for you. A multitude of promises in the Father's Good Book belongs to you.

Take a few moments and remember how God has worked in your life. Recall past circumstances: the narrow escapes, economic hardships, the loss of loved ones, broken relationships, disappointments, and failures. Now, remind yourself that God is faithful. Thank Him for what He has brought you through in the past and for what He has promised to do for you in the future.

Because God's great love for us never changes, we need to develop an appreciation for the magnitude of love He expresses toward us. Throughout the Bible, God allowed His children to experience moments (or even seasons) of difficulty. But nowhere does it ever indicate that His love was diminished in the least during any of those ordeals.

Now, let's go back to the book of Acts, when Paul was stoned, dragged out of Iconium, and left for dead. After that traumatic encounter, the Bible says, "He rose up, and came into the city" (14:20b). Now, let's meditate on this. Paul went right back into the same city he had just been stoned and dragged out of. Stoning in biblical times was a form of execution. Surviving a stoning would be comparable to stepping out of the electric chair or walking out of the gas chamber.

I have heard that stones used in this form of execution were not like those you would skip across the surface of a pond. These stones likely ranged in size from as big as a fist to as large as one's head. And often the stoning didn't cease until the victim's body was covered with the lethal missiles. There was Paul's body, bloodied and bruised, appearing lifeless. Then suddenly he dragged himself up to his feet and went right back into that same city?

Certainly, the road that led *into the city* also led *out of the city*. Perhaps after the stoning Paul was disoriented and simply got turned around. Perhaps one of the stones had found its mark and had addled his brain. Could it possibly be that he simply recalled the words from a passage such as Psalm 27:5-6?

> For in the time of trouble he shall hide me in his pavilion: in the secret of his tabernacle shall he hide me; he shall set me up upon a rock. And now shall mine head be lifted up above mine enemies round about me: therefore will I offer in his tabernacle sacrifices of joy; I will sing, yea, I will sing praises unto the LORD.

When you feel like you have been flattened by the trials of this life, run to God for help. He will give you the same resilience that He gave the Apostle Paul. If somehow the music stops during your big performance, you can throw back your head and keep on singing. When you are tempted to feel guilty over past mistakes, drop that heavy load, freeing yourself of its clutches, and trade it in for the freedom that Jesus gives.

When feeling sorry for yourself has left you looking for a hand-out, throw up your hand and let Jesus pull you up. If you've been disabled, paralyzed by fear, kick those crutches to the curb, and start stepping to the beat of different drummer. Just keep in step with Jesus. When and if you experience a setback, don't worry. *Jesus can turn every test into a testimony.* He'll give you the power to rebound, pick yourself up, dust yourself off, and start all over again.

EMBRACE YOUR DAY

Today is a great day to stage a comeback, don't you agree? If life has dealt you a low blow, bringing you down to your knees, always remember—you don't have to stay down. With the help of God, you can pull yourself up, brush yourself off, and press on.

On that note of victory, we'll close today's encounter and conclude this movement in God's symphony of love. Remember, though, God is your strength and your song. As we spend a few moments in prayer, let's make the prayerful words of "Out of the Depths" by the great hymn writer Martin Luther our own:

Dear heavenly Father,

I call to You from deepest need,
O Lord, hear my request.
I know I've sinned in word and deed,
But now I'm in distress.
Please overlook my errant ways,
And gaze at me with tender grace,
And help me fix this mess.
In You, dear Lord, I place my trust,
I've soured on self-reliance.
Your Spirit arms each one of us
To slay our taunting giants.
Your promises prove strong and true,
And I'd be nothing without You.
I pledge my full compliance.[2]

Father, may every setback always drive me to come back to You. In Jesus' name,
Amen.

Think About His Love

In spite of disappointments, setbacks, and times of despair, God's love for you never, ever changes. Just think about that for a bit today. Nowhere in the Bible does it ever indicate that God's love diminishes during times of difficulty. Use this wonderful promise as a launching pad to propel you to your next victory.

Read About His Love

There came thither certain Jews from Antioch and Iconium, who persuaded the people and, having stoned Paul, drew him out of the city, supposing he had been dead. Howbeit, as the disciples stood round about him, he rose up, and came into the city: and the next day he departed with Barnabus to Derbe. (Acts 14:19-20).

Really work hard at memorizing this powerful passage because as you commit it to memory, it will pierce your subconscious mind and then present itself to you again in times of distress. Oh, yes, like Paul and so many others who have gone before us, you will discover the truth of Psalm 46:1: "God is our refuge and strength, a very present help in trouble."

Pray About His Love

Don't let guilt, self-pity, fear, or any other deceptive tool of the enemy keep you from knowing, without a doubt, that you are loved, forgiven, fearless, and free. Now, read Romans 8:26-39, and let it lead you into prayer. Then as you go about your day, offer up prayers of thanks to the Father for His unending, never-failing, overcoming love.

Be About His Love

Has the bottom ever dropped out of your plans, leaving you holding the bag—only to have Jesus come and deliver you? Share this "*test*-imony" with your spouse, your children, or a friend today. It will encourage them to hear it and encourage you to share it with everyone you know.

DAY 18

MAKE A BIG DIFFERENCE

Never worry about numbers. Help one person at a time
and always start with the person nearest you.[1]
—Mother Teresa

You are the salt of the earth; but if the salt loses its flavor,
how shall it be seasoned? It is then good for nothing but
to be thrown out and trampled underfoot by men.
—Matthew 5:13 NKJV

By His power, God has divinely "seasoned" you to make an amaz-ing difference in this world for His glory.

As a young girl watching Grandma in the kitchen I was amazed how she could put together a recipe without using meas-uring cups or measuring spoons. When making biscuits, for exam-ple, she would scoop some flour into a bowl with her hand, pour in some baking powder or baking soda, add a dash or two of salt, toss in some bacon fat or lard, and pour some buttermilk into the mixture. She would blend it all together, knead it briefly, roll it out, and then cut the dough with the rim of a coffee cup or mason jar. Then she would place the flat discs of dough on a greased pan, pop it in the oven, and *presto-whammo*, there in front of your eyes were beautiful golden-brown, light-as-a-feather biscuits.

Decades after Grandma died, I acquired a bread-making machine. I was determined to have a healthy diet despite the convenience of manufactured foods, which are full of preservatives, food coloring, and long lists of substances—the names of which I cannot pronounce. In my first attempts at bread making, I noticed the recipe called for 1½ teaspoons of salt, but since I understood that salt waterlogs the tissues, it robs calcium from the body, it paralyzes the 260 taste buds in the mouth, it is a heart poison, it increases irritability of the nervous system, it is a deadly poison to all fowl, and it is a leading cause of high blood pressure, I decided to eliminate salt from the bread recipe.

I dumped the ingredients, minus the salt, into the bread maker, pushed the buttons, and smiled. Within a short time, the yeasty smell of baking bread filled the house, and my mouth watered for the taste of a warm slice of buttered whole wheat bread.

During the baking process I peeked at the loaf through the glass top of the machine and noticed that the loaf had risen magnificently. My excitement increased. The timer indicated that within the hour the bread would be ready. I had plenty of time to dash to the store to get some unsalted sweet creamery butter and some strawberry preserves. Shortly after my return, the bread machine signaled that the baking process was complete.

When I raised the lid, to my dismay, I discovered that the loaf that had risen so majestically had fallen and had become a tough, gnarled lump. The color was golden, the taste was bearable, but the texture left a lot to be desired. I read the troubleshooting section of the owner's manual and discovered that the problem, most likely, was a lack of salt. A little salt can make a big difference.

God calls us to be "salt," to make a big difference in this world for Him.

Life's Most Important Ingredient

In Matthew 5 Jesus preached one of His greatest sermons, which we now refer to as the Sermon on the Mount. The message is revolutionary. Even today, it turns the world order upside down—first with a section we call the "Beatitudes," when Jesus began by saying, "Blessed are the poor in spirit, for theirs is the kingdom of heaven" (v. 3).

Later, in Matthew 19:24 (NIV), when Jesus told the disciples it would be easier for a camel to go through the eye of a needle than for a rich man to be saved. The next verse says they were "greatly astonished," asking Jesus, "Who then can be saved?" This is yet another example of how Jesus looked at traditional wisdom and turned it inside out.

Jesus looks at the despised stations in life and calls them "blessed." Going back to the Sermon on the Mount, Jesus promised that those who mourn would be comforted, that the meek would inherit the earth, that those who hunger and thirst for righteousness would be filled, and that the merciful would obtain mercy (Matthew 5:4-7). Then a little later He said,

Blessed are you when they revile and persecute you, and say all kinds of evil against you falsely for My sake. Rejoice and be exceedingly glad, for great is your reward in heaven, for so they persecuted the prophets who were before you. You are the salt of the earth; but if the salt loses its flavor, how shall it be seasoned? It is then good for nothing but to be thrown out and trampled underfoot by men. (vv. 11-13 NKJV)

In a world filled with violence, hatred, selfishness, pride, deception, and greed, as blood-bought believers in Jesus Christ, we are called upon to season this unsavory mix. There is only *one ingredient* that can change this bitter brew, and it is the most important ingredient: *love*.

Years ago, early in my music ministry, I was invited to sing in Ft. Lauderdale, Florida. Up until that time, Charles and I had been driving by car to our engagements that were, for the most part, no more than two to three hours from home. However, this trip would mark the first time we would board an airplane to travel to a concert date. We were extremely excited to be going to another state to share our music ministry.

Our host not only flew us to Ft. Lauderdale; he also sent a chauffeur-driven limousine to pick us up from the airport. Needless to say, Charles and I were simply beside ourselves when the driver ushered us to his long black limo. He swung open the door for us and motioned for us to step inside. Then he stored our bags in the massive trunk and took us on the scenic route to the hotel where we would be staying.

Our eyes widened like kids on Christmas morning as we took in all the luxurious scenes along the harbor. Gorgeous homes lined the shore while huge private yachts sailed the crystal blue ocean waters. Enjoying the view, my husband and I remarked to each other that we could really get used to this kind of treatment.

As the driver pulled onto the property where the luxury hotel was located, my eyes glanced up, all the way to the top of the tall skyscraper-like building where we'd be spending the night. I marveled at the meticulous landscaping that lined the drive.

It was then that I saw something out of the ordinary that is still etched in my memory right up to this very moment. Nestled among the neatly trimmed shrubs was a homeless man, asleep on a cardboard box. I couldn't believe my eyes. This scene of the homeless man lying on a piece of cardboard juxtaposed to the high-rise luxury hotel full of nice, clean beds sent my head spinning. I felt a huge nudge from the Holy Spirit, giving me permission to enjoy the advantages I had been given, but never to get too comfortable.

After the car pulled up to the front door of the hotel, we walked over to where I had seen the man sleeping. Charles and I wanted to help him in some way. We were even willing to offer him a room for the night, but the attendants had chased him off the property. Not long after that, I was inspired to write a song called, "Show Me How to Love." It serves as a vital reminder to every believer that *love* is the ingredient we add to the mix:

> *You didn't have to leave the glory of Heaven*
> *But You became a simple man*
> *You didn't have to serve the poor and afflicted*
> *But You touched and healed their brokenness*
> *No greater love has been given*

You became the ultimate sacrifice
Create in me the heart of a servant
Let this be my soul's desire

Show me how to love
In the true meaning of the word
Teach me to sacrifice
Expecting nothing in return
I want to give my life away
Becoming more like You
Each and every day
My words are not enough
Show me how to love[2]

Christ has assigned us, as believers in His name, the great task of adding love to this world's bitter mix. He has given us the mission of making the world a little bit more like heaven on earth.

The Power of Love

Perhaps it would be beneficial at this point to pause and define *love*, because in our English language this small word has many meanings. We love French fries and fast cars. We love our family and friends. We fall in love and we make love. In Greek, the language of the New Testament, there are four words to express that for which we have only one word in English:

Agape: affection or benevolence

Thelo: to delight in, desire, or be disposed toward

Phileo: to be a friend of[3]

Eros: to be sexually attracted to[4]

The *Tyndale New Bible Dictionary* gives the etymology of the word *agape* and defines it as "that highest and noblest form of love which sees something infinitely precious in its object."[5]

In 1 John 4:8 (NKJV) the writer says, "He who does not love does not know God, for God is love." When we come to fully understand this simple statement—"God is love"—we take hold of the eternal power that changes the world.

The world has yet to learn that love is more powerful than weapons of mass destruction or drones, unmanned aircraft that can identify and destroy a single target. Warfare might change the landscape. War can even change behavior. *But love changes the heart.*

In His wonderful Sermon on the Mount, Jesus taught that we should love our enemies. He told us to pray for those who misuse us (a revolutionary idea then, when Israel was struggling under the iron rule of the Roman Empire). (See Matthew 5:44.) Now that the threat of terrorism causes us to walk barefooted through airport check points, we see that the power of love still has a lot to confront.

Love is a weapon that often goes untested during times of war. In spite of popular opinion I have heard this nation gives less than 1 percent of its budget to foreign aid, while military spending is 19 percent.[6] I wonder what would happen worldwide if we were to build schools, roads, and bridges; provide safe drinking water and sanitation, and feed the world's hungry instead of destroying millions of tons of food. I wonder what the global outcome would be if this nation was totally committed to being the salt of the earth.

Well, it's unlikely U.S. foreign aid will ever equal the military budget; however, in the kingdom of God, love is the primary weapon of war. The power of love, intertwined with the gift of grace, dismisses all faults and guilt and gives a poor, desperate, and downcast world the hope it so desperately needs.

Within this framework, Jesus urges us to love one another so that the world will know we are His disciples (see John 17:20-23). It is in this framework as well that John drew a sharp distinction between the words *agape* and *phileo* in Christ's conversation with Peter on the shores of the Sea of Tiberias (John 21:15-17).

Upon closer examination of this passage, we see Peter's willingness to use the words *phileo se* (I am your friend) rather than *agapo se* (I love you unconditionally). The *Tyndale New Bible Dictionary* says, "It is difficult to see why a writer of such simple Greek as John should have used two words in this context unless he intended a distinction be drawn between their meanings."[7]

It seems apparent that John, who was an eyewitness of that conversation between Peter and Jesus, simply records Peter's reluctance to make an unconditional commitment. When the Lord asked, "Do you love me?" Peter answered, "I am your friend." (Remember that Peter was talking to the risen Christ, who had demonstrated to the fullest extent His love [*agape*] for all humanity at Calvary some forty days earlier. He had done so in spite of unbelievable humiliation, degradation, horrendous torture, and death.)

Now, our Lord was standing as *Love personified* asking Peter for a full commitment, in response to the love He had extended. His admonition to Peter to "feed my sheep" was a direct instruction for him to "make a big difference" as he ministered to others. The word of God sets the standard for us to love one another today—whether it is by teaching the word (as it was in Peter's case) or just lending a helping hand to someone in need. Our heavenly Father admonishes us to make a big difference in our world.

In Matthew 5:41, to demonstrate the power of love, Christ told the multitude: "Whoever compels you to go one mile, go with him two" (NKJV). During this time in their history, Jews were under the crushing oppression of the Roman Empire. If a Roman soldier approached a Jew on the road, the Jew could be compelled to carry the soldier's equipment for one mile. Jesus was telling the multitude, "When you get to end of that mile, keep on walking."

It takes about fifteen minutes to walk a mile. In my opinion, although the first mile shows the authority of the Roman soldier over the burden bearer, when that person voluntarily carries the equipment for the next mile, the volunteer assumes more control. The longer this burden bearer willingly carries the soldier's load, the more he or she is empowered, and the authority of the soldier is weakened in equal measure. For that distance, that second mile, the servant seizes the power. In another setting, the Apostle Paul says this general principle is much like pouring "coals of fire" on the enemy's head. (See Romans 12:19-20.)

But the key word here is *willing*. If you offer to do above and beyond only to get an advantage over someone else, your motive is wrong. Jesus was speaking of having a love for God that causes you to rise up in His love and demonstrate it to those who need it most. That's what I call power! That's what I call making a difference.

Another parable in the Gospel of Luke shows us how to demonstrate this *agape* love. Jesus explained it quite vividly when a lawyer tested him, asking: "What must I do to inherit eternal life?" Jesus put the ball back in the lawyer's court: " 'What is written in the Law?' he replied. 'How do you read it?' " (See Luke 10:25b-26 NIV.)

The lawyer quoted the law, which he knew inside out, " 'Love the Lord your God with all your heart and with all your soul and with all your strength and with all your mind'; and, 'Love your neighbor as yourself' " (v. 27 NIV). Jesus replied, "You have answered correctly. . . . Do this and you will live [eternally in the kingdom of God]" (v. 28 NIV) Then Luke says, "But he [the lawyer] wanted to justify himself, so he asked Jesus, 'And who is my neighbor?' " (v. 29 NIV).

It is worth noting here that a person only seeks to "justify himself" when he knows he is not justified, when he is well aware that he has come up short of God's perfect standard.

So, this lawyer realized that he had fallen short in upholding the law, and like a good lawyer, he began to split hairs with Jesus by asking Him to define terms. Jesus shared with him the parable of the good Samaritan, in which he not only defined *neighbor* but also painted a picture of love that transcends religious, ethnic, social, and racial divides, as well as educational and economic differences.

At the conclusion of the story Jesus told this Jewish lawyer to duplicate the behavior of a Samaritan—a member of a mixed-race people whom the Jews despised. The Lord ended the conversation by telling him, "Go and do likewise." (See Luke 10:30-37 NIV.)

Jesus is saying the same thing to us today.

We are living in an age of preemptive military strikes, where the silent rule is, "Do unto others *before* they do unto you." We must rise to the challenge and show God's love in a time when the gap between rich and poor has deepened and widened broadly; when racism still peeps into the window of the human heart; and when one person's well-being is based on another's misery.

Christ is telling us that, like that good Samaritan, as we journey through this life in our day-to-day experiences (and we don't have to go out of our way, by the way), we can embrace someone who has suffered an attack from the enemy. We can take time from our busy schedules to become actively involved in the welfare of our neighbor. We can show concern. We can speak kind words. We can commit our resources. We can "go" into the harvest field, or we can "send" someone else.

We can express real, *agape* love to another person who, like us, has been created in the image of God. And that image, as John simply describes, is *Love*. (See 1 John 4:7-8.)

Finally, just as I discovered in my bread-baking experience, it doesn't take a large amount of salt to achieve the desired results. Actually, in comparison to the other ingredients, the amount of salt is less than all the rest, but that little bit of salt makes a huge difference!

So it is with love. Often, it's the little things that count the most. Call the widow down the street, and take her grocery list with you when you go shopping. Call the single mom who is working two jobs and tell her you'd like for her kids to come over for pizza with yours. When you've cranked up your snow blower to clear your sidewalk, don't stop at the property line. When you've harvested your vegetable garden and eaten all you can, and canned all you can't, call your neighbors across the street and offer them some vegetables.

Showing love is not complicated. Grandma said when she lived as a sharecropper in the Deep South, she never knew of the Great Depression until she heard about it on the radio. The family lived on a river, and Grandpa caught fish and kept them alive (in the river) in a big wood-framed box covered with fence wire. They had a vegetable garden and some chickens. One of their neighbors had a milk cow, and another neighbor had hogs; another raised sugar cane and pressed molasses.

When Grandma needed butter, she'd tell one of the kids, "Take Miss Sally a dozen eggs and tell her to send me some butter." Sometimes a neighbor would send some lard, bacon, or ham in exchange for fresh fish. Coffee, flour, and cornmeal largely comprised the shopping list because they lived in *community* and because they loved one another.

It didn't matter if the children squabbled or if the adults disagreed; on Sunday morning all the adults piled into a mule-drawn wagon and headed to church. The children put their Sunday shoes on the wagon and played barefoot along the route to the country church, which was two or three miles away. Grandma said as they drew near the little church they could hear singing from its open windows, and the wagonload of worshipers would join in the song before they ever arrived.

Like the lyrics of my song "Show Me How to Love," those country folks not only understood what real *agape* love was all about; they truly lived out the principles of the Scriptures. In their own simple way, they showed the world how to love in the true meaning of the word.

Not long ago I heard someone say, "There's so much trouble in the world. Somebody needs to do something." Oftentimes we feel helpless to effect change in this great big world of ours, and we feel that our "little bit" makes no difference. However, the words of the English author and Anglican cleric Sydney Smith reveal what is actually true: "It is the greatest of all mistakes to do nothing because you can only do a little. Do what you can."[8]

Doing what you can while seasoning your actions with the love of Christ is the greatest gift of all. It's never too late to show real love.

EMBRACE YOUR DAY

For the past three days we have seen how the power of God's love *working in you* can make a world of difference. Whether it's in taking a huge step of faith, bouncing back from a setback, or letting God use you to add the sweet love of Christ to a very bitter world, you must remember that you are an ambassador of Christ. You represent Him here on the earth. It's up to us—you and me—to do something.

We've come to the close of another *Embraced by God* concert theme. My friend, *God's power in you is accessible!* It is, you know. All you have to do is *ask* and Jesus will give you the compassion you need to put His love on display. Then, He'll give you the opportunity to share it. Tomorrow we'll begin our last theme: "God's Promise in You Is Incomparable." This variation of our love theme will be our last together.

Our time is almost up, so let's make the most of it. I'll meet you back here tomorrow. But before we end this session, let's pray once again. Let's call upon Paul's prayer for the church at Ephesus in Ephesians 3:14-21 and make it our prayer for one another:

For this cause I bow my knees unto the Father of our Lord Jesus Christ, of whom the whole family in heaven and earth is named, that he would grant you, according to the riches of his glory, to be strengthened with might by his Spirit in the inner man; that Christ may dwell in your hearts by faith; that ye, being rooted and grounded in love, may be able to comprehend with all the saints what is the breadth, and length, and depth, and height; and to know the love of Christ, which passeth knowledge, that ye might be filled with all the fulness of God. Now unto him that is able to do exceeding abundantly above all that we ask or think, according to the power that worketh in us, unto him be glory in the church by Christ Jesus throughout all ages, world without end. Amen.

Think About His Love

Today, ponder the difference that just a little bit of salt can make. In the same way that salt brings out the flavors of foods, being salt in a world that has lost its savor will bring out the beautiful essence of the love of God. Always think about God's love, but don't hesitate for a moment to show it. Opportunities are all around you, my friend. As you *think about His love*, turn to others and share the love of Christ today.

Read About His Love

"You are the salt of the earth; but if the salt loses its flavor, how shall it be seasoned? It is then good for nothing but to be thrown out and trampled underfoot by men" (Matthew 5:13 NKJV). We've eaten a lot of tasty, nutritious food at the Father's table today. Try this exercise: go back through today's devotion and read the scriptures only. Slow down and reread where needed, and be sensitive to the leading of the Holy Spirit. Now, come to Jesus in prayer.

Pray About His Love

What has the Lord quickened in your heart to pray today? As you come to Him in prayer, ask the Lord to help you demonstrate His *agape* love to others. Where you may have had trouble being salt in the past, lay these heavy burdens down, and pick up His easy yoke. Now, pray earnestly for everyone God brings to your heart, that their lives will be seasoned with His love, especially as He demonstrates it to them through you.

Be About His Love

Remember, you are an ambassador of Christ. You are on display as you represent Jesus in your home, in the workplace, on the city bus, at the grocery store, on the expressway—wherever you go, the love of Christ goes with you. *Will you make yourself available to be used by God today?* Pray for a specific opportunity to represent Jesus in some way. Pay attention . . . you won't want to miss an opportunity because in God's kingdom little things carry a lot of weight! Finally, after you make a big difference in someone's life today, make sure to give God the glory, and thank Him for empowering you to do it.

THEME SEVEN

GOD'S PROMISE IN YOU IS INCOMPARABLE

O Christ, in thee my soul hath found,
and found in thee alone,
the peace, the joy I sought so long
The bliss till now unknown.

I sighed for rest and happiness;
I yearned for them, not thee;
But while I passed my Saviour by,
his love laid hold on me.

Now none but Christ can satisfy,
none other name for me;
There's love and life and lasting joy,
Christ Jesus, found in thee.[1]
—Emma Frances Bevan

People have often asked me if I experience stage fright before I sing or speak. After giving that question a good deal of thought, I have concluded that my propensity to be afraid or nervous onstage is drastically reduced if I am prepared. Hours and hours of prayer, practice sessions, and performances have equipped me to be at my absolute best. Fear is banished. Anxiety is squelched. All that remains is that great sense of anticipation and dependence on Jesus that allows me to say, "I can't wait to do my thing for God!"

God has equipped each of us with gifts and talents to accomplish His specific will and purpose for our lives with ease. There's nothing more fulfilling than traveling in the lane where you know you are assigned. When you are confident of God's call on your life, you will not be concerned about the gifts and talents of others. You will not be jealous or envious of their success, comparing yourself to them. Rather, you will find that you can celebrate them, instead.

Over the next three days we will pump up the volume on your life assignment. God's promise within you is limitless, boundless, and inexhaustible. It's running over with power according to Ephesians 3:20, which we just prayed together at the close of our sixth concert theme. As you walk in your assignment, my friend, God will do "exceeding abundantly above" your greatest dreams, according to His mighty power that is at work within you.

Just as a cook stirs a wonderful pot of flavorful homemade soup that's been simmering on low heat atop the back burner of the stove, the Lord desires to reach down to the bottom of your heart and stir your gifts from the bottom up, releasing all of your Godlike potential.

Now, we have reached our final movement in the Father's symphony of love. The finale is at hand. Are you ready to take part? The spotlight can be an intimidating place, but not if you're prepared. Do you sense the Lord moving you from the shadows backstage? Is He leading you out, front and center, to deliver your lines and sing your big solo? *Get prepared to do your part!* The Lord needs you. So, surrender your gifts anew and afresh today. Lean in and pay attention, my friend. God wants you to focus on your own set of skills to be displayed on the world's stage. Get ready! This is your moment in the spotlight!

FOR THE NEXT THREE DAYS, THINK ON THESE THINGS:
Because God loves me, He has bestowed upon me gifts
and talents to use for His glory. I will make myself available to Him.

DAY 19

ENCOURAGE YOURSELF

I have found there are three stages to every great work of God: first it is impossible, then it is difficult, then it is done.[1]
—Hudson Taylor

It came to pass, when David and his men were come to Ziklag on the third day, that the Amalekites had invaded the south, and Ziklag, and smitten Ziklag, and burned it with fire; and had taken the women captives, that were therein: they slew not any, either great or small, but carried them away, and went on their way. So David and his men came to the city, and, behold, it was burned with fire; and their wives, and their sons, and their daughters, were taken captives. Then David and the people that were with him lifted up their voice and wept, until they had no more power to weep. And David's two wives were taken captives, Ahinoam the Jezreelitess, and Abigail the wife of Nabal the Carmelite. And David was greatly distressed; for the people spake of stoning him, because the soul of all the people was grieved, every man for his sons and for his daughters: but David encouraged himself in the LORD his God.
—1 Samuel 30:1-6

The task can never be too hard, or times too tough, for you to encourage yourself in God.

Have you ever been faced with so much discouragement that your only response was to cry? I don't mean you responded with a whimper or a whine. I mean, has your heart ever been so broken that your only outlet was to wail with grief? I know this feeling of uncontrolled sadness all too well.

I shared briefly with you in our devotion on Day 6 about the first few nights I spent alongside my husband's hospital bed after he had suffered a stroke. That first night Charles was in the cardiac intensive care unit was one of the longest nights of my life. Sleep deprived but vigilant, I guarded him closely as he lay in that hospital bed, fighting for his life, hanging in the balance between life and death. I was fighting for him, too, standing in the gap for him with every breath he took.

The thought of our children losing their father, our grandchildren losing their Papa, or me losing my husband of more than thirty years was more than I could take. As the hours turned past midnight and into the wee hours of morning, I tried my best to stifle my tears. But as the hospital ward grew silent and Charles lay still, tears welled up. I tried with all my might to hold back the flood of anguish welling up in my throat, but the wave of distress would not be stopped.

Overwhelmed with grief and stung by fear, I dashed to the bathroom that was inside my husband's private room. Too overcome to turn on the light, I grabbed a large bath towel, covered my face to muffle the sound, and heaved gut-wrenching sobs of grief there in the darkness. I stayed in that dark bathroom prayer closet until I had no more tears left in me.

Oh, dear friend, it is in midnight hours such as these when I am so glad I know Jesus in a real and personal way. Without Him and the comfort of His sweet Holy Spirit, I don't know what I would have done. It is amazing how powerful, yet peaceful, the presence of our Lord is when we need Him most.

With God, You Are Never Alone

First Samuel 30:1-6 tells us that David and his troops came home to Ziklag, only to find everything they held dear completely wiped out. The wicked Amalekites had raided the town, setting it on fire. Then they took the women and children and everyone else, young and old alike, as their prisoners. When David and his soldiers returned to find their homes smoldering in ruins and all of their loved ones gone, the Bible says these mighty men wept until they had no more power to weep.

The word *discouragement* does not begin to describe the condition of David and his men. As their leader, David even had to endure the threat of his own troops turning against him in the wake of this horrendous mess. In spite of it all, the Bible tells us in the sixth verse "but David encouraged himself in the LORD his God."

There was no one around who would or even could encourage David at this point. So, David did for himself what no one else could do for him.

Do you have deep disappointments that weigh heavily in your heart? Have your hopes and dreams literally gone up in smoke? Are you feeling the deep pain and sting of suffering a great loss? Take comfort, my friend. You don't have to wait for others to speak the encouraging words you long to hear. You can speak over yourself and like David did—*encourage yourself in the Lord your God.*

How do you begin? Keep reading, dear one. Soon you will be filling your own heart with the encouragement you need.

Because we are spiritual beings who are engaged in spiritual warfare, the enemy's priority is to wound or kill our spirit. Sadly, he is increasingly successful in the world today. At various times in our lives, we can all experience episodes of stress, unhappiness, sadness, or grief. Often when we suffer a personal tragedy like the loss of a loved one, a severe difficulty like a divorce, or the loss of a job, we may feel deeply depressed. Most of us are able to deal with these kinds of situations in a productive way.

Clinical depression, however, goes far beyond experiencing grief or a feeling of sadness. This illness can challenge your ability to perform even routine daily activities. In the extreme, depression may even lead to suicide. I have read that clinical depression is among the fastest growing mental illnesses in our nation, affecting about nineteen million Americans every year. It is estimated to contribute to half of all suicides.

It is also projected that about 5 to 10 percent of women and 2 to 5 percent of men will experience at least one major depressive episode during their adult lives. It seems that depression doesn't limit itself to primarily one demographic group. It affects people of every race, age, gender, and income level, regardless of their religious background. As a result, the use of antidepressants is widely on the rise, and support groups and various therapies abound—but the number of depressed individuals continues to grow.[2]

So, what is the solution for us and for the millions who are suffering under this yoke of oppression? While medication serves its purpose, God's Word serves as the remedy for whatever ails us. Let's go back to David a moment. In 1 Samuel 29, just before David and his men returned to find Ziklag spoiled by the Amalekites, another enemy of Israel, the Philistines, remembered God's favor upon David's life (vv. 3, 5).

My point is this: as God brings you to center stage, tapping your gifts and abilities and using you to advance His kingdom, stay on the alert. Watch and pray because the enemy can recognize God's hand upon your life; he'll do whatever he can to wound you and stall your progress.

But God! Our enemy, the devil, is a liar and a defeated foe. Though he may attack us by stealth, doing his best to hit us hard and unexpectedly, hoping his wicked scheme of discouragement and depression will pull us under, *we only need to stand in faith and remember*—God has already gone before us and paved the way to victory. Father God is working *all things together* for our good—*because we love Him* and are "the called according to his purpose" (Romans 8:28b).

Here are a few points to remember as God uses you more and more to do great exploits in His kingdom. When those moments of grief and discouragement come, I know you'll discover God has made a way for you.

Remember What God Has Done in the Past

In Psalm 137, God's people, the children of Judah, had been released from Babylonian captivity. Yet they recalled the horrific and depressing experience they encountered at the hands of their captors. They remembered the enemy's taunting requests to "sing us one of the songs of Zion" (v. 3b). In the next verse, God's heart-broken people responded rhetorically: "How shall we sing the LORD's song in a strange land?" In other words, "How can we sing at a time like this?" It was a time of national spiritual depression.

Likewise, Jesus' stunned disciples must have felt this over-whelming sadness, confusion, and fear on that day when His mutilated body was laid in the tomb. This was no time for gaiety or even the consideration of future endeavors; there was only a sense of intense hopelessness. This brings to my mind the conditions that gave birth to the Negro spiritual, which was conceived in oppression, hatred, degradation, and estrangement, yet has become a powerful genre that brings glory to God.

You see, God has placed a harp deep within the human soul. So, even though you may not be able to carry a tune or play an instrument, the harp in your soul is an instrument of joy, light-heartedness, and true worship. In every circumstance, as you call upon God and lift up your heavenly instrument in praise, it will carry you into His presence. This harp in you can even take a mournful tune and bring encouragement to a severely downcast soul.

A song with such a soul-stirring melody comes readily to mind; it was written by Clara Ward. I remember it best as it was sung by the late, great Mahalia Jackson. It simply says, "And my soul look[ed] back and wonder[ed] how I got over."[3] Even when remembering difficult times, you can encourage yourself by look-ing back and reviewing your history with God. Regardless of the circumstance, you will find that God has a perfect track record. Truly, He cannot, and will not, fail you.

The Apostle Paul, who experienced beatings, stoning, imprisonment, snake bites, shipwrecks, and other physical discomforts, wrote to the church at Corinth: "We are hard pressed on every side, yet not crushed; we are perplexed, but not in despair; persecuted, but not forsaken; struck down, but not destroyed" (2 Corinthians 4:8 NKJV).

As you look back over your life, consider just for a moment the things God has brought you through in recent days. Doesn't it do your heart good to remember God's faithfulness and goodness to you, even in the midst of life's challenges?

I think satan understands the power of remembering what God has done in our lives. It is for this reason I think he intensifies his attack on new believers who haven't yet established a spiritual track record with the Lord. Recently, I had a phone conversation with a young lady whom God has delivered from drug addiction. She is currently struggling with spousal infidelity, but still seemed quite excited about the new life she had found in Christ.

I asked rather tentatively why her husband's infidelity didn't seem to bother her very much. She said, "Oh, yes, it bothers me a lot; but when I think about how God took me off drugs cold turkey . . . no counseling, no twelve-step program, no gradual withdrawal—and I had used drugs since I was fourteen years old and now I'm twenty-eight—I realize this is trying to pull me back into that world of addiction and violence. But I know if God can deliver me from drugs, cold turkey, with no side effects, there ain't nothing God can't do. So, even if my marriage seems doomed, even if my husband leaves me for another woman, even if I am struggling to forgive his infidelity, I know if God can do all of these things for me, then I know that He can give me the strength I need to be victorious in this too."

I listened to this new believer who was baptized only a few months ago, the mother of three beautiful children, whose marriage is under severe attack. I listened to her praising God for what He has brought her through, in spite of the situation she is currently facing. When I hung up the phone, I felt a shout coming on and said out loud, "You go, God!" Then I began to reflect on the storms God has brought me through, and my spirit soared in worship. I sat right there at my desk and had church all by myself!

Consider What God Desires to Teach You

When we "encourage ourselves" like David did in Ziklag, not only should we look back at what God has brought us through, we also should look inward. We should ask ourselves what God is trying to teach us, how He is trying to change us, and how He is attempting to mold us into the image of His Son. Introspection can be a difficult process because the image we see in the mirror usually looks pretty good from our own biased perspective. It is much easier to see the faults of others than our own. Before we can fully enjoy the benefits of lifting up our own countenance, we must first recognize the problem that has brought us down.

I know a Christian couple who began dating last year. She is an accountant, and he is a journalist. He is a wordsmith and she is a number cruncher. Her language skills are not as sharp as his, and he is more concerned with the analytical process than getting to the bottom line. She told me they both loved the Lord and believed God had ordered their steps to meet, but their personality differences and their personal idiosyncrasies (which may seem small and insignificant to others) kept them at odds.

In their casual conversations, she felt as if each sentence she uttered was being scrutinized. He'd often ask, "What do you mean by that statement?" And she would rephrase her thoughts, trying to clarify an intended meaning. Then he would retort, "But that's not what you said originally. Why don't you say what you mean?" Conversely, he took great pains to give a detailed explanation to what she considered to be simple and practical questions. She found herself tuning out or telling him, "Why don't you just get to the point?"

Their fragile relationship was on the verge of being fatally fractured, although they claimed to love one another deeply. Then one Sunday morning as they sat together in church listening to the pastor's sermon, he spoke of God's grace extended through His love for humanity. The conclusion of the sermon was that God's desire is for believers to extend grace to one another.

The pastor spoke of the parable of the unmerciful servant in Matthew 18:23-35, in which a king forgave one of his servants a debt of ten thousand talents. However, this same servant went out and found one of his fellow servants, who owed him a hundred pence, roughed him up, and had him jailed in spite of his pleas and promises to pay.

My friend told me that as the pastor concluded the message she and her boyfriend, without saying a word, looked at each other with tear-streaked cheeks, strongly convicted of their lack of grace toward each other. They knew the condition of their relationship was a disgrace to God. After hearing the message, instead of pointing an accusing finger at each other, they saw themselves reflected in the words of Scripture.

Perhaps the greatest obstacle to introspection is getting over the notion that we are without fault. Once we overcome that obstacle, however, it is greatly encouraging to take a look at what God wants us to become. How valuable it is to understand that little by little, God is bringing us, often kicking and screaming, to a place of great joy and completeness.

Consider How God Is Moving in the World Around You

One of my students in the college songwriting class I teach is a young single mother. She is often stretched and stressed by working, going to school, and taking care of her pre-school-aged daughter. One day after class, she stayed behind and openly shared her challenges with me:

> *It was an idyllic morning in early March. The forsythias were in full bloom. The morning sunshine was brilliant and warming. Spring had successfully wrested control from the icy grip of a winter in the Tennessee mountains, and the earth was responding with new growth and bird songs. I had dropped off my four-year-old at*

preschool after one of those mornings when it seemed nothing was going right . . . when it seemed I had gotten up on the wrong side of the bed.

It was a morning when I had forgotten to put coffee on the grocery list and there wasn't even enough to brew one full cup, so I skipped coffee. It was a morning when I had washed a load of clothes, then discovered, after the fact, that the water temperature setting on the washer was inadvertently turned to "hot," and before I finished my morning shower, the water ran cold.

It was a morning when one of the tires on the car looked low and when I drove to the gas station to put some air in the "soft" tire, I heard the telltale hissing sound of my car's right front tire going flat. What a way to start the day! It was one of those mornings when you feel you should have just stayed in bed.

But then it happened. On the return trip from the pre-school, I was heading east with the morning sun. It was not quite high enough for the car's visor to block it out. It was nearly blinding my vision when I stopped at a red light. I was full of attitude by now, even disgusted with the morning sun that caused me to squint at the traffic light, which I could hardly see because of the glare.

Then I noticed this person in the cross-walk. It was a young guy, maybe in his midtwenties. Apparently he was afflicted with muscular dystrophy because he laboriously made his way across the street using two crutchlike appliances, half-dragging his lower torso along. Then I looked more closely and saw on his face a grin that stretched from ear to ear, as his head wobbled loosely with his stumbling gait. What a smile!

He wasn't grinning at me. He didn't even look in my direction. His countenance reflected the pure joy of living. And there I sat in my automobile grumbling over a lack of coffee, a lukewarm shower, a soft tire, and sunshine in my face. The Holy Spirit convicted me immediately. I was not walking, although I was perfectly capable.

No, I was riding in an automobile, which (although it was not new)
was paid for, and (although it had a leaky tire) I had money enough
to get it repaired.

Not only had I dressed myself this morning, but my four-year-old
as well; and I was not struggling alone on my journey through life, but
had the joy of parenting a young child. And finally, I realized that the
same sunshine that caused me to squint and complain brought hilarity
to this person, to whom life had dealt a much tougher hand.

I marveled at what I had just witnessed. A car behind me honked.
The light had turned green. God had used a complete stranger, but
a fellow traveler, to save me from a day of discouragement, and
some days later, there are moments when I still see that infectious
grinning face.

Quite frankly, I haven't had a bad morning since. Many times,
we can encourage ourselves by simply looking around. My
mother used to admonish us to eat lima beans by telling us about
the starving children in other parts of the world. I reasoned that
no loving parent would present a starving child with a plate of
lima beans. I could look to the images of a war-torn foreign country or to the face of a starving child to remind me of how good
God is to me. But more often, I usually don't have to look any farther than my own front door to know how richly blessed I am. I
simply need to look around.

Remember Just How Big Father God Is!

In her book *Holding On to Hope*, Nancy Guthrie describes in profound detail the pain and discouragement she, her husband,

David, and their family experienced after two losing two infants to Zellweger syndrome. In the midst of deep despair they held on to the hope that can be found only in God's promises.

Nancy writes very candidly,

> Sometimes what God has allowed into our lives is so bitter that we're hurt and angry and don't even want to talk to Him about it. But where does that leave us? On our own. No resources, no truth to dispel the despair, no hope. The truth is, there is no comfort to be found away from God; at least, there is no lasting, deep satisfying comfort . . . only the truth of God's Word, the tenderness of His welcome, the touch of His healing presence can bring the kind of comfort we crave.[4]

Nancy's words remind me of how David must have felt while standing amidst the awful devastation at Ziklag. Confronted by one of the most difficult circumstances in his life, David chose to look beyond his circumstances to a great big God. As he looked beyond himself, he found the strength to press on in the face of tremendous adversity.

Many believers have recited the words from 1 Samuel 30:6: "But David encouraged himself in the LORD his God." Here are some other powerful passages from God's word to remind you just how big God is, so you'll always remember—even in the midnight hour—both who and whose you are:

1 Peter 2:9 . . . you are part of God's "chosen generation."
John 13:35 . . . you are one of Jesus' disciples.
John 15:14 . . . you are Jesus' friend.
Isaiah 49:16 . . . you are engraved on the palms of His hands.

Matthew 5:13 . . . you are the "salt of the earth."

Matthew 5:14 . . . you are the "light of the world."

Romans 8:37 . . . we are "more than conquerors" in Christ.

Numbers 13:30 . . . we are "well able" to overcome our enemy.

Meditate on the Word of God

When life's circumstances keep you up all night, remember the promises of God. And when you remember them, *meditate on them*. The word *meditate* implies a moving of the lips or to converse with oneself. (That's why I encouraged you to "chew, chew, chew" on God's word in our devotional reading exercise on Day 6.) In other words, a great way to meditate on God's word is through self-talk, or talking to yourself concerning your situation—rehearsing God's promises, not your problems. When you meditate on God's word, you are reminding yourself of what you know to be true about God. So, like David, let your meditation be about how good God is and how able He is to work on your behalf. Psalm 1:1-2 says:

> Blessed is the man that walketh not in the counsel of the ungodly, nor standeth in the way of sinners, nor sitteth in the seat of the scornful. But his delight is in the law of the LORD; and in his law doth he meditate day and night.

Whether you are walking along the hallway to an appointment, standing in a long line at the DMV, or sitting down to catch a twenty-minute catnap, keeping your mind on the Lord will cause you to be encouraged, productive, and fruitful. Discouragement will tell you that the whole world is against you and nothing is going to work out. Encouragement, on the other hand, will tell you that Jesus, who is always on your side, is much greater than a whole world against you.

Oh, yes! Even when the fallout of warfare is all around you, and even if no one is standing with you, *God has made a way*. You can encourage yourself in the Lord, just like David did, because "the joy of the LORD" is your strength (Nehemiah 8:10).

EMBRACE YOUR DAY

Sometimes, by choice or by design, there may come a time in your life when there will be no encourager to physically comfort you or lift you up with edifying words. There may be no cheerleader to rally you on. There may be no preacher to motivate you and no choir to lead you in a song of praise.

When the dark night of the soul drives you into your prayer closet, cry out to God, even if you've cried until you can cry no more. Take all the time you need in that solitary place. While you are there, talk to God and listen to Him. When you come out, talk to yourself; meditate about everything God has said and shown you in His word.

When you have given your situation fully over to God, you will emerge much stronger, remembering no one can encourage you the way you can encourage yourself.

We are at the end of another session and nearing the end of this wonderful and enriching concert experience. My hope is that with each passing day, you are realizing just how much God loves you and that His great favor is operating in every area of your life. Before you rush off to do other things today, let's pause and thank our God who encourages us:

Dear heavenly Father,
It is with great humility that I approach Your throne. I thank
You, dear Father, that I can find everything I need in You. My

friends and loved ones are indeed a blessing. I am much richer because they are in my life. But when they leave and go home, they do not leave me lonely . . . because You are still with me. Even in my lowest moments, thank You, Lord, that I need not look to anyone but You to supply my deepest need for encouragement. Please help me to meditate on Your word instead of my circumstances. Today, as I encourage myself, meditating on Your promises, I will be ever mindful of Your great love for me. In Jesus' name,
Amen.

Think About His Love

The ability to encourage yourself is a precious gift from God. Think about how His love for you is so great that He made a way for you to receive help directly, and only, from Him. Remember and meditate on a few of the things Father God has done for you in the past. Then write a few thoughts in your journal.

Read About His Love

It came to pass, when David and his men were come to Ziklag on the third day, that the Amalekites had invaded the south, and Ziklag, and smitten Ziklag, and burned it with fire; and had taken the women captives, that were therein: they slew not any, either great or small, but carried them away, and went on their way. So

David and his men came to the city, and, behold, it was burned
with fire; and their wives, and their sons, and their daughters,
were taken captives. Then David and the people that were with
him lifted up their voice and wept, until they had no more power
to weep. And David's two wives were taken captives, Ahinoam
the Jezreelitess, and Abigail the wife of Nabal the Carmelite.
And David was greatly distressed; for the people spake of stoning
him, because the soul of all the people was grieved, every man for
his sons and for his daughters: but David encouraged himself in
the LORD his God. (1 Samuel 30:1-6)

Read and meditate on this passage.

Pray About His Love

There are times when a situation is so complex that you aren't
even sure how to pray. No problem. The Holy Spirit can pray for
you. When you are in a situation where you can't find the right
words, God understands. Thank Him for giving you the beautiful
promise in Romans 8:26: "The Spirit also helpeth our infirmities:
for we know not what we should pray for as we ought: but the
Spirit itself maketh intercession for us with groanings which cannot be uttered."

Be About His Love

How can you practice the habit of encouraging yourself this
week? Jot down a few examples in your journal as they come to

mind. Your entry might look something like this: *Instead of speaking negative words about my weight, I will encourage myself with the truth that God says I'm beautiful. He will help me make better choices concerning the things I eat. According to Philippians 4:13, "I can do all things through Christ who strengthens me"* (NKJV).

EQUIP YOURSELF

Go, spread the Saviour's love
Go, tell His matchless grace
Proclaim salvation, full and free
To Adam's guilty race

We wish you, in His Name
The most divine success
Assured that He who sends you forth
Will your endeavors bless[1]
—Mrs. Vokes

Whatever you do, work at it with all your heart,
as working for the Lord, not for men, since you know
that you will receive an inheritance from the Lord as a reward.
It is the Lord Christ you are serving.
—Colossians 3:23-24 NIV

God has enabled you to accomplish great things.

I can't believe it, dear friend, but our time together has almost come to a close. One more day and we will draw the curtain for the last time and turn down the lights on this amazing demonstration of God's great love for us. Joining you at this place each day has been such a blessing to my soul. I believe the best is still yet to come for you. Long after we complete this *Embraced by God* encounter, the blessings of God will continue to overtake you. God's promise from 1 Corinthians 2:9 comes to my mind:

> Eye has not seen, nor ear heard,
> Nor have entered into the heart of man
> The things which God has prepared for those who
>   love Him (NKJV)

Our final three-day theme together will remind you that because God loves you, He has given you gifts and talents to do great things in His name. You are His masterpiece, pregnant with incredible promise to effect change in the world around you. God has placed you on the earth at just the precise time you are needed. It is no mistake that you are alive and on the earth at this specific moment in history. God wants to use you!

We have established these truths in days past, but let me remind you again. God loves you with a deep abiding love. He has great plans for you. His plan is to prosper you, not to do you harm. He wants to fill your days with enduring hope. In spite of what you read or what you may hear others saying, I want to encourage you to anticipate the many ways God will use you in the days to come.

There is also great promise in you for personal growth and change. With each passing day as you linger in God's embrace, you can become a better version of the person you were yesterday.

I once met a lady during the break at a conference where I was speaking. At the session just prior to meeting her, I had been teaching about how important it is for us not to worry. She said to me, "I've always been a worrier. My mother was a worrier. My grandmother was a worrier too. I guess I'll always be a worrier."

Before I could chime in, another lady standing nearby added her insight. She said, "If you had a broken toe and had to walk on crutches, you wouldn't be satisfied to walk on crutches for the rest of your life, would you? No, you'd get that toe fixed! You can get that worry problem fixed too!" All I could do was laugh and add, "Amen, sister!"

"We are more than conquerors through him that loved us" (Romans 8:37)! We never have to succumb to feelings of helplessness or remain stuck in life's dead-end situations. Jesus always offers us a better way. Whoever says that we can't grow and change is simply not telling the gospel truth.

In fact, as believers who aspire to become more and more like Jesus Christ, we must never stop growing toward excellence. Becoming who Christ has called us to be is our life's goal. We must take hold of His promises and *live out the promise* within us. If you are doing anything less than your absolute best for the cause of Christ, it is mediocrity. Ephesians 5:15-16 presents this challenge beautifully. Read it with me:

> Look carefully then how you walk! Live purposefully and worthily and accurately, not as the unwise and witless, but as wise (sensible, intelligent people). Making the very most of the time [buying up each opportunity], because the days are evil. (AMP)

Be Fearlessly Obedient to God

One such woman who was not satisfied with the way things were was Jochebed. As God would have it, her name means "Jehovah-gloried."[2] Certainly Jochebed's life was a demonstration of God's glory, for she is highly esteemed as one of the greatest mothers in the Bible. Having possessed commendable character traits as a godly woman, she and her husband hold a well-deserved place of prominence in God's divine Hall of Faith in Hebrews 11:23.

God equipped this woman with great wisdom, courage, complete trust in Him, a dedication to her family, and a heart of total selflessness. These admirable qualities would alter the course of the entire Israelite nation. Because she stood on God's promise, the entire nation rose to greatness, in spite of a wicked pharaoh's edict to annihilate them.

Jochebed proves that when we use our gifts for God, He always finds a way to express His glory through them.

Before we look more closely at the qualities Jochebed possessed and then take a look at yours, let's first see what the word of God says about the situation she faced. Starting in Exodus 1:22, on into Exodus 2:1-10, we read concerning this historic event:

> Pharaoh charged all his people, saying, Every [Hebrew] son that is born ye shall cast into the river, and every daughter ye shall save alive. And there went a man of the house of Levi [Amram], and took to wife a daughter of Levi [Jochebed]. And the woman conceived, and bare a son: and when she saw him that he was a goodly child, she hid him three months. And when she could no

longer hide him, she took for him an ark of bulrushes, and daubed it with slime and with pitch, and put the child therein; and she laid it in the flags by the river's brink. And his sister stood afar off, to wit what would be done to him. And the daughter of Pharaoh came down to wash herself at the river; and her maidens walked along by the river's side; and when she saw the ark among the flags, she sent her maid to fetch it. And when she had opened it, she saw the child: and, behold, the babe wept. And she had compassion on him, and said, This is one of the Hebrews' children. Then said his sister to Pharaoh's daughter, Shall I go and call to thee a nurse of the Hebrew women, that she may nurse the child for thee? And Pharaoh's daughter said to her, Go. And the maid went and called the child's mother. And Pharaoh's daughter said unto her, Take this child away, and nurse it for me, and I will give thee thy wages. And the woman took the child, and nursed it. And the child grew, and she brought him unto Pharaoh's daughter, and he became her son. And she called his name Moses: and she said, Because I drew him out of the water.

Now, let me clarify a little about Israel's background in Egypt up to this point. Remember from our devotion on Day 15 that Joseph ultimately became a great leader in Egypt, second only to Pharaoh (Genesis 41:38-45). While Joseph was alive (before a new king arose over Egypt in Exodus 1:8), the pharaoh he served did very little to control the growing Israelite population. In fact, Exodus 1:7 says, "The children of Israel were fruitful, and increased abundantly, and multiplied, and waxed exceeding mighty."

But after the death of Joseph, the new pharaoh was not as favorable. Fearing a population explosion and the possibility that the Jews could potentially overtake Egypt, he made life unbearable for them. They set taskmasters over the Jews who were as hard as nails. The Hebrew slaves found themselves under tremendous, and increasing, hardship as they built cities and worked in Pharaoh's fields making mortar and bricks and doing every kind of hard labor to build the Egyptian empire. Even under these conditions, the Israelites continued to thrive. (See Exodus 1:8-14.)

Now, we come back to where we started with the story of Jochebed in Exodus 1:22. To control the population, Pharaoh ordered that all newborn Hebrew boys be murdered. It was into this situation that Moses was born. With the help of her husband and two older children, Jochebed kept her little baby boy hidden for three months. Can you imagine how difficult it must have been for this mother to keep her baby hidden in the house? Surely, her newborn son (whom Pharaoh's daughter ultimately named Moses) cried as heartily as any other baby. No doubt, Jochebed kept all windows and doors tightly shut, even in what might have been sweltering heat, for fear that his cries would be heard by a nosy neighbor and her secret be exposed.

In my mind's eye, I can see her panic-stricken face with every knock at the door. As baby Moses grew, it likely became increasingly difficult to keep him hidden. With her back against the wall, Jochebed faced a very difficult decision.

Take Bold Steps of Faith

Has your back ever been against the wall? Have you ever stood toe-to-toe with the difficult task of having to make an excruciating life-or-death decision? We will turn to Jochebed to see how God equipped her to stand strong in the face of a compromising culture.

It's interesting how many similarities there are between that culture and ours. Just as God called a woman named Jochebed into the spotlight, He is moving you out of the shadows of the backstage to play a big role in today's session. So, let's see what you can glean from this great woman of God.

First of all, you must decide to obey God. Pharaoh's orders were clear. Throw all Hebrew baby boys into the Nile River. There is no telling how many mothers' hearts were shattered and how many newborn boys lost their lives to this dastardly order. Jochebed refused to obey this wicked order from this evil leader. She chose to obey God.

Confronted by this difficult decision, Moses' mother did an unusual thing. (And I don't think Jochebed came by this idea on her own.) She got the idea to put her baby in a wicker basket and place him among the reeds of the dangerous, crocodile-ridden River Nile. This idea did not originate from anywhere in this world, my friend. It was divinely inspired by God.

To any mother, this drastic decision would seem totally ridiculous. However, God in His divine design knew exactly what He was doing. It is obvious to me that Jochebed did what *she knew* God instructed her to do. Above every heart-wrenching circumstance she faced, this brave woman obeyed God. Then she trusted Him to handle the rest. Isn't that the epitome of obedience?

You must do the same. When the enemy tries to put you in a

chokehold, seek God and do what He tells you to do, regardless of how unconventional His instructions may be. Then leave the rest to Him. God will complete His plan, doing what only He can do.

In 1984 when my growing concert calendar began to compete with my middle high school teaching job, common sense said, "Hang on to the job." My practical head knowledge reminded me that my husband had recently quit his job to start a new business. The pressures of meeting the needs of our growing family tempted me to rely on the security of my paycheck, as well as the health-care and retirement benefits the school system provided.

For a solid year, I nursed a newborn and mothered another active elementary school-age son. I taught private piano and voice lessons. I held down my teaching job. I tried to keep up with a growing music ministry. Is it any wonder that I almost collapsed from exhaustion in the process? Of course, my husband did all those things that great fathers do. But there are some things that only a mother can accomplish.

I sought God with all my heart. He led me to follow Him, step off the conventional path, and trust Him for the rest. After I quit my job, I found that He provided everything we needed. All of our family's needs were gloriously met. The bills got paid. God even sent someone to contribute enough money for health care for the first year of our new music ministry!

Now, after pursuing this calling for more than half my life, I can truly say there is nothing more fulfilling than doing what I firmly believed God had called me to do. I can honestly share that I love what I do and I do what I love. *Someone said if you love what you do, you'll never work a day in your life.* Amen! Truly, God is faithful! As you move into your calling, remember as I do what David shared in Psalm 37:25:

> I was young and now I am old,
> yet I have never seen the righteous forsaken
> or their children begging bread. (NIV)

Second, to equip yourself for the days ahead, you must depend on God. Exodus 2:2 (NKJV) says that Moses was a "beautiful child." I love that! Every baby is beautiful to his mother, but this baby was especially beautiful. In Acts 7:20, Moses is described as being "exceeding fair." Then in Hebrews 11:23 (NIV), Moses is described as being "no ordinary child." Moses was beautiful to his mother, but it's obvious that God smiled upon him in a special way.

Jochebed loved her baby, and he grew until he could no longer be kept a secret. Exodus 2:3 reveals that she had to resort to a drastic measure to save her child. She did what many mothers since then have had to do in order to save the lives of their babies—she gave her cherished child away. Oh, the anxiety she must have felt in her heart! With no idea where or how the baby would end up, Jochebed had to do an excruciatingly difficult thing. Only God could have helped this obedient woman carry out such a difficult task.

I have a friend we'll call Kaye, who adopted a sweet baby girl many years ago. I leaned on Kaye for her valuable insights on the adoption process. This is the powerful testimony she shared with me:

Some people will look at the natural birth mother, the one who gave her baby away, in a very negative light. But as a mother of an adopted child, I view this woman as tremendously courageous, and I consider the act of giving her baby up for adoption as entirely selfless. While she recognized her inability to provide everything that our precious daughter needed, she also recognized my family's ability to provide and meet her needs in every way. She said, "In my situation, our daughter would not have had a safe and loving Christian upbringing; she would not have had the benefits of a Christian education, and most of all, she may not have come to know Christ as Savior in her youth. The gift of adoption is one of the greatest gifts our family could ever receive."

Some people think you must come to the place where you have complete and total peace before acting on a decision. I believe Moses' dear mother must have had many second thoughts before releasing her baby to what appeared to be an unknown fate. But again, it occurs to me that nothing ever occurs to God.

For this reason, we can do nothing in and of our own strength. *Like Jochebed, we are able to do what we are called to do, when we are commanded to do it, solely because God empowers us to do it.*

I am reminded of a passage I taught my children to memorize, so they could call upon it when facing times of difficulty. I recommend it to you today. It is found in the book of Isaiah:

Fear not, for I am with you;
Be not dismayed, for I am your God.
I will strengthen you,
Yes, I will help you,
I will uphold you with My righteous right hand. (41:10 NKJV)

Third, you must determine to uphold godly values. You must care about the things God cares about. The principles of honoring one's faith and family shine through like brilliant stars in this God-story. The evidence that Jochebed loved the things that God loves was reflected in the lives of her amazing children. Aaron became the first high priest of the nation of Israel. Miriam was a gifted poet, musician, and lead worshiper. Moses, the deliverer of the Israelites, became one of the greatest leaders the world has ever known.

What a legacy this woman produced! All of her children grew to fame and notoriety.

We see in this situation that her little daughter Miriam, probably around age ten at the time, was much like her mother. Although she was young and maybe a bit naïve, she exhibited great godly wisdom when suggesting that her own mother be the one to nurse little Moses, after Pharaoh's daughter discovered her baby brother in the river.

It is clear that Jochebed placed her faith and family first. It is clear, as well, that her children followed in her footsteps. Many years later, God would equip Moses to lead the Hebrew nation out of Egypt. He would equip Aaron to be an eloquent spokesperson for Moses and their people, and He equipped Miriam to bless and encourage the Israelites just when they needed it most. Surely, God's promise in each of them proved to be incomparable.

Do What God Has Equipped You to Do

What has God uniquely equipped you to do? If challenging the laws of an evil national leader or leading a nation out from the bonds of slavery seems way over your head, not to worry. As we have discussed on numerous occasions, God has a unique assignment for you. If you know what that assignment is, don't let fear, pride, pretense, or a need for approval get in your way. Rather, remember the Apostle Paul's encouraging words:

> Whatever you do, work at it with all your heart, as working for the Lord, not for men, since you know that you will receive an inheritance from the Lord as a reward. It is the Lord Christ you are serving. (Colossians 3:23-24 NIV)

You can accomplish great things for Christ because He has empowered you to do what He's called you to do. Your attitude as His child and willing servant should be one not of pressure or obligation, but of privilege. True servants don't say with dread, "Ugh! I have to do this." Instead, they say with joy, "Oh! I get to do this!"

If you are still seeking God for your assignment, begin asking Him right now to give you opportunities and occasions to serve Him. John Wesley, a great preacher and a humble servant, lived by an incredible motto. Let his words motivate you to find God's assignment for your life and get to it. This is what he said:

> *Do all the good you can,*
> *By all the means you can,*
> *In all the ways you can,*
> *In all the places you can,*
> *At all the times you can,*
> *To all the people you can,*
> *As long as ever you can.*[3]

You may need to start small, but start today. Remember, God is not looking for superstars. He is looking for servants. If you're not sure what that looks like, just take a long look at Jesus. Do what He did. Jesus will show you how to serve Him by loving others. Often, Jesus did small things in a great way. He served the sick. He cared for children. He cooked simple meals for His friends. He enjoyed great conversations. No assignment is too basic when you put your heart in it.

Sweet friend, our time is up for today. Tomorrow we'll spend one last session together. Until then, remember that God created you and placed you on this earth for a purpose. It is with that purpose in mind that God has given you the means to accomplish it. Starting today, add Galatians 6:9 to your list of encouraging scriptures: "Let's not get tired of doing what is good. At just the right time we will reap a harvest of blessing if we don't give up" (NLT).

It's a privilege to pray with you today. I know that God will use you to do either great big things or small things in a great big way. Whatever you do for Him, do it with joy! Right now, join me in prayer:

Dear loving Father,

I thank You, Lord, that You have equipped me to serve You by serving others. My request of You today is that You would save the lost in the world around me. Comfort those who mourn. Raise up those who have fallen. Give shelter to those who are fighting the elements. Feed the hungry. Clothe the naked. Visit the sick and the prisoner. Love the unlovable and touch the untouchable. Lord, befriend those who are lonely. To accomplish these great tasks—use me to help You. In the name of Your precious son, Jesus, I pray these things. Amen.

EMBRACE YOUR DAY

Think About His Love

Look back over the past few day days, and chronicle how God has equipped you to fulfill your special assignment. Does a significant opportunity or two come to mind? If you completed one or both of them, how did it make you feel? Remember, small things done in a great way are vitally important to God; they are equally significant as what people might consider to be big opportunities. Think about how God has filled you with promise to make a profound difference in this world for Him.

Read About His Love

"Whatever you do, work at it with all your heart, as working for the Lord, not for men, since you know that you will receive an inheritance from the Lord as a reward. It is the Lord Christ you are serving" (Colossians 3:23-24 NIV). As you meditate on this passage and commit it to memory, think about Jochebed. She certainly didn't do what she did to receive the accolades of men. Rather, against human wisdom and likely her own emotions, she believed the word of the Lord and put her beautiful son in the Nile River. Now personalize this verse. I'll get you started: "*Whatever I do, I will work at it with* *all **my** heart, as working for the Lord, not for men . . ."* Keep going, my dear friend. Rehearse this promise until it's bubbling up in your heart.

Pray About His Love

Throughout the day, actively seek the Lord concerning how you may serve Him by loving others. Remember, our world is in a love crisis. You are uniquely equipped and filled with promise to shed His love abroad in simple ways. As you spend time with the Lord in prayer, ask Him to help you overcome any fear or apprehension that could keep you from joyfully carrying out His work today.

Be About His Love

Jesus told His disciples in Matthew 28:18-20,

> I have been given all authority in heaven and on earth. Therefore, go and make disciples of all the nations, baptizing them in the name of the Father and the Son and the Holy Spirit. Teach these new disciples to obey all the commands I have given you. And be sure of this: I am with you always, even to the end of the age. (NLT)

Oh, yes, God's promise in you is incomparable. What part can you play today to help further His Great Commission? God's assignment for you today may be as brief and simple as letting someone who is in a hurry get ahead of you in traffic. It may mean committing to share your God-story before a small group. Whether your opportunity is a difficult task or something you could do with your eyes closed and your hands tied behind your back, commit this opportunity to the Lord and ask for His help to accomplish it with excellence.

DAY 21

ENVISION YOURSELF

The tragedy of life is not that it ends so soon,
but that we wait so long to begin it.[1]
—W. M. Lewis

Those things, which ye have both learned, and received, and heard,
and seen in me, do: and the God of peace shall be with you.
—Philippians 4:9

Your life is a reflection of who Christ is in you.

Our twenty-one-day endeavor has almost come to an end. The time has gone by so quickly, hasn't it? Pretty soon, we'll be singing the closing benediction. But before we do, we have to tie up a few loose ends. This is a very important day—because completing these twenty-days of being *Embraced by God* marks a brand-new beginning for you.

This very moment could be a defining one if you allow it to be. You could close this book and say, "That was nice." Then pick up where you left off twenty-two days ago. But instead, you could say, "That was then and this is now . . . and starting now, with the help of God, I will live like I know I'm God's favorite." From this moment forward you can know, beyond the shadow of any doubt, that

> *You are deeply loved by God, without condition.*
>
> *You are complete in Him, lacking nothing.*
>
> *You are never alone; God is with you.*
>
> *Your needs are all met because God has supplied them.*
>
> *You have a specific assignment to complete.*
>
> *You are equipped with power to carry out that assignment.*
>
> *Your God is faithful to complete the work He started in you.*

You've read a specific passage from the word of God each day for the past three weeks. You've been encouraged, challenged, and inspired. Your life is consecrated, your thinking is more stimulated, and your heart is more motivated to be the person God wants you to become. With this review in mind—now that you've heard all these things—let me ask you this question: *What will you do with what you have heard?*

As we have met each day, we have given God's word priority, looking to Him to give us the wisdom we need for everyday living. The word of God is your textbook for life, teaching you God's principles and precepts. It's your owner's manual, revealing the intricacies of how you are wired and put together. It's your navigation system, pointing you to true north, leading, guiding, and directing you through life to God's intended destination. And it's your source of comfort when life is cruel and discouraging.

God Wants You to Have "Good Success" in Life

Oh, yes! As you "observe" the word of God, like Joshua did, and many other heroes of the faith who have gone before us, you will experience "good success" in life. Let us remind ourselves of this inspiring promise:

> This book of the law shall not depart out of thy mouth; but thou shalt meditate therein day and night, that thou mayest observe to do according to all that is written therein: for then thou shalt make thy way prosperous, and then thou shalt have good success. (Joshua 1:8)

A "prosperous" way and "good success"—aren't they what you want from life? I know I do. In the third chapter of the book of Philippians, Paul helps us hone in on our life's goals by comparing who we were *back then* to who we are now. He proclaims that his old life, even with his pedigree and personal accomplishments, paled in comparison to life in Christ:

> If anyone else has reason to put their confidence in physical advantages, I have even more:
> I was circumcised on the eighth day.
> I am from the people of Israel and the tribe of Benjamin.
> I am a Hebrew of the Hebrews.
> With respect to observing the Law, I'm a Pharisee.
> With respect to devotion to the faith, I harassed the church.
> With respect to righteousness under the Law, I'm blameless.
> These things were my assets, but I wrote them off as a loss for the sake of Christ. But even beyond that, I consider everything a loss in comparison with the superior value of knowing Christ

Jesus my Lord. I have lost everything for him, but what I lost I think of as sewer trash, so that I might gain Christ and be found in him. (Philippians 3:4b-9a CEB)

In essence, Paul was reminding us that we can do *all the right things* for *all the wrong reasons*. We can hold onto our stuff and miss Christ and everything He has for us. We can be born into the right family, observe all the rules, be devoted to our church, and basically be good people. But apart from knowing Christ, all of that is worthless.

The Apostle Paul gave us permission to use his life as an example of what it really looks like to follow Christ without missing a beat. He told us to *stand firm*, another military term, meaning to stand our ground out on the battle front: not to be moved by popular opinion or shaken by what's going on around us.

I once heard a preacher use the term *flat-footed*. I like that analogy. Can you get a mental picture of a holy soldier standing flat-footed, with great intention, upon the truth of God's word? I believe you can. Having done this, you can then make the determination not to change your stance, but to stand firm according to Philippians 4:1: "Therefore, my brothers and sisters whom I love and miss, who are my joy and crown, stand firm in the Lord" (CEB).

Do you sense Paul's deep passion for us—members of the church body today—as he called his fellow Christ-followers "brothers and sisters . . . my joy and crown"? Paul wanted them, and I'm sure all who would come after them, to develop a like passion for the body of Christ. I am certain he would want us to get this message today because if we don't get it—understanding that we are all a part of something much bigger collectively than we are individually—we will succumb to the pressures of our culture and fail our mission.

Going back to chapter 3 of Philippians, Paul established the fact that he was in this endeavor for the long haul. He was in it to win it. I'm with Paul. How about you? This mighty man of God said,

> Brethren, I do not count myself to have apprehended; but one thing I do, forgetting those things which are behind and reaching forward to those things which are ahead, I press toward the goal for the prize of the upward call of God in Christ Jesus. (Philippians 3:13-14 NKJV)

Paul admitted that he was a work in progress—that we all are for that matter—and he admonished us not to compromise our faith or lower our standards while we are on this road to becoming like Christ. So keep your eyes on the prize. In other words, keep your gaze fixed and your mind made up. Don't think like the world, act like the world, walk like the world, or talk like the world.

God Wants You to Stand on What You Know

If you belong to Jesus, then stand up and be counted. Too often we are led by our feelings. A number of times throughout the book, I have reminded you to stand on what you know, not on what you feel. If the devil can control your feelings, then he can control how you live. So, make up your mind now that you will not be swayed by your emotions; instead, you will stand on what is reliable, trustworthy, faithful, genuine, and sure.

When you stand on truth, you stand on the only thing that doesn't change, and that is the word of God.

Years ago, I began writing a list of things I know to be true about God. Today, I am still adding to that list. It's quite a faith-building assignment, and I recommend you establish a list of your own. Allow me to share a few statements from my journal:

I know the word of God is true.
—*John 1:1*

I know God is love.
—*1 John 4:7-8*

I know all things work together for good.
—*Romans 8:28*

I know God is for me.
—*Romans 8:31*

I know God is faithful.
—*Deuteronomy 7:9*

I know greater is He who is in me than he that is in the world.
—*1 John 4:4*

I know God owns it all.
—*Psalm 24:1*

I know God is able.
—*Ephesians 3:20*

 I know that nothing can come between me and God's love
for me.
—*Romans 8:38-39*

I know that Jesus was crucified on a rugged cross for my sin.
—*Matthew 27:50*

Now, hear me, dear friend. *There's plenty I don't know—but what
I do know makes all the difference in the way I live.* I am so passionate about standing on what I know, rather than what I feel, this
divine inspiration came to me complete with a song. We sing this
song as an anthem at the conclusion of every "Embrace Worship
Celebration for Women" that I'm able to lead. Women stand all
over the room declaring these truths we shared at the beginning
of Theme Three:

> *I know that You are God*
> *I know You're on Your throne*
> *I know Your love embraces me*
> *And I am not alone*
> *I know that You are able*
> *To keep what I've committed*
> *Unto You against that day.*
> *I know, I know, I know.*[2]

God Expects You to Walk in Unity with Others

Then, Paul reminded us in the fourth chapter of Philippians that it's imperative we *stand together*:

> I beseech Euodias, and beseech Syntyche, that they be of the same mind in the Lord. And I intreat thee also, true yokefellow, help those women which laboured with me in the gospel, with Clement also, and with other my fellowlabourers, whose names are in the book of life. (vv. 2-3)

These two women worked side by side with the Apostle Paul in the work of the gospel, but somewhere along the way, they had a disagreement. Now, it's fine to disagree, but when that disagreement becomes a distraction that leads to dissension, discord, and division, it sets back the cause of Christ and dishonors the Lord.

We will never be effective for Christ as long as we are fussing and bickering, refusing to work together. Our enemy knows that we can do much more together than we can do apart. And if he can keep us divided, fighting among ourselves, then he doesn't have to lift a finger.

We do the work of the enemy ourselves when we carelessly tear down a brother or sister in the Lord with our words or actions. Let us realize this is one of the most deceptive tricks of the enemy, designed specifically to destroy us from within. *We must walk together and work together.*

I heard a great story concerning Jimmy Durante, a popular comedic entertainer of the twentieth century. Once when he was asked to perform in a show for World War II veterans, Mr.

Durante said that his schedule was extremely tight and that if he came, he'd only be able to stay for a few minutes—just long enough to perform a short monologue. Then he would have to leave to meet other appointments. But when Mr. Durante got out onstage, the strangest thing happened. He went through his short monologue, but the cheers and applause from the audience compelled him to lengthen his performance from five minutes to ten and then to twenty minutes.

Finally, after thirty minutes, Mr. Durante took his bow and exited the stage. Backstage, someone stopped him and asked, "What happened? I thought you had to leave after a few minutes." Mr. Durante replied, "I did have to go; I'll show you the reason I stayed. You can see for yourself. Just look down in the front row." Sitting in the front row were two soldiers. Both had lost an arm in the war. One soldier had lost his right arm, and the other soldier had lost his left. Together, they were able to applaud for him loudly and clearly for the entire show.[3]

My dear friend, that is the perfect picture of unity! If we stand together in humility and thankfulness before God—acknowledging all our names appear together in His wonderful Book of Life—then we can settle any confrontation with the power of God's love. In this earthly battle, we are complete in Christ as we stand together.

Paul concluded in Philippians 4:9 by compelling us to put these things into practice: "Keep putting into practice all you learned and received from me—everything you heard from me or saw me doing. Then the God of peace will be with you" (NLT).

Years ago when I was a young piano student, I was instructed to practice thirty minutes a day. *The Baptist Hymnal* was my first piano method book. At the time, as a six-year-old, while my friends played kickball in the street, I was confined to the family den to practice my piano lessons. With my mother listening from the kitchen, I was assigned to practice those same hymns over and over again to the point of pure drudgery. A few decades later, all of that practice has proved to be quite beneficial.

In the same way, if we get in the habit of putting "these things" Paul mentioned into practice, we will grow together to become the church—the glorious, interdependent, and victorious spiritual body—Father God has called us to be.

Take Up His Armor . . . "Stand in There" for Jesus!

My mother, Mrs. Georgie Wade, is a great and godly woman. She's the mother of five brilliant children, of which I am the middle child. She served with my father, Pastor George W. Wade, as the founding first lady of the church where I grew up.

One Mother's Day weekend twenty-five years ago, Mom and I had the privilege of recording a mother-daughter interview for a radio station. Near the close of the interview, the host of the show asked my mom if she had some parting words. Mom is like E. F. Hutton. When she speaks, we lean in and listen. Mom said some words I will never forget. I'll leave these words with you now:

People will often try to encourage you by telling you to "hang in there." But when people tell you to "hang in there," don't listen to them: because when you are hanging in there, you're vulnerable to your circumstances. You're exposed to the elements. You're at risk and susceptible to your weaknesses when you're hanging in there. The position of hanging paints the picture of dangling by a thread or by a noose. That's not the position you want to be in. You *never* want to hang in there! As believers, we are never commanded to hang in there. Instead, we are commanded to *stand in there!* As Ephesians 6 tells us: "Wherefore take unto you the whole armour of God, that ye may be able to withstand in the evil day, and having done all, to stand" (v. 13).

My mother said it best. Don't hang—stand! We don't need to hang in there. That is what Jesus did for us. He was hung high and stretched wide, so we could stand strong on the truth of God's word!

EMBRACE YOUR DAY

At the end of our time together, I want you to never forget when times get tough (and you know that's the way life is), sometimes God will put your trouble out there "on the stage" for the whole world to see. If you've rehearsed your lines, you'll know what to say when the spotlight is on you. This is your moment to shine, my dear friend. Make your Father proud.

I want you to remember: *you can't be who you want to be without being who God made you to be.* On an ongoing basis, review your calling and constantly let God nudge you into the place you were meant to fit best. Make your Father's name famous in the earth.

Last, always remember whose you are. You are nothing without Christ, but with Him you can do great things in His name. *He loves you passionately because you're His favorite.* Live like it, dear one. Don't settle. Don't compromise. Your faith in Christ is rooted and established in love, and nothing you have done or ever will do can ever change this fact!

Life is brief. Richard J. Needham reduces the "seven stages of man" to a short sentence: spills, drills, thrills, bills, ills, pills, and wills.[4] Life is short. Live each day with the keen awareness of God's love for you. *Maintaining this attitude will take intent.* This kind of mind-set doesn't just happen. You must cultivate it, reminding yourself that each day is a blessing and your best and brightest days are still ahead of you. I want to pray for you once again before we wrap things up:

Dear heavenly Father,

You are amazing, God. Thank You for being right by my side these last three weeks and for showing me how much You love me. Thank You for the gift of living life on purpose and for a purpose. What a gift that is! Help me to live my life according to Your plan. Let my life be a love song, a continual, sweet-smelling sacrifice of praise to You.
In Jesus' name,
Amen.

Think About His Love

Just think about everything we have covered together. Consider how wonderful it is to be truly, deeply, and completely *Embraced by God.* As a believer in Jesus, remember this all your days. Never compromise your love for and faith in Him. God is here with us right now, and He will always be there, encouraging and challenging you to stand firm on the truth of His word. As you consider God's love today, thank Him that though everything around you may change, His word will remain a constant, powerful force in your life.

Read About His Love

"Those things, which ye have both learned, and received, and heard, and seen in me, do: and the God of peace shall be with you" (Philippians 4:9). Let this tasty morsel be the icing on the cake of God's bountiful banquet of love. Let's do a familiar exercise

together one more time. Say with me, *"Those things, which **I have**
both learned, and received, and heard, and have seen in **God's word**
over the past twenty-one days, I will do: and the God of peace shall
be with **me all the days of my life.**"* Excellent job! Would you care
for another generous helping? Don't be shy. Go for it!

Pray About His Love

Standing firm on what you know, instead of what you feel, requires
maturity. In the days ahead, ask God to grow you up so that you
will not be moved or shaken by the slightest wind that comes
along. Thank Him for making you both a hearer and a doer of His
word, according to Matthew 7:24-27—that He is establishing your
faith on a "rock" and not on sinking "sand." Finally, as you pray
about His love today and every day hereafter, ask the Holy Spirit
to lead you daily in intercession for others, for this is where God's
incomparable promise, both in and through you, is released.

Be About His Love

This is no time to experience stage fright, my friend. This final
movement in God's symphony of love is about to close. It has
encouraged, equipped, and *envisioned* you to go out and make a
world of difference. Any propensity you may have had to be
afraid or nervous onstage should now be drastically reduced
because you have spent twenty-one glorious days being *Embraced*

by God. You are fully prepared to go out on the world's stage and do your thing for Him. Your gifts have been thoroughly stirred up from the bottom up. It's time to stand in the spotlight for Jesus. The Lord needs you, dear one. So, move assuredly and unashamedly into your assignment: your unique "lane" of purpose in God's kingdom. Your life will count for eternity as you share it with others.

THE ENCORE
A LEGACY OF LOVE

Some of us have great runways already built for us.
If you have one, take off! But if you don't have one,
realize it is your responsibility to grab a shovel and build one for
yourself and for those who will follow after you.[1]
—Amelia Earhart

Summing up: Be agreeable, be sympathetic, be loving, be
compassionate, be humble. That goes for all of you, no exceptions.
No retaliation. No sharp-tongued sarcasm. Instead, bless—that's
your job, to bless. You'll be a blessing and also get a blessing.
Whoever wants to embrace life and see the day fill up good,
Here's what you do: Say nothing evil or hurtful;
Snub evil and cultivate good; run after peace for all you're worth.
—1 Peter 3:8-11 THE MESSAGE

Congratulations! You have made it all the way through our heavenly Father's symphony of love. Let me be the first to applaud you for completing this unique concert experience: from the starting overture sounding off our seven concert themes, all the way through the big finale. Now, let the encore begin! The best concerts always have them, you know. I can't think of a better way to wrap up spending three wonderful weeks, twenty-one incredible days, of being *Embraced by God*.

Today is a landmark day—one that is full of hope, promise, and new beginnings—because you have just completed a series of life-changing discoveries about the love of God. Now, it is my earnest prayer and expectation that you have gained a deeper understanding of your place in God's eternal legacy.

The days ahead will present you with many opportunities to put what you've experienced into practice. You have so much to look forward to. No matter what tomorrow may bring, remember God loves you and there is no need to fear the future because God is already there. He will give you just what you need, exactly the way you need it, at the precise moment you need it.

At this moment, and each moment hereafter, you should be gloriously confident that everything in your life is in His sovereign care because you have been *Embraced by God*.

Dear one, this is *really* the last day we'll spend together in this capacity. Although we'll end our *Embraced by God* fellowship at this time, the love of Christ will keep our hearts united. Though the words *the end* may appear after the final scene of a movie, for us as believers in the Lord, our closing is only the beginning. So, before we power down the sound system, turn off the spotlight, and close the curtain for the last time, I want to send you off with a few encouraging words.

Keep Sowing in Love

Here's the first thing I want you to take with you. Your love relationship with God is alive and active. It must be cultivated on a daily basis. So, to maximize your relationship with Him, you'll need to *keep sowing* to this vital relationship. The more "good seed" you sow, the more you'll grow. Just keep on giving. You will find that the more you give, the more God and people will give back to you. Our greatest joy in serving Christ comes by serving others. And as you refresh the lives of others, you will discover your own life being refreshed.

How does this work? First of all, remember, you're either a missionary or a mission project. The difference between the two is that missionaries know what it means to develop a lifestyle of giving. Just like a body of water grows stagnant if it has no outlet, the same is true of your life. Even if your efforts are small, little things will make a big difference. Missionaries understand this well.

I remember one day, I was on my way to speak to a group of women. While on the road I decided to drive through at a fast-food restaurant and grab a cup of coffee. As I was moving through the drive-thru, the Lord prompted me to buy lunch for the person in the car behind me. I didn't know who he or she was. I didn't know what the person had ordered. I just obeyed the Lord's prompting and told the clerk that I wanted to bless the person behind me by buying his or her lunch. I paid for it and drove off.

It's always interesting how things can work out when we obey God. Yes, I got blessed by this act of kindness, and I believe the person behind me was blessed. But I would also like to think the clerk working the drive-thru that day was affected as well. But that's not the end of the story.

The next day I was on my way back home again and went through another restaurant drive-thru to order a quick lunch. When I pulled up to the window to pay, I had misplaced my credit card and I didn't have any cash. The nice clerk at the window said, "Well, today, ma'am, your lunch is on the house!" He gave me my lunch for free! This is what you can expect when you sow into the lives of others.

It's easier now than ever before to share your love for Christ. Begin at home—in the house or apartment where you live, in your hometown, your home church, or your home school. Sharing from a heart of love is the nature of God's economy. No matter where you are, opportunities will always present themselves.

Christian singers often seek my counsel when desiring to jump-start their music ministries. They want suggestions on how to get started and get their ministry up on its legs. I always emphasize at our "Inner Circle" gatherings for musicians that instead of waiting for a big break or spending a lot of money on promotion, simply find a place to serve. As long as there are hospitals, homes for drug rehabilitation, jails and prisons, and senior assisted living facilities, there will always be places to minister God's love.

Sow! Give! Volunteer to visit one of these places on a Sunday afternoon. Tell some humorous stories to give folks a chance to enjoy some laughter. Sing some fun songs that everybody knows. Conclude by telling your own God-story. Then watch what happens.

This doesn't mean you'll always get paid monetarily, but I have found that one thing always leads to another. People who work in places like these are also involved in your community and their church. You never know when or where they may call on you to serve in another capacity. This is the key—always be ready and willing to serve. Listen to what Jesus told Peter and the other disciples in Mark 11:22-24. His counsel still stands today:

> Embrace this God-life. Really embrace it, and nothing will be too much for you. This mountain, for instance: Just say, "Go jump in the lake"—no shuffling or shilly-shallying—and it's as good as done. That's why I urge you to pray for absolutely everything, ranging from small to large. Include everything as you embrace this God-life, and you'll get God's everything. (*THE MESSAGE*)

Keep Growing in Love

Here's the next thing I want you to take with you. As long as there are life and breath in your body, you have the call from Christ to *keep growing*—to grow deeper, richer, and fuller in God's love. I mentioned in "The Overture" that life coaches and therapists suggest it takes twenty-one days to establish a new habit. So, if this practice of reading the Scriptures, praying, and meditating on God's Word is new for you, then you should be well on your way to establishing this as a new habit.

Take a look around you right now. Maybe you can spot a silk flower or a silk plant somewhere nearby. Silk plants are available in every color, shape, size, and texture, and they are becoming more and more popular these days. You can find them everywhere: in the mall, in airports, and in church. Silk plants are even being used in wreaths and floral arrangements for weddings and funerals.

But there's one element that silk plants just don't have. *Life.* They may look like the real thing, but if you move in for a closer look, if you touch a leaf or flower with your hand, or lean in to inhale its fragrance, you'll be sorely disappointed. You'll know immediately, it's an imposter. It's a fake, a phony.

While artificiality may work well for silk plants, there's no place for this characteristic in the life of the believer. Your spiritual life comes from staying connected to God and His word. You know the value of meeting with God by now, so continue this spiritual discipline for the next twenty-one days and then twenty-one days after that. Keep going and you'll keep growing!

This life-giving commitment is the greatest investment you can make in sustaining your love relationship with God. It's this discipline that fine-tunes your heart and life, spurring you on to maturity.

Before you can ever be effective in serving God publicly, you must practice His presence by serving Him privately. This is the mark of true maturity. Listen to these words from the Apostle Paul; they reflect his heartfelt desire to see every believer grow up in Christ:

> No prolonged infancies among us, please. We'll not tolerate babes in the woods, small children who are an easy mark for imposters. God wants us to grow up, to know the whole truth

and tell it in love—like Christ in everything. We take our lead from Christ, who is the source of everything we do. He keeps us in step with each other. His very breath and blood flow through us, nourishing us so that we will grow up healthy in God, robust in love. (Ephesians 4:14-16 *THE MESSAGE*)

Keep Going in God's Love

The third thing I want to leave with you is this. Some days you'll be tired. Other days you'll experience disappointments. Still on other days you may be discouraged. It's on days like these you'll just need to keep going. Just keep walking. Keep putting one foot in front of the other and keep moving forward. Keep walking in the love that God has for you.

See yourself as He sees you—loved beyond your capacity to imagine, saved from your sins, healed from all diseases, delivered from the bondages of sin, and free to live the life He has planned for you. When you really take hold of this life-changing truth, it will impact the way you think and ultimately the way you live.

Keep reminding yourself over and over again that you are loved by God. It's great that you love God. This is the first commandment God gives us. *But once you lay hold of how much God loves you, you will grasp a life-changing truth.* I love the fact that John, the author of the book that bears his name, considered himself to be the disciple whom Jesus loved! (See John 13:23; 19:26; 20:2; 21:7, 20.) John knew something that we must know deep down inside, something that we must celebrate each and every day. *He knew that to love God was one thing, but to be loved by God, to be considered God's favorite, changes your life forever.*

Dear one, don't let anything come between you and God's love for you. Don't let guilt separate you. Don't let shame separate you. Don't let your past mistakes separate you. Nothing, beloved friend! Don't let anything separate you from God's love. Listen to the Apostle Paul's victorious statement. I encourage you to memorize this powerful passage:

> Do you think anyone is going to be able to drive a wedge between us and Christ's love for us? There is no way! Not trouble, not hard times, not hatred, not hunger, not homelessness, not bullying threats, not backstabbing, not even the worse sins listed in Scripture. . . . None of this fazes us because Jesus loves us. I'm absolutely convinced that nothing—nothing living or dead, angelic or demonic, today or tomorrow, high or low, thinkable or unthinkable—absolutely nothing can get between us and God's love because of the way that Jesus our Master has embraced us. (Romans 8:35, 37-39 *THE MESSAGE*)

I want to tell you one last story about my dad, Pastor George Wade. He was a great preacher, pastor, prison chaplain, college professor, and public servant. Like the Apostle Paul said of himself, Dad was all things to all people that he might win some. (See 1 Corinthians 9:22 NKJV). He and my mother, Mrs. Georgie Wade, were married almost fifty years and served diligently together in one church for nearly forty years. I learned how to serve God and the church by observing their tireless example.

Dad passed away almost twenty-five years ago. He left a great legacy: an insatiable appetite for the things of God, an enviable passion for His word, and an undying love for His church. Long after his death, Dad still encourages me to do great things for God and for people.

It is from his example that I want to inspire you. Dad died on March 4, 1987. Even today his victorious "home going" challenges us to *march forth*—to never give in to the pressure from the world around us, but to *march forth* and press on in the gospel. Keep putting one foot in front of the other with diligence, determination, and love.

You see, my friend, God will use you to make an eternal difference if you make yourself available to Him. You may feel like saying, "Well, I'm just an ordinary person. I'm nobody special. God couldn't possibly use me." And apart from Christ, you'd be absolutely correct in saying that. The Bible says that you can do nothing without Him. But as you yield yourself to Him, placing your life in His loving, capable hands, you find yourself being the perfect candidate to be used by God to do extraordinary things.

God is looking for someone just like you to spread His love in the earth.

It All Comes Back to Love

Everything begins and ends with God's great love for you. According to 1 John 4:7-8, love originated in the heart of God, and there would be no love without Him—for *He is love.*

Starting tomorrow, when you get up out of bed, start your day by saying this, *"God, I don't deserve it, but thank You for loving me the way You do. Help me to love You with all my heart. Then give me the power and the desire to love everyone I come in contact with today: with this kind of love!"*

The message of unconditional love is God's absolute favorite message! You can journey through life unaffected by it, taking His love for granted, or you can walk in this unbelievable gift, allowing it to impact every area of your existence. The choice is yours.

In a world where far too many people have forgotten about God, and even more have forgotten that He loves them, determine to be one of those who will rise high above the crowd and shouts from the mountaintop: *There is a great big God and His love is available for the whole wide world!*

So, the next time you hear the words *God loves you,* I hope you ponder for just a little while the great price that was paid for you to be *Embraced by God.* May this awesome promise reduce you to a humble heap of eternal gratitude. That's exactly what happens to me when I pause and consider His love.

Dear friend, I pray you come to understand this powerful truth in an ever-increasing way. Just think about it. Of the seven billion people on the face of the planet, God loves you as if you were the only one to love. You are constantly on his heart and mind. He finds you beautiful, valuable, and acceptable. He takes great pleasure and finds tremendous delight in you. May this truth forever rock your world! And as you walk it out day by day, returning the Father's embrace, may you never, ever be the same.

Now, let's close our encore with a brief excerpt of another song I wrote with my good friend Donna I. Douglas. It simply tells our Father we are "So Grateful" for His love. This song is so appropriate for our final moments together in His embrace, don't you think? Because, my friend, this is how we should posture our hearts each day. As the symphony plays this final melody and before the curtains close, I pray these words will resonate in your heart toward God all the days of your life. Now, lift your voice and sing with me:

> *You are holy and amazing*
> *Such a High and Mighty God*
> *That You created all from nothing*
> *Makes me humbly bow in awe*
> *I see the beauty of creation*
> *All around me every day*
> *Lets me know I'm in Your presence*
> *You take my breath away*
>
> *So when you say You love me*
> *More than all the grains of sand*
> *And that You're thinking of me*
> *Because I'm etched upon Your hand*
> *And what it cost to know me*
> *I don't pretend to understand*
> *Just how someone like me*
> *Could be loved by You*
> *But I'm so grateful to You Jesus, that it's true*
> *So grateful that You do . . .*[2]

HOW TO RECEIVE CHRIST AS SAVIOR

Receiving Jesus Christ into your heart and life is the "first note" of God's beautiful love symphony. When you make this vitally important decision to receive and embrace His love, your life will never be the same. So many incredible and unforgettable new experiences are ahead of you in your brand-new life with the Lord.

If you would like to receive Christ as Savior, you can make this decision at any place or at any time. So, why not do it right now? Begin by giving these important facts your utmost consideration:

God loves you and wants to have a personal relationship with you! Revelation 3:20 says, "Behold, I stand at the door and knock. If anyone hears My voice and opens the door, I will come in to him and dine with him, and he with Me" (NKJV).

The Problem: Because of sin, everyone in the world has been born spiritually dead. Romans 6:23 says, "For the wages of sin is death; but the gift of God is eternal life, through Jesus Christ our Lord."

The Promise: Jesus will forgive us of every sin, promising us eternal life with Him in eternity! First John 1:9 tells us, "If we confess our sins, he is faithful and just to forgive us our sins, and to cleanse us from all unrighteousness." Added to this, Jesus promised in John 14:1-3,

> Do not let your hearts be troubled. Trust in God; trust also in me. In my Father's house are many rooms; if it were not so, I would have told you. I am going there to prepare a place for you. And if I go and prepare a place for you, I will come back and take you to be with me that you also may be where I am. (NIV)

The Prayer: To receive Jesus Christ as Savior, you can pray a prayer like this: *Dear Lord Jesus, I confess that I am a sinner. I invite You to come into my life and forgive me of all my sins. I believe that You were crucified, that You died, and that You rose again for my sin. Jesus, I want to be the person You designed me to become and be with You from this moment forward. Thank You, Lord, for loving and saving me! Amen.*

If you prayed this prayer and meant it with all your heart, you are now a Christian. *Welcome to the family of God!*

Now, won't you join me in God's embrace? Just go back to "The Overture" where you left off on page 22. The first concert theme is about to begin!

Author Notes

Theme One

1. Thomas Kelly, "Glory, Glory Everlasting," http://saintsserving .net/song.php?id=166.

Day 1

1. Frederick M. Lehman and Meir Ben Isaac Nehorai, "The Love of God," http://www.cyberhymnal.org/htm/l/o/loveofgo.htm.
2. Max Lucado, *Grace for the Moment: Inspirational Thoughts for Each Day of the Year* (Nashville: J. Countryman, 2000), 29.
3. Galatians 2:6 in *Matthew Henry's Commentary on the Whole Bible.* (Austin: WORDsearch, 2005).
4. Frederick C. Mish, *Merriam-Webster's Collegiate Dictionary, 10th edition* (Springfield, Mass: Merriam-Webster, 1993), 1113.
5. Babbie Mason, "I Love You, I Do" May Sun Publishing/ASCAP, 2011. Admin. by Babbie Mason.

Day 2

1. Charles Haddon Spurgeon, www.spurgeon.us/mind_and_heart/ quotes/g2.htm.
2. Mark Twain, *Classic Wisdom for the Good Life,* ed. Bryan Curtis (Nashville: Thomas Nelson, 2000), 163.
3. Frances R. Havergal and Henri A. C. Malan, "Take My Life and Let It Be." *The United Methodist Hymnal* (Nashville: The United Methodist Publishing House, 1989), 399.

Day 3

1. Alexander Woollcott, http://quotationsbook.com/quote/32234/.
2. Sir Isaac Watts, http://fosterroadchurch.org/church/wp-content/ uploads/2011/03/032211.htm.

Theme Two

1. Babbie Mason, "I Love You, I Do," May Sun Publishing/ASCAP, 2011 Admin. by Babbie Mason.

Day 4

1. Frank A. Clark, http://en.thinkexist.com/quotes/frank_a._clark/2.html.
2. Babbie Mason, "Each One, Reach One" (Nashville: Word Music/ASCAP, 1990). Admin. by Word Music, Nashville, Tennessee.
3. Clara T. Williams, "Satisfied," *The Baptist Hymnal* (Nashville: Convention Press, 1991), 539.

Day 5

1. William Arthur Ward, http://en.thinkexist.com/quotes/William_Arthur_Ward/.
2. Thelma Wells, *God Will Make a Way* (Nashville: Thomas Nelson, 1998), 80.
3. Anne Steele, "My Heart Demands," www.hymnary.org/hymn/CHUU1858/page/178.

Day 6

1. Ralph Waldo Emerson, http://thinkexist.com/quotation/finish_each_day_and_be_done_with_it-you_have_done/11827.html.
2. Babbie Mason, "You Are Not Alone," May Sun Publishing/ASCAP, 2011. Admin. by Babbie Mason.

Theme Three

1. Babbie Mason, "I Know," May Sun Publishing/ASCAP, 2011. Admin. by Babbie Mason.

Day 7

1. Helen Keller, http://en.thinkexist.com/quotes/Helen_Keller/.
2. Leena Rao, "What 20 Minutes on Facebook Looks Like," http://tech

crunch.com/2010/12/31/what-20-minutes-on-facebook-looks-like-1m-shared-links-2-7m-photos-uploaded-10-2m-comments/.

3. "Loneliness Linked to High Blood Pressure," http://psych central.com/news/2010/03/19/loneliness-linked-to-high-blood-pressure/12275.html.

4. "Desolate" (8074, "shamem," Heb.) in *The New Strong's Exhaustive Concordance of the Bible: A Concise Dictionary of the Words in the Hebrew Bible* (Nashville: Thomas Nelson, 1990).

5. Donna I. Douglas and Babbie Mason, "In All of His Glory" (Nashville: Word Music, Inc./BMG Songs, Inc. Pamela Kay Music, 1990). Admin. by EMI Christian Music Publishing/ASCAP.

6. Elizabeth Scott, "Serene," www.hymnary.org/hymn/PH1878/page/404.

Day 8

1. Adoniram J. Gordon, http://en.wikipedia.org/wiki/Adoniram_Judson_Gordon.

2. Edward McKendree Bounds, *Prayer and Praying Men* (London: George E. Doran, 1921), 63.

3. Eddie Carswell and Babbie Mason, "Trust His Heart" (Nashville: Causing Change Music, Word Music/ASCAP, 1989). Admin. by Word Music/Dayspring Music.

4. Frank Laubach, www.christian-prayer-quotes.christian-attorney.net/.

5. Adoniram J. Gordon, http://en.wikipedia.org/wiki/Adoniram_Judson_Gordon.

Day 9

1. Eugenia Price, www.inspiration-for-singles.com/Christian-quotes.html.

2. Dennis Bratcher, "Ba'al Worship in the Old Testament," www.cri voice.org/baal.html.

3. Donna I. Douglas, "He'll Find a Way" (Marietta, Ga: C. A. Music/ASCAP, 1985).

4. John Ryland, "O Lord, We Would Delight in Thee," www.stem publishing.com/hymns/ss/243.

Theme Four

1. John Newton, "Quiet, Lord, My Froward Heart," www.hymn lyrics.org/lyricsq/quiet_lord_my_froward_heart.html.

Day 10

1. "Using Your Failures," www.angelfire.com/fl5/hleewhite/2samuel1127usingyourfailure.html. Accessed 11/13/11.
2. "The Golden Archives: McDonald's Sandwich Hall of Fame," http://blog.paxholley.net/2007/08/21/the-golden-archives-mcdonalds-sandwich-hall-of-fame/.
3. Corrie Ten Boom, "Goodness of God," www.sermonillustrations.com/a-z/g/god_goodness_of.htm.
4. Eddie Carswell and Babbie Mason, "Trust His Heart" (Nashville: Causing Change Music, Word Music/ASCAP, 1989). Admin. by Word Music/Dayspring Music.

Day 11

1. Charles Swindoll, http://thinkexist.com/quotation/courage_is_not_limited_to_the_battlefield_or_the/298490.html.
2. Adrian Rogers, "Detours, Dead Ends, and Dry Holes," www.sermonsearch.com/content.aspx?id=14423.
3. Mario Andretti, http://en.thinkexist.com/quotes/Mario_Andretti/.

Day 12

1. Thomas Kelly, "How Sweet to Leave the World Ahwhile," www.hymnary.org/hymn/PH1878/69.
2. "Worshipping Wrong Gods in the Right Way!" www.nnedaog.org/sermons/sercom1.htm.
3. "Slavery in the United States," http://en.wikipedia.org/wiki/Slavery_in_the_United_States.
4. Anita Renfroe and Babbie Mason, "Come Away, My Beloved" (Nashville: Centergy Music [BMI]/Praise and Worship Works [ASCAP], 2001). Admin. by BMG Copyrights Management, New York, NY 10016.

Theme Five

1. Babbie Mason, "I Believe," May Sun Publishing/ASCAP, 2011. Admin. by Babbie Mason.

Day 13

1. Doris Mortman, http://en.thinkexist.com/quotes/Doris_Mortman/.

2. Johann Sebastian Bach, "Soli Deo Gloria," http://revelation4-11 .blogspot.com/2009/05/js-bach-soli-deo-gloria.html.

Day 14

1. John Newton, "Let Worldly Minds the World Pursue," www.hymn ary.org/hymn/RH1858/92.
2. Tony Evans, *Tony Evans' Book of Illustrations* (Chicago: Moody, 2009), 172–73.

Day 15

1. Dr. Charles L. Allen, www.searchquotes.com/search/?searchf =Charles+L+Allen&sbut.x=11&sbut.y=11.
2. Beth Moore, *Get Out of That Pit.* (Nashville: Integrity, 2007), 147.
3. Tony Sutherland. *GRACEWORKS* (Atlanta: Tony Sutherland Ministries, 2011), 231.
4. Andrew Stanley, *North Point TV with Andy Stanley,* North Point Community Church, 4350 North Point Parkway, Alpharetta, GA 30022, www.north point.org.
5. Edward Mote, "My Hope Is Built," *The United Methodist Hymnal* (Nashville: The United Methodist Publishing House, 1989), 368.

Theme Six

1. John Newton, "Be Gone, Unbelief, My Savior Is Near," www.oremus.org/hymnal/b/b004.html.

Day 16

1. Amy Carmichael, "Flame of God," www.womenofchristianity.com/ ?p=481.
2. Babbie Mason, "All Rise!" (Marietta, Ga: C. A. Music/ASCAP, 1985). Admin. by Music Services, Nashville, TN.
3. Babbie Mason. "Steppin' Out on the Water." Copyright © 1998/ASCAP. Admin. by Integrated Copyright Group, Nashville.

Day 17

1. Anonymous, http://thinkexist.com/quotation/fall_seven_times _and_stand_up_eight/147984.html.
2. Based on Martin Luther, "Out of the Depths," www.hymn ary.org/hymn/UMH/515.

Day 18

1. Mother Teresa, www.life-changing-inspirational-quotes.com/mother-teresa-quotes.html#Action.
2. Babbie Mason, "Show Me How to Love" (Nashville: Word Music/ASCAP, 1988).
3. John 21:15–17, *agape* (25, Gk.); *thelo* (2309, Gk.); *phileo* (5368, Gk.) in *Strong's Talking Greek and Hebrew Dictionary* (Austin: WORDsearch, 2005).
4. J. D. Douglas II and Norman Hillyer, *eros* in *Tyndale New Bible Dictionary*, 2d ed. (Leicester, England: Universities and Colleges Christian Fellowship, 1982), 711.
5. Agape in ibid.
6. Barbara Crossette, "Foreign Aid Budget: Quick, How Much? Wrong," www.nytimes.com/1995/02/27/world/foreign-aid-budget-quick-how-much-wrong.html?scp=1&sq=February%2027,%201995&st=cse; U.S. Military Budget, en.wikipedia.org/wiki/Military_budget_of_the_United_States.
7. Douglas and Hillyer, "Phileo se" in *Tyndale New Bible Dictionary*.
8. Sydney Smith, http://en.thinkexist.com/quotes/Sydney_Smith/.

Theme Seven

1. Emma Frances Bevan, "O Christ, in Thee My Soul," *Voices United* (Etobicoke, Ontario: The United Church Publishing House, 1996), 630.

Day 19

1. Hudson Taylor, http://en.thinkexist.com/quotes/J._Hudson_Taylor/.
2. "Depression," accessed November 17, 2011, www.emedicine health.com/depression/article_em.htm.
3. Clara Ward, "How I Got Over." Admin. by ASCAP.
4. Nancy Guthrie, *Holding On to Hope* (Wheaton, Ill: Tyndale House, 2002), 51.

Day 20

1. Attributed to Mrs. Vokes in *The Psalmist: A New Collection of Hymns for Use of The Baptist Churches* by Baron, Stowe, and S. F. Smith (Philadelphia: American Baptist Education Society; Boston: Gould and Lincoln, 1870), 462.
2. Exodus 6:20, *Jochebed* (3115, Heb) in *Strong's Talking Greek and Hebrew Dictionary* (Austin: WORDsearch, 2005).
3. John Wesley, http://en.thinkexist.com/quotes/John_Wesley/.

Day 21

1. W. M. Lewis, http://thinkexist.com/quotes/w._m._lewis/.
2. Babbie Mason, "I Know," May Sun Publishing/ASCAP, 2011. Admin. by Babbie Mason.
3. "Jimmy Durante," http://bible.org/illustration/jimmy-durante.
4. Richard J. Needham, "The Seven Stages of Man," http://bible.org/illustration/seven-stages-man.

Epilogue

1. Amelia Earhart, www.consciouslivingfoundation.org/quotations OnSuccess.htm.
2. Donna I. Douglas and Babbie Mason, "So Grateful" (Did My Music/ASCAP, 2009. Admin. by BMG Copyrights Management, New York, NY 10016; May Sun Publishing/ASCAP, 2011. Admin. by Babbie Mason.

Purchase the music of Babbie Mason at www.babbie.com

EVERYTHING
An inspiring collection of worship songs written and delivered as only Babbie Mason can. Includes: *Everything, Let Your Fire Fall, Come Thou Fount, Strong Tower, God Will Open Up the Windows*, and more.

MY BEST SO FAR, VOLUME ONE
Features the timeless classics that have made Babbie Mason a quintessential gospel music artist. Includes: *Each One Reach One, God Has Another Plan, With All My Heart, Love is the More Excellent Way, All Rise, Standing in the Gap*, and more.

MY BEST SO FAR, VOLUME TWO
More classic favorites from Babbie Mason, this collection features songs the church has come to love such as: *Pray On, Trust His Heart, It Must Be Love, Carry On, Jesus the One and Only, To the Cross, Stop By the Church, Shine the Light, In All of His Glory* and more.

CHUCK ROAST (DVD)
This LIVE concert pays tribute to love, marriage, and Babbie's husband, Charles, letting you on the inside of their marriage of more than three decades. The contents will cause side-splitting, hilarious, and contagious laughter as you get to know Babbie, Charles, and the Mason family up close and personal.

TREASURED MEMORIES
Paying beautiful homage to the African American worship experience, this LIVE worship service, recorded in Babbie Mason's hometown of Jackson, Michigan, features the soulful, heartfelt hymns and spiritual songs of days gone by, featuring The Barrett Sisters, Willie Rogers, Inez Andrews, Georgie Wade, and more. Songs include *Near the Cross, Come and Go to That Land, Old Ship of Zion, Yes, Jesus Loves Me, What A Fellowship*, and more.

THE INNER CIRCLE

Babbie Mason and her husband, Charles, host their own exciting music conference, The Inner Circle, drawing on almost three decades of music ministry and business experience to encourage and mentor those desiring to jump-start their own endeavors. The Inner Circle is packed full of tools and tips for launching a music ministry, writing great lyrics and music, making a great CD on a not-so-great budget, vocal care, critiques, and internet marketing techniques. Babbie features many of her friends in the music industry who join her for this encouraging weekend conference. Hear from producers, writers, arrangers, vocal coaches, entertainment attorneys, web masters, and Christian artists. Guests have included Helen Baylor, Carol Cymbala (director of the Brooklyn Tabernacle Choir), Charles Billingsley, Ron Kenoly, Morris Chapman, Pastor William Murphy, Kenn Mann, Donna Douglas, Turner Lawton, Eulalia King, Cheryl Rogers, and more!

Find out more at www.babbie.com

Embrace: A Worship Celebration for Women, is a ninety-minute, interactive concert with a purpose. In an atmosphere of worship and an attitude of joy, Babbie Mason invites women to step away from life's responsibilities, breathe out, let go of the challenges they face, and receive the love, validation, and comfort that every woman needs. At every *Embrace* concert, women experience exciting worship music, God-honoring testimonies, the fellowship of Christian sisterhood, and a huge dose of encouragement, all in an atmosphere where women can encounter the unconditional love of God.

Babbie Mason says, "I've had the privilege of being a part of women's ministry from the local church to the national stage for a long time now. And wherever I go, I meet women who are in desperate need of encouragement. Too often women are discouraged, depressed, and defeated. Women need to know that they really matter to God, and that He has a great big plan and we're all in it. I'm so honored that God would give me the music and the opportunity to lead women in worship at each of these encounters. *Embrace: A Worship Celebration For Women* was created to give women the opportunity to bask in the deepend of God's love and receive healing for our hearts."

Inspired by her new and uplifting book, *Embraced By God,* Babbie Mason presents the companion CD *Embrace.* Encouraging and God-honoring, each song resonates with the themes of the book, underscoring the powerful messages of God's grace, acceptance, and forgiveness. The songs from the CD also serve as a backdrop for Babbie Mason's worship concert, *Embrace: A Worship Celebration for Women.*

Send some love to a special someone with Babbie Mason's *Embrace* note cards. Each blank card allows you to write your own sentiments of hope and encouragement. Each box contains twelve cards and envelopes.

For more information go to www.babbie.com.